AND ALSO TEACH
THEM TO READ

AND ALSO TEACH THEM TO READ

Y tambien enséñeles a leer

by Sheryl L. Hirshon
with Judy Butler

Photographs by Larry Boyd

LAWRENCE HILL & COMPANY
Westport, Connecticut 06880

Published in the United States of America by
Lawrence Hill & Company, Publishers, Inc.
520 Riverside Avenue
Westport, Connecticut 06880
2 3 4 5 6 7 8 9

Library of Congress Cataloging in Publication Data

Hirshon, Sheryl L.
  And also teach them to read = Y tambien enséñeles
a leer.

  In English.
  1. Literacy—Nicaragua—History—20th century.
  2. Education, Rural—Nicaragua—History—20th century.
  3. Hirshon, Sheryl L.   4. Teachers—United States—
Biography.   5. Teachers, Interchange of—Nicaragua.
  6. Teachers, Interchange of—United States.   I. Butler,
Judy, 1940-   . II. Title.   III. Title: Y tambien
enséñeles a leer.
LC155.N5H57   1983   374'.012'097285   83-18370
ISBN 0-88208-170-5
ISBN 0-88208-171-3 (pbk.)

Manufactured in the United States of America

DEDICATION

This is for you, the children and half-grown children I had in my classes in the United States. This is for you, with the light in your eyes and nowhere to shine it.

I would think of you all sometimes in my endless solitary walks from one end of the valley to the other. I would think of how you would have loved to be here as brigadistas, of how good you would have been. I'd see you here, proud in your uniforms and singing, working under the hot sun and growing strong with the knowledge that at last you were doing something important, something real. Knowing that you could teach. Knowing that you could help.

You will probably never get this chance to test your strength, to share the crazy exuberance that accompanied your Popular Literacy Army. Most likely no one will ever tell you that your country needs you, all of you, for a very special task of building.

So I think of you, the light dying slowly in classrooms and fastfood restaurants and in other armies very different. I wish that somehow you could have been here with us.

It's also for the literacy brigadistas of all Nicaragua, whose light could—and did—illuminate a whole continent. And for the peasants, the real heroes of the story. And for you Chico, and Manuel, and you Matías, wherever you are.

I guess it's basically for all of us.

CONTENTS

FOREWORD

Not very long ago, in a Central American country that few people in the United States had ever thought about, a dictatorship was overthrown. Suddenly, Nicaragua was news. In bits and pieces we Americans learned that the Somoza family had ruled for nearly half a century, following U.S. Marine occupation for most of the twenty years before that. If we stayed with the saga, we learned another important name—that of the peasant leader, Augusto César Sandino. Sandino's guerrilla movement, formed in the late 1920s, had fought for the cause of Nicaraguan nationalism. In 1933, he won a partial victory: the U.S. government financed the creation of a Nicaraguan national guard, put it under the control of Anastasio Somoza García, and brought the Marines home. But within a short time, Sandino was led into a trap and assassinated on orders of the new strongman. Successive U.S. administrations would continue to finance the Somoza dynasty for the next forty-five years as sons succeeded father, amassing more and more wealth and drawing their corrupt base of support ever narrower. Bribery replaced due process, and dissent became synonymous with death. Elections, when they were held, were a travesty.

By July 19, 1979, the Sandinista National Liberation Front (FSLN)—named after this nationalist patriot—had organized an entire people to overthrow the second generation of the Somoza family tyranny. Few had believed it would be possible, except the handful of Sandinistas that had been patiently organizing in the rural highlands for nearly twenty years. But by the end, the Somoza family's insatiable greed became its nemesis. The small middle class and even many alienated business owners joined the ubiquitous peasants and landless poor who were the heart and soul of the Sandinista movement.

Facing an armed population that would not be turned back, the Somoza dynasty collapsed. On July 17, Anastasio, Jr., and his close allies abandoned their ranches and factories, grabbed what they could, and fled northward on a special flight to Miami. Others in his circle commandeered boats and followed across the sea. Within two days, the remnants of his National Guard were routed, and the euphoric guerrillas, now numbering in the thousands, marched tattered but triumphant into Managua, the capital. An ocean of people greeted their arrival with frenzied cheers and thousands of red-and-black Sandinista banners.

The war in Nicaragua was over. The revolution was just beginning.

The Sandinista revolutionaries inherited an underdeveloped, underpopulated country, the capital city of which had been flattened by an earthquake in 1972 and never rebuilt. Now other cities, too, were in ruins. Factories were twisted skeletons of rusting steel, stucco row houses were roofless shells, destroyed by Somoza's aerial bombing, the gaping remains of their common walls pockmarked from strafing. Almost 50,000 Nicaraguans had been killed and 100,000 more wounded, out of a population of 2.5 million. Forty thousand children had been orphaned, and 200,000 families left homeless. In the countryside, crops had gone unplanted or untended or had been pounded flat; three quarters of a million people were dependent on food assistance. The immediate tasks of survival were immense.

The longer term picture wasn't much brighter. Nicaragua's economy, like many in Latin America, was skewed toward an excessive reliance on agricultural exports. Little of the fluctuating profits went into developing domestic industry and even less into meeting social needs. Even basic foodstuffs had to be imported; malnutrition stalked the land. The average Nicaraguan looked forward to a life-span of under fifty-two years; the infant mortality rate exceeded 12 percent, and illiteracy stifled more than half the population. The country was so disorganized from the war and from decades of neglect that many of these facts weren't even known until later.

And if all this weren't enough, the country was bankrupt. Somoza had left only $3.5 million in foreign exchange in the Central Bank. What he hadn't stolen or destroyed, he and his cronies had already mortgaged to the local banks, including their control of about a third of the country's enterprises. Banks, enterprises, and mortgages all fell to the state. Somoza also bequeathed the revolution a foreign debt of $1.6 billion, the largest per-capita debt in Latin America at the time.

Where to start? How to begin to change the legacy of so many years, to fill the deep ruts—psychological as well as economic—of so much destruction?

What they decided to do was to teach everyone to read and write. Even as bulldozers began to clear the rubble and seeds were distributed for the new planting, the Sandinistas declared a literacy crusade.

It was announced within a month of the victory; and eight months later the whole embattled country was mobilized to achieve it. Not five months after that the Nicaraguans could announce to a startled world that they had—once again—done the impossible. They had reduced the illiteracy rate from 50 percent to 12 percent, making theirs the third most literate country in Latin America, after Cuba and Argentina.

This is the story of that war, a war on ignorance.

It's also the story of one rural community and of the twenty-five brigadistas—in this case, all young boys from the capital—who taught 123 peasants to read. Furthermore, it's the story of the changes that the literacy process brought to the community and to the brigadistas themselves. In this aspect, the events, conflicts, and successes in one tiny rural zone mirrored those that were taking place all over the country.

It's also, to some extent, my story. I'm not a Nicaraguan and, like many North Americans, barely knew where the country was until the drama of the revolution brought it into the headlines. Born and educated in the United States, ultimately in Oregon, I had spent three years after graduation from college teaching in alternative high school programs. Then after a year of travel in Latin America, I had returned to a Title I program, also at the secondary level, described as "containing social problems." I soon realized that the phrase meant the kids were the problem, not the society, and that the task was to contain them. Since I didn't see much value in this containment theory, I decided to try something different. I'd read about the Cuban literacy experience, and had dreamed of someday being a part of such a movement. I was twenty-nine when I actually got the chance.

I arrived in Nicaragua with a reporter friend six weeks after the victory, motivated by sympathetic curiosity. Fearing hostility, I encountered only exuberance; anticipating chaos, I discovered an underlying order that was the realization of a dream the Sandinistas had nurtured for many years in the mountains. The air was electric with excitement.

I found that I couldn't merely look on as the Nicaraguan people marshaled to rebuild their shattered country. Nor could I go back home to a world of hopeless social projects, defeated before they began. There were already rumors of a literacy campaign; I decided to stay, hoping I might be useful.

My actual participation in the literacy crusade was the result in part of a series of lucky coincidences—of being in the right place with the right skills at the right time. So it was that I, together with volunteers from countries all over the world, joined the more than sixty thousand Nicaraguan brigadistas who stepped forward to teach their peasant sisters and brothers to read. I'll always be grateful to those Nicaraguans who helped me to gain acceptance, trusting me at a time when the United States government was already beginning to work to undermine their revolution.

Although I draw heavily on my own experiences, and at times on my actual field diary, this book is mainly about the Nicaraguan people as they struggle to free themselves from a tyranny far more tenacious than that of the Somozas. Illiteracy is a social disability having effects that go far beyond being unable to read. Illiteracy breeds a sense of social inferiority that permeates how people think, not only about things, but about themselves in relation to others. Authoritarian rulers throughout history have understood this, manipulating the helplessness of their subjects as much through paternalism as through raw power.

The literacy crusade was one expression of the Nicaraguan revolution's determination to give power to the people, to make them actors in their own social destiny. And it also taught them to read.

BOOK ONE

MARCH
The Arrival

Brigadistas' Hymn

Ever onwards, Brigadistas,
Staunch guerrillas of the
Literacy Crusade.
Your machete is the primer
To kill ignorance and error
With just one fell swoop.

Ever onwards, Brigadistas,
Many centuries of ignorance
will fall
We'll erect our barricades
Of notebooks and blackboards,
Let's go onwards
To the cultural revolt,

Fists on high! Books open!

Everybody's in the national
Crusade
We'll earn our destiny
As children of Sandino
Bringing clarity where there
Was only darkness before.

CHAPTER 1
Beginnings

And the day came that had been awaited for several centuries. The day of obligation and commitment. The day to say "Basta ya"—that's enough—to ignorance. The day to teach reading and learn reading. On the face of our people was the joy of a new dawn. Came the day of pencils and notebooks, the day of fists high and books opened. Came the day of the farewell and the beginning, of the hope of a whole people looking for light.

FROM *ENCUENTRO 16*, MAGAZINE OF THE CENTRAL AMERICAN UNIVERSITY, MANAGUA, NICARAGUA

It was March 23, 1980—the first day of the Nicaraguan Literacy Crusade. Departure Day for sixty thousand Nicaraguan high school and university students and their teachers—all bound for the remote rural zones of their sparsely settled country.

The streets were suddenly full of kids, hysterical with excitement. The parks were one solid mass of brigadistas, and the high schools were another. Freshly ironed uniforms—gray tunics and new blue jeans—as far as the eye could see. It was the Popular Literacy Army off to war, amid the carnival atmosphere that any troop deployment brings with it.

To a people who had just experienced all the horrors of real war, this was a day of redemption. It was the start of the children's crusade, a gigantic postwar catharsis. Boys kissed girls. Mothers cried. Vendors did a record business in ice cream. Last chance to find out what detachment your friends were in, to see whether anyone you knew from another part of the country was coming through, to strut in front of the ones who would be staying behind.

To anyone who didn't know what was going on—if any such person still existed after all the months of planning and publicity—it must have seemed that the world had gone mad. Or, perhaps, that the film of their recent revolutionary triumph—trucks jammed with euphoric young soldiers converging on the capital—was being run in reverse. Dumptrucks loaded with brigadistas were now pouring *out* of Managua, on their way to the mountains in the north, the rice fields in the south, the jungles in the east. As they entered towns along the way, they circled the streets, while horns honked and people waved frantically and the kids screamed slogans.

> *In the mountains we swear to smother*
> *the ignorance that we uncover.*
> *EPA, EPA...Ayyyyyyyyy-Pah!**

Where had it all begun? It was hard to pinpoint a day. While the official announcement had been issued in August 1979, a month after the triumph, the idea of the literacy crusade had been born in the mountains many years before. Several of the generals in Sandino's army had learned to read during their struggle for sovereignty in the nineteen-twenties, as had guerrilla leaders of the Sandinista National Liberation Front (FSLN) nearly half a century later. More than one young fighter had received his first experiences in *"conscientización"* by working in literacy programs with the poor. The first point in the section on culture and education of the FSLN's political program, written in 1969, was a "massive campaign to immediately wipe out illiteracy." And now, a decade later, it was happening.

But it was Carlos Fonseca Amador, a founder of the FSLN and its leading theoretician, who had been the inspiration. In the words of Tomás Borge, the only founder still alive: "Germán Pomares [another founding member, himself a campesino who learned to read and write during the struggle] and I were training a group of peasants, various young men and a woman. We were teaching them to dismantle and reassemble the Garand, the M-1 carbine and the .45 caliber pistol. Carlos arrived and instructed us, 'And also teach them to read.'"†

Now, four years after his death in combat, Fonseca's offhand words appeared on billboard after billboard. There was his solemn, bespectacled face and the now-famous phrase, *"Y tambien enséneles a leer."* The war against ignorance was on.

But it was one thing to discuss the teaching of reading and quite another to mount an all-out literacy crusade. The former is a question of books and classrooms, methodologies and techniques; the latter one of highly complex logistics. A literacy crusade means the col-

---

*Ejercito Popular de Alfabetizacion (EPA)—the acronym of the Popular Literacy Army.
†Tomas Borge, "Carlos, El amanecer ya no es una tentación," reprinted in the Havana literary magazine, *Casa de las Americas*, May–June 1980, no. 114.

lecting of statistics—going out and finding the people who are illiterate, whether they live in the poorest urban neighborhood or the most sparsely settled region of the mountains. It means finding methods and teachers that will be effective with the people, working with them in whatever hours they can spare from other labor. It means training, transporting, supplying, and lodging an army of volunteer teachers, establishing a communications network, collecting more statistics. It means mobilizing thousands of people for the kind of collective effort generally mounted only in wartime.

The only real precedent had been the Cuban experience, twenty years before. But the Cubans hadn't begun their literacy campaign until their revolution was two years old, and they had evolved it over several years, not in the mere five months that the Nicaraguans had programed. Nor had Cuba suffered such massive war damage; nor did it have such rampant illiteracy or such vast expanses of sparsely settled land. And no country could have been more disorganized or more bankrupt than the Nicaragua of 1979.

Nonetheless, right before our eyes, the impossible was happening. March 23, 1980—eight months and four days after the Sandinista victory—before the world's television cameras and the assembled international dignitaries, Father Fernando Cardenal—a Jesuit teacher and the crusade's official director—was vowing to put an end to illiteracy in Nicaragua. And all the brigadistas were echoing his vow with their cry of "*Venceremos!*" We will win!

Literacy is fundamental to achieving progress and it is essential to the building of a democratic society where people can participate consciously and critically in national decision-making. You learn to read and write so you can identify the reality in which you live, so that you can become a protagonist of history rather than a spectator.

FATHER FERNANDO CARDENAL, S.J., FEBRUARY 1980*

A few months before the July 1979 triumph of the revolution, a Junta of National Reconstruction had been formed in exile in Costa Rica. It created several working groups to prepare a governmental plan, as well as the plans and programs of the various ministries. Among

---

*Quoted in Valerie Miller, "The Nicaraguan Literacy Campaign," in Thomas W. Walker, ed., *Nicaragua in Revolution* (New York: Praeger, 1982).

these was the educational working group, which drafted a program for the literacy crusade.

Within days after the victory, Father Fernando Cardenal, brother of the poet Ernesto Cardenal, was charged with responsibility for the crusade. A team of five young people with little pedagogical training but with experience in the liberation struggle set about studying different methodologies of basic adult education. They also analyzed the experiences of literacy campaigns throughout the world—Cuba, Peru, Guinea Bissau, São Tomé, and others. The renowned Brazilian educator, Paulo Freire, whose theories on educating the illiterate of the third world were very influential, paid a personal visit in October.

In the end, the project, like the insurrection itself, followed no one model slavishly. It adapted and amalgamated what seemed appropriate to the Nicaraguan reality.

"La Cruzada Nacional de Alfabetización"—a national literacy crusade. The idea was deceptively simple. All those who were at least twelve years old and had received at least a full primary education would be trained to teach all those over ten who had received none.

Adults with family responsibilities, housewives, and younger students would give evening classes to small groups in their own cities or neighborhoods. Others—for reasons of mobility mainly secondary and university students—would be dispatched to the isolated rural zones, areas which had never known teachers or schools. Lodged in the large haciendas or in the peasants' own homes, they would do manual labor with their students during the day and teach reading and writing in the evenings or whenever possible. At the end of five months of intensive study (Spanish being much more regular phonetically than English), the basics would be mastered. All over Nicaragua, the previously illiterate would be reading, writing, and doing basic math.

The ramifications of the project, however, were far from simple. The crusade would bring together the educated and the inarticulate, the committed and the passive, to learn from each other. It was a learning process that would in no way be confined to primers and syllables.

The poor, traditionally sunk in ignorance and passivity, would be learning that the circumstances of their lives *could* be changed—but only when they themselves analyzed what was necessary and possible and organized themselves to make it happen—"to become a protagonist of history rather than a spectator."

It is no accident that so many of the third world's rural poor are illiterate. When lands are in the hands of the few and profits from their plantations depend on large numbers of docile and dependent field hands, there is neither incentive nor encouragement for education; certainly, few peasants would be given technical or managerial responsibilities. Furthermore, the paternalistic, authoritarian political structures of such countries have little use for the participation of the rural or urban work force. Its demands tend to seriously conflict with those few landowners and businessmen in whose interests such systems have developed.

For this reason, another crucial aspect of the crusade was that the "teachers"—generally students from the more privileged sectors of society—would be sharing the lives of Nicaragua's most destitute. In so doing, they would also come to understand the need for fundamental social and economic change in the country. Through this, the Sandinistas hoped to forge a strong union between peasants, students, workers, and urban poor, and to empower and orient these people to see themselves as the inheritors and the beneficiaries of the revolution. They would surely demand profound changes; that was what the overthrow of Somoza had been all about. They needed to understand the political impact of those changes, and they needed to be technically equipped to implement them.

Such a project can be extremely threatening—to those who stand to lose some of their privileges. Surely it was for this reason that none but a popular revolutionary government had ever attempted such a thing. For the Sandinistas it was an urgent political priority, and it would not be without its detractors. Roberto Saenz, one of the crusade's planners and currently Vice Minister of Adult Education, had had four years of experience teaching literacy in semiclandestinity. "It is a political project with pedagogical implications," he explained, "not a pedagogical project with political implications. There are no neutral projects, not in Nicaragua, not in the United States, not anywhere. Every social project carries with it an ideology—in order to maintain a system, to reproduce a system, or to sustain a process of profound change."*

The decision, then, to launch the literacy crusade at the earliest possible date was no whim. With the triumph still fresh, the country was bursting with idealism, with mutual good will. International interest and support, too, were at a peak; for a few more months, Nicaragua would be a favorite child. But the Sandinistas knew that

---

*Interview with Roberto Saenz, June 1982.

this honeymoon wouldn't last forever. Before the tenuous anti-Somoza coalition began to pull apart, it was crucial to seize its momentum, to harness its energy in another common struggle—a struggle whose result would help to consolidate the revolutionary process.

There were other reasons, too, for starting quickly. The war had been traumatic. What better way for young people to make the transition from the violent, nightmare past than to plunge into a profound and positive activity, one honoring the heroes and martyrs of the liberation struggle. And, finally, the carrying out of such an ambitious mobilization would increase the people's respect both for themselves and for the capabilities of their new government.

Matagalpa, the small mountain city where I was living, whence I would be dispatched, was enjoying more than its fair share of carnival and chaos. It was capital of a mountainous department of the same name, some eighty miles northeast of Managua, having a population of 95,000 and an illiteracy rate of 71 percent, the third highest in the country. So the city became the jumping-off point for thousands of brigadistas, and they had been flowing in from Managua since the day before. Now, grouped together with local students who were also awaiting placement, they filled every possible corner of the ample central plaza.

"When are we going?" "Let's get moving!"

Restlessly they fidgeted in their various squadrons, while from the atrium of the cathedral an already hoarse official was struggling to be heard. "Attention! Your attention, please! The 'Ricardo Morales Squadron' from St. Lucas's school, advisor Mrs. Leona Castillo, has been assigned to the hacienda El Tepeyac on the road to El Tuma. Please gather your group and get ready to board the truck."

Where is it? What road? Which truck? "Please, compañeros," the official pleaded from the stairs. "We're doing the best we can to get the transportation organized. Be patient."

"We want to inform the 'Arlen Siu Squadron' from the Rubén Darío Secretarial College that you will not be leaving until tomorrow." Groans from the kids; smiles from already frayed teachers. Another day at home nursing anxiety and frustrated anticipation.

The crusade office, like every other facility in Matagalpa, was filled to capacity. I pushed my way though the mass of teachers still awaiting placement. "Have you figured out where I'm going yet?" I asked Lazo, the skinny, long-haired clerk behind the desk.

"Ah, sí," he responded with maddening calm. Among a crowd of teachers having family problems, health problems, needing to be here, there, anywhere but the outlands, one unattached foreigner was easy to take care of. As a member of the special teachers' corps, the "Red and Black," named for the colors of the FSLN flag, I'd sworn to go wherever they sent me—presumably to the remotest, most godforsaken region of the country. "You're going to be a technical advisor—supervising a squadron of brigadistas in one of the communities outside Muy Muy. The commission office in Muy Muy just called to ask for more advisors. Got your photos?"

"What? Photos? Oh, sure." And there it was. My official identity card with "Destination: Muy Muy" typed on the back. I was in. I ran to show friends waiting outside, hiding a sharp disappointment. Muy Muy was a small town a mere two hours away, connected to Matagalpa by good gravel roads. And though they said I'd be sent out from there to a more isolated community, it seemed just a bit too close, too easy.

My group of brigadistas was on the way from Managua, I was told, and I'd meet them later. In the meantime, I could hop a pickup truck out to Muy Muy with a few teachers and members of the commission who were headed that way. "Fine with me," I said, and went off in search of a ride.

As quickly as it had come, my disappointment was gone. As the crowded pickup bumped down the highway, I gazed euphorically at the postcard-blue sky and the humping hills. Land so rich and empty. Is there anywhere a land as empty as Nicaragua? Dust borne on the hot summer wind caked my face.

During the insurrection, we had learned to take unimaginable risks and to dare against what seemed impossible odds. We learned about organizing and to trust and appreciate people's extraordinary capacity for daring, creativity and perseverance. We were confident, therefore, that we could translate that spirit into the basis for the Literacy Crusade but, in August, we just were not quite sure how.... In one year, we learned a lot.

FATHER CARDENAL*

It had all seemed to happen in such a hurry. Now, as the truck to Muy Muy bumped on—past a sleepy town and on into more dusty

---

*Quoted in Valerie Miller, *op. cit.*

mountains—I reflected back on the process that had gotten us here. First, the brief announcement in August 1979 and the setting up of a tiny, three-room alcove in Managua's civic center. Within six weeks this little center had mushroomed into four full suites of offices, each with its own staff and its own assignment. Divided into teams for publicity, financing, training, and technical preparation, the crew began to tackle the most urgent details: adapting the chosen method for use by untrained volunteer teachers; designing a primer and a simple teacher's manual; finding an efficient way to train thousands of volunteers on all levels; deciding on a practical uniform and a list of minimum basic supplies for each brigadista; fabricating, borrowing, or just plain begging these supplies; planning an organizational network to unite all the rural areas with the city; working out a motif for the crusade to go with the national and international publicity; designing statistical reporting forms. International cooperation abounded in the headquarters office. The staff included one person each from Chile, Costa Rica, Honduras, Peru, and Puerto Rico; two each from Argentina, El Salvador, and Uruguay; three from the United States; and four each from Colombia, Cuba, and Spain. But we hadn't any money! Where would the money come from?

The first job was to find out exactly how many illiterates there were. Typically, such a census takes several years to prepare, and it costs millions to employ data gatherers and analytical specialists. UNESCO (United Nations Educational, Scientific, and Cultural Organization) offered to help with technicians and money, but the Sandinistas couldn't wait: this was a people's war. By October thousands of high school kids were tramping immense distances through the muddy countryside recording names, ages, educational levels, occupations, interest in learning, convenient times for teaching, and, simultaneously, if among the people there were those who wanted to teach, what day, what time, and where. The census was carried out in just one month, for less than $10,000.

How simple it would have been to process all this information by computer, but there were only fifteen of them in the whole country. Using them would have brought financial activity to a halt, so the students processed the questionnaires on the floor of an auditorium. A UNESCO specialist who came from Paris to help plan the census was incredulous when she discovered that it had already been completed. Her evaluation of the results indicated that the technical limitations had had minimal effect on the accuracy of the data.

The reality uncovered by this census was alarming. It revealed approximately 722,000 illiterates over the age of ten—just a bit more than half of the canvassed population. Of these, 21 percent were adolescents between ten and fourteen years of age, a damning indictment of the educational system under Somoza. Illiteracy was especially concentrated in the underpopulated zones of Jinotega, Matagalpa, and Zelaya—the north-central and eastern departments—and in the rural areas in general. Teaching this population, applying the ideal student-teacher ratio of five to one, would require about 120,000 volunteers. Even raising this ratio in deference to the difficult realities, some 25,000 volunteer teachers would be needed within the cities and towns, and some 60,000 more would have to be prepared to spend five months in the countryside.

The census confirmed what the original crusade staff had already suspected. If it were to be a success, the literacy crusade would have to call once again upon a special sector of the country, Nicaragua's youth. What other group was educated enough, patient enough, idealistic enough, and free enough to leave their homes for five months?

It was time, then, to begin organizing the literacy army. High schools were the main recruitment centers, followed by universities, and even—at their own insistence—the fifth and sixth grades. Shock waves echoed through middle-class homes with their traditional, tightly knit family structures as one by one the children presented their requests—or ultimatums. "Mom, sign this paper. I'm going on the crusade."

For a while, it seemed there would never be enough participants, as some Nicaraguan parents looked askance at the prospect of their children marching off to "the jungle." But the propaganda campaign built—marches, hikes, fund-raising dances, slogan contests, music—and, nourished by the kids' own enthusiasm, the needed response began to come.

"Si eres Cristiano / Alfabétice a tu hermano"

If you're a Christian / Teach your brother to read.

"Con Carlos y Sandino / Alfabetizaremos al obrereo y al campesino"

With Carlos [Fonseca] and Sandino / We'll teach the workers and peasants.

The Popular Literacy Army (EPA) was to be made up of units grouped by age and sex, and, where possible, from the same school or other institution. Thirty brigadistas made up a squadron, four squadrons a column, and all the squadrons in one municipality a brigade. Each squadron would have its student leader and second in command, selected from the squad itself. The column leaders would be members of the Sandinista Youth, and they in turn would form part of the high command of each brigade. The squadrons would eventually be dispatched to one of six "battle fronts"—geographic divisions based on the actual fronts of the final insurrection against the dictatorship. Each squadron bore the name of a martyr of the revolution, an important battle, or a famous international figure.

This use of the military metaphor was highly deliberate. First, it built enthusiasm, conferring on the young participants, most of whom had not actually fought in the revolution, a piece of the revolutionary mystique. At the same time, it underlined the seriousness of the mission, linking the literacy campaign with the ongoing political revolution; the enemy now was ignorance. And, finally, it was the most natural model for a general mobilization. Only within a military framework had the moving of so many people in organized units ever before been undertaken.

Of course, neither the kids in the EPA nor their urban counterparts could work without supervision. Their teachers, ten thousand in all—all the primary and secondary teachers in the country—would be accompanying them throughout the crusade as technical advisors, like myself. These educators comprised the first and only group of draftees in the war against illiteracy; as the announcement was made, there was a collective holding of breath. How would the nation's teachers react to this unprecedented new assignment? Leaving their families, putting on blue jeans, and marching off to the countryside— it wouldn't be fun for those who were used to wearing high heels and teaching little children in classrooms. As a group, educators had lived in relative comfort under Somoza. While generally sympathetic to the revolution, they had never been a particularly vocal or combative sector. Some would even feel professionally threatened—the educational process was being turned on its head. How could teachers preserve their status and privileges if their own students were teaching the country to read?

Yet, like the kids, like the parents, there they were, joining in. They were led by ANDEN, the National Association of Nicaraguan Educators, which had been given organizing and coordination responsibilities. With genuine sincerity and an idealism that few would have suspected, they began preparing to teach their "campesino brothers and sisters." Solemnly studying the new techniques, absorbing the new facts, the new perspectives, puffing red-faced up hills on periodic training hikes, the teachers, too, were earning the title of heroes and heroines.

Then it was February. Little by little, the crusade had built, until it was nothing short of a national mania. The crusade offices had spread out into departmental and then municipal branches. There were offices in remote mountain areas where even radios were unknown. Each rural area linked to a small town which linked to a city, all the way back to Managua. And in every area of whatever size there were constant reminders—talkathons, fund-raisers, posters, parades of brigadistas. Even the matchboxes were special—each one bearing a letter of the alphabet with a picture indicating the corresponding sound. No one could so much as light a cigarette in the *"año de la alfabetización"*—the year of literacy—without being reminded of it.

The newspapers carried special daily reports of the fund-raising efforts. "OAS donates $220,000." "Swedish labor unions promise 50,000 lanterns." "Support from the government of Iraq." Nicaraguans learned a new geography as, daily, countries they had never heard of responded to their nation's plea. Meanwhile, within the country itself, kids sold banners, T-shirts, buttons, and Certificates of Patriotic Contribution. Factories such as the Industrial Bread Cooperative of Managua volunteered one day of production for every month of the crusade. Even at the level of the tiny, impoverished local communities, fiestas were held to raise "pennies for pencils." While they were still far, far from raising the $20 million that was the crusade's estimated cost, it appeared that the project would at least be able to move forward.

> *You will be a catalyst of the teaching-learning process. Your literacy students will be people who think, create and express their ideas. Together, you will form a team of mutual learning and human development. . . .*
> CARLOS CARRIÓN, FSLN REPRESENTATIVE
> TO THE LITERACY CRUSADE*

Then it was time to begin the final preparations—the training and the mobilization. The training workshops were impeccably planned two-week sessions with agendas posted in advance. They covered every-

---

*Ibid.

thing from methodology to malaria symptoms, from sanitation to statistics. We discussed the goals of the crusade, practiced teaching by role-playing, simulated the debates we hoped the lessons would encourage, developed songs and sociodramas and practiced collective problem-solving. The stress was on creativity. We learned that there were other tasks for us, too, in this once-in-a-lifetime mobilization. We were to provide an example of better hygiene habits to people who did not make the connection between this and health; we were to collect folklore traditions and note local flora and fauna. We were also to keep a field diary of all our most significant experiences. This idea had come from the valuable journals kept by some of the guerrillas during the years of struggle.

We also contemplated the discipline that would be required of all of us. Privately, but with the knowledge that it was no secret, we each contemplated our own fears as well. What if the water was contaminated where they sent me? Could I survive on just tortillas and beans? Would the counterrevolutionaries really attack as they threatened? What if I got malaria? Would I be courageous enough to stay the five months? Few among us had not lost a relative, a friend, a neighbor; this was the chance of the survivors to pay homage to these dead, to make their own contribution and commitment to the future. For these young inheritors of the revolution, it was a rite of passage.

The workshops were conducted in geometric fashion: 80 outstanding teachers received the initial training; each of these "multipliers" taught 30 more; the resulting 2,400 trained the rest of the nation's teachers; and these teachers, at last, trained the student brigadistas. Each workshop broke into smaller groups for maximum participation in the discussions, with the teachers keeping a low profile. In early March, all schools were closed, making it possible for everyone to attend the training workshops. In this way, it was hoped that some last stragglers might still pitch in.

The final lists were drawn up—who would be stationed in the city, who in the countryside, and who in the emergency child-care centers made necessary by the five-month school closing. The last brigadistas were still signing up—some for adventure, some for dedication, and some because it was said that all who taught in the crusade would pass their own school year. It looked as if there would be enough volunteers.

Finally, the specific placements were arranged. Names of censused illiterates were paired with the various squadrons of brigadistas, ten illiterates per brigadista, thirty brigadistas per squadron. Provinces that had an excess of potential alphabetizers would supply brigadistas to those that had a deficit. In general, younger boys and female students would be sent to areas where the population was centralized, mainly the state farms and the large haciendas, while the older male students would be scattered in zones where isolation was the norm. And the special "red-and-black" squadrons who had volunteered for hardship duty would go wherever they were sent.

Night after night, the offices of the literacy crusade were filled with tired volunteers, painstakingly copying the scrawled census data: names, squadrons, locations, potential hosts. Faces of the curious ringed them as they wrote. "Where am I going?" "Have you got us placed yet?" Parents had been promised information on the exact location of their children's placement before their departure. This meant the preparation of thousands of additional individual tags, the name of a brigadista and the address of his or her peasant host on every one.

Then, before anyone could, turn around, it was The Day, time to go. The mobilization of the brigadistas out to the countryside had been planned for weeks. All transport, all normal activity in the country, virtually stopped. Every bus was commissioned, every government vehicle, every large truck, and as many small private ones as could be begged. Since it was summer,* most of the roads were passable; only the Atlantic coast contingent needed boats and biplanes to reach their destinations. Some of the peasants in the Pacific region, however, lived in such remote areas that there were no roads. To reach them, donkeys and horses had to be borrowed or the brigadistas would have to pack in on foot.

The students were to be dispatched in their columns of 120 to the departmental capitals, there to be reloaded into trucks bound for the municipal centers. From there, they would be parceled out to the rural communities where members of the local militia would guide them to their homesites. Roads were jammed for days.

The plan encompassed all the mass organizations and every willing body in the country, from cooks to uniform-makers to drivers to armed guards. Suddenly, as in wartime, everybody was very impor-

---

*Nicaragua has two seasons—dry, or "summer" (December to May) and wet, or "winter" (May through November).

tant; and as at such times of crisis, nearly everyone responded to the call. People also came from more than fifty other countries; in some cases they were sponsored by their governments, in some by solidarity groups, and in some, like mine, they had come on their own. And now here I was, being helped off the back of a pickup truck onto the cracked sidewalk of Muy Muy.

DIARIO DEL CAMPO

Monday, March 24

Muy Muy, a westernish town of wide low buildings. A several-horse town dusty and hot in the late afternoon. Official population 2500; it seems like less.

Where are the troops, captain? I walk from the baking plaza to the Hotel Very-Very (all the townspeople seem to know that "very" is Engglish for *muy*) and back again to the new offices of the Municipal Literacy Commission, where there are only questions without answers. Where will we put the brigadistas if they come tonight? What if they sent them all on Río Blanco by mistake? Are all the lodgings confirmed in the communities? Are you sure they told you the kids would be here later today? Anyway, they're not sending us enough. Should we send a telegram now to Matagalpa asking for more, or should we wait to confirm the census?

Lazo arrives from the Matagalpa office, does some intermediate calculations and I'm marked for El Jícaro, together with a teacher named Estela. Off he goes again, leaving the office staff still in confusion.

The brief burst of excitement caused by our arrival has already worn off. The afternoon grows hotter and sleepier as I wait and watch blankly. Dirt streets with no cars, a wilted market, and a few tired passers-by. It's a county seat in Iowa on a summer afternoon a hundred years ago. It feels like I'm on the wrong set.

Night now. There are stars and a meeting by lamplight. Muy Muy doesn't have electricity, although some of the shops have their own generator hookups, offering dim beckoning lights and cold drinks from the refrigerator, glass jars of sweets, and bored, aging women behind the counters. Not much to offer.

So we lay our mats out on the bare floor of an empty house, just Estela and me now. There's utter silence in town, and when I blow out this candle it'll be completely dark. Sleep, then. Wait and see.

CHAPTER 2
El Jícaro

Nicaragua is an underpopulated country. Roughly the same size, and even shape, as Wisconsin, it has only half as many inhabitants.

The majority of Nicaragua's 2.5 million people live in the relatively settled strip of humid flatland bordered on one side by the Pacific Ocean and on the other by a range of mountain highlands. This is the agricultural heartland of a country that has little other wealth. It is dotted with volcanos, a few major cities, and vast tracts of cotton, sugar cane, and rice. Those plantations abandoned by the fleeing Somocistas or by Somoza himself have been turned into state farms or peasant cooperatives. The rest remain in the hands of wealthy private landowners. In the very center of this fertile swath is Managua, the sprawling capital. To the northeast is León and to the southeast Granada, picturesque colonial cities that were the strongholds of feuding political parties in the independence period.

Directly northward from Managua, foothills soon become cool highlands, growing ever steeper as they spread into Honduras. Here the hillsides are quilted with rich, velvet-green patches of coffee bushes. To the south, the mountain range narrows to run down along the eastern bank of Lake Managua—itself nearly the size of tiny El Salvador—makes a left-hand turn at the Coast Rican border and deposits itself in the Caribbean. Beyond the range to the east begins the sprawling department of Zelaya, a maze of rivers and jungle lowland stretching all the way to the sea. This is the part—commonly referred to as the Atlantic coast but really more than half of Nicaragua's land mass—that the Spanish colonizers spent three centuries trying to wrest away from its combative Indian inhabitants and their British protectors.

Muy Muy lies in almost the exact geographic center of the country. A two-hour drive southeast of the city of Matagalpa, it's still in the foothills. The rolling landscape is dry but fertile, pleasant but undramatic, livable but not wealthy. In these foothill areas, large expanses of land have been given over to cattle grazing. Between and among the large- and medium-sized ranches are thousands and thousands of small tracts, land from which tenacious peasants coax a bit of corn and beans, and on which they wage a daily struggle for survival.

REPUBLICA DE NICARAGUA

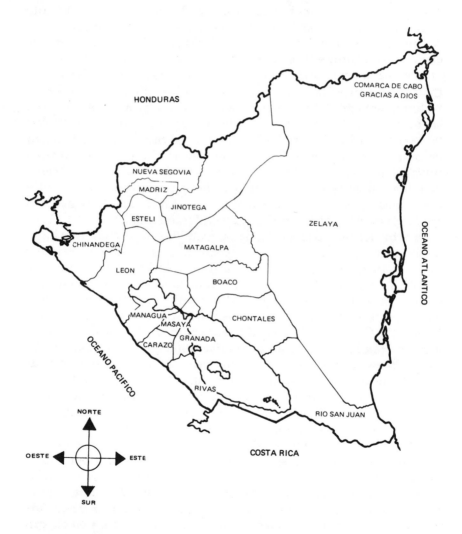

HONDURAS

COMARCA DE CABO
GRACIAS A DIOS

NUEVA SEGOVIA

MADRIZ

JINOTEGA

ESTELI

ZELAYA

CHINANDEGA

MATAGALPA

LEON

BOACO

MANAGUA

MASAYA

CHONTALES

CARAZO

GRANADA

RIVAS

RIO SAN JUAN

OCEANO ATLANTICO

OCEANO PACIFICO

NORTE

OESTE

ESTE

SUR

COSTA RICA

Because the area around Muy Muy had never been prosperous enough to attract Somoza and his followers, or mountainous enough to shelter guerrillas, it had remained almost unaffected by the war and the revolution. There had been refugees, of course, but no combat; rumors, but no substantial changes. A few Somocista holdings had been confiscated, and their cattle operations were now being run by the state. But in these nine months little had changed for the handfuls of workers who tended the herds. For the most part, life continued as before. Farmers lucky enough to have eight-, ten- or even two- hundred-acre plots continued to work them with the help of family members. The less fortunate led their lives as before, as *mozos*—permanent hired hands on the one-thousand-acre ranches— with perhaps an acre or two lent them to raise a subsistence crop of beans and corn. Theirs had been the deadest of dead ends before— no land, no school, no future. Even now, the revolution had brought only a faint shadow of hope—a law requiring a minimum wage of 25 córdobas ($2.50) a day, and the end of the dreaded National Guard. And now a new song on the radio:

> *Campesino, learn to study,*
> *Campesino, learn to read.*
> *Campesino, if you read and study,*
> *It will be yours all the land you seed.*

Before the March sun had sharpened its mid-morning edge, another teacher, Estela, and I had arrived at our final destination. For the first time, and the last, I rode into El Jícaro on a truck, not even suspecting what a rare event it was. From Muy Muy, we had rattled on back toward Matagalpa—fifteen minutes along the highway, a sudden turn off to the right, a series of curves, and a quick fork along a sluggish river. The pickup banged past some seven or eight small houses and pulled up in front of a tiny, pristine brick schoolhouse set smack in the middle of a pasture.

"That's my school!" Estela announced with pride as she hopped off the truck. Kids were already running out from the various shacks to surround her. "The teacher's here!" "*Hola, maestra!*" Hi, teacher!

"You're lucky you're with me," she informed me abruptly. "I've been teacher in this area for a year and a half and I know the zone. That's an advantage others don't have. And this is a good community, really good people. I don't know about the crusade in other places, but you're going to have it easy here, you'll see."

"*Hola, mi amor.*" She had turned to one of the hopping children. "How's your grandmother? Can you ask her to get Migdonio for us? Tell her the teachers need to borrow him for the day. And tell her I send her a hug and a kiss. I'll be over later. How is she? OK? Good, get along, then."

"Poor lady, she lost her husband last month after fifty years of marriage. He was a really great man, Don Chico;* too bad you couldn't have known him. Now let's see how this poor neglected school looks. The community built it with their own money and we inaugurated it just last January. That was some party, it was."

Still talking, she opened the door into a small square room. A table and forty wooden desks were carefully arranged on the dirt floor, and fresh blue paint adorned the door and windows. Though bare, it was better kept than many city schools I'd seen.

"Nice," I murmured.

"Isn't it? Freddy; is your mother home? She's not at the river? Good. Listen, let's go over to Doña Amelia's to eat while we wait for Migdonio. Have you eaten breakfast? I'm starved."

"Yes, we're going over to your house, *amorcito,*" she announced to the small boy named Freddy, who wriggled with excitement. "Let's just leave the stuff here. We have to go all the way to Wapá today, at the other end of the zone. Who knows what time we'll be back. We should borrow some horses, maybe for tomorrow. Can you ride? Well, you'll have to learn. Wait until you see the winters here. Sometimes you can't even get around on a horse. Mud up to your knees around here, and out in Wapá, in the lowlands by the rivers, it's even worse. Well, that'll be your job. Community supervisors don't have to do quite as much moving around as the technicial advisors, thank God. Anyway, I'll help you do this census. We have to confirm the October data and make sure we can lodge all the brigadistas when they come. You're lucky you're with me, all right. Ready for some food before we get started?"

Short, straight auburn hair efficiently framed Estela's light-skinned face, exaggerating her darting brown eyes. The whole wiry package seemed filled with energy. She was thirty-six and had three children.

---

*The polite form of address used in the countryside consists of Don or Doña with the person's first name.

"That's all we wanted," she had confided to me during the truck ride. That was a rare statement from a Nicaraguan woman. Without explaining what had happened to the other half of "we," she had chatted on amiably about herself. Her home was in Managua—"San Judas, the most combative neighborhood in the city." Her mother still lived there, ravaged by diabetes and with both legs recently amputated, the result of loss of circulation. After teaching for sixteen years in Managua, Estela had decided to try the rural zone.

Her voice was startlingly low and loud for such a tiny person, and her manner slightly intimidating despite the joking, easy manner. What was her role here in the community? How would we get along? Her previous reputation would have a great effect on how the crusade and the brigadistas—and I—were accepted here. For the moment, she was our link to community tradition. As I started down the road after her, in the wash of her nonstop conversation, I did feel lucky. At least someone here knew what she was doing.

After breakfast we began walking across a landscape as vast and empty as a daydream. Just beyond the school we left the road. Before us were only burnt hills and herds of cows as far as the eye could see. The countryside surprised me a little. This could be eastern Oregon, or southern Ohio, with its humping hills and dry grass. Far off to the right, the river painted a green swath through all the shades of brown and charred black stubble of last year's crops. Migdonio, a round-faced youth of about eighteen led us, scratching his stomach and chuckling as Estela and I struggled to keep up.

There would be a shack and then nothing, another shack and more nothing, and maybe three shacks together and then more nothing. At each of them we stopped and, while Migdonio rested in the shade, began our work.

"Good morning. How are you, Señora? Good? Good." Pause. "We're here because of the alphabetization. You've heard of it, haven't you? Fine. Well, first of all, we need to confirm the census they did last October. Did they come by here? Good, well...."

It was a routine we'd practiced in the training workshops. We'd done role-playing with everyone from hostile landlords with machetes to women with sick children, but despite the rehearsals, I suddenly got stage fright. I sat dumbly and, while Estela talked, tried to take in this new world.

The shacks were ancient and unpainted, with corroding zinc roofs and dirt floors. Generally, a wooden partition marked off the sleeping area, where the lineup of hammocks, boards, *tijeras,** and, rarely, a bed, gave mute evidence of the family's economic status. In the main room or just off to one side was the kitchen fire, unventilated but for a window opening, with its *comal*—a flat earthenware pan for cooking tortillas—and the inevitable pot of soaking corn. Close by were a hand mill and a heavy stone for grinding. The corn itself was seldom far away. Piles of the dried, unhusked ears filled roofed storage areas or spilled out into the main room itself. Clearly, these were the items that took precedence; whatever space that was left was for sitting.

Some of the huts boasted a rude table with stools; others merely a bench against the wall. A water jug, a few dishes—there was almost nothing else to be seen in the way of possessions. Despite the crowds of children, there were no toys. No pictures on the walls, no glass in the windows, no curtains or mirrors, and, needless to say, no books. The overall effect was one of monastic simplicity.

Outside, it was busier. Chickens, dogs, and sometimes pigs ran free. Although some of the yards had small fruit trees or flowers, these were the exception. In most, the children and animals had picked the area clean. Oddly, I could see no sign of cultivation, only miles and miles of pastureland.

We were highly visible as we moved across this plain, and long before we approached each house, I could hear the children screaming the news. The little ones watched us with huge absorbent eyes, mute behind their mothers. The older ones ran to join us until soon we were something of a mob on march across the prairie of Wapá.

The sun baked the sense out of my head; I lost all awareness of movement. By midday I was far too sunburnt and exhausted to accept any of the food or drink that was unfailingly produced for us—the oranges, hot tortillas, beverages of toasted cornmeal, watered and sugared. The eyes that watched us were solemn, silently taking notes and making unfathomable judgments. "Impenetrable as stones," Che Guevara had once said of Latin America's peasantry.

Came the moment in our speech when we had to ask the big question: "We don't know yet whether boys or girls will be coming, but... would you possibly be willing to take in a brigadista?" I squirmed in my chair—it seemed such a terrible imposition. For one thing, it

---

*A cot formed of a minimal frame crossed by strips of sacking. It opens and closes, scissors fashion, hence the name *tijera*, or scissors.

just didn't seem possible that these shacks could fit another person. For another, it was only too clear that food was severely limited. How could these poor peasants feed a hungry teenager?

Yet the response was almost universally sympathetic. "I think so," most of them said, or "Maybe we can." Some suggested a neighbor who had more room, and some wanted to consult with their men or women. In several houses the lineup of potbellied children—a clear sign of malnutrition—was evidence enough that the question would be superfluous. But most of the replies were positive. Like the people in the cities, they were eager to participate. They'd like a pretty girl brigadista, they joked, but they'd settle for whoever came.

In one minuscule shack, a small, delicate-looking man named Chavelo Cruz assured us with great intensity that we could count on him for whatever we might need. There were seven children counting on him already, and it looked like there'd be eight within the month, yet he refused our suggestion that the brigadista stay somewhere else. "No, it's more convenient here. I know how to read a little, but the children need to advance." Another of the shacks was 99 percent full of corn, but here, too, the campesino we met, a tall, dynamic young man named Arturo, was eager for a brigadista. He questioned us closely about every phase of the crusade, revealing a restless intelligence that set him apart from his neighbors.

"We have to go as far as old Sí-sí-cómo-no's place," Estela remarked several times as an exit line, provoking delighted giggles from her audience each time.

"What's that?" I asked her later.

"Oh, a local resident with the regrettable custom of repeating certain expressions to excess." Her answer wasn't very enlightening, yet in the expression, in the snickers, there was something a bit furtive. Whoever he was, he didn't seem to be anyone's favorite.

We were on our way back, crossing the wooded stretch, when we met him—a wiry old man, white-haired and graceful on his horse. Shadows of the somber *chilomate* trees slanted past us as Estela stopped to chat, joking about the fiesta last January. Why hadn't he wanted to dance with her? "Sure, right," he repeated playfully at pauses, turning to spit on the ground. He obviously found her flirtatious kidding delightful, but when the conversation turned to the loan of horses, his laughter became slightly forced, and it was his turn to pause. "Why don't you ask someone back at the other end, closer to you," he finally answered. Abruptly he turned and rode off, leaving in my mind a frozen image—the late afternoon light through the trees, the vast presence of prairie, the curiously dominating figure, now growing smaller in the distance. The stillness was broken by the howling of Congo monkeys. So that was the popular Mr. "Sure-sure-why-not."

By six o'clock the sun had set and we were still walking, guided now only by thin clear moonlight and by Migdonio's sure instincts. We made our way up a long hill capped by a leaning tree whose branches were a lacy silhouette far in front of us. I trudged forward doggedly, moving by pure willpower.

"Where are we? Is this the gate to the school?"

"No, we have a ways to go yet," explained Migdonio. "This is the uphill path back to El Jícaro. I'm taking you here so you'll know it when winter comes and the lower road floods." Estela groaned. I was too tired even to do that.

At last they reappeared, the school and the brick house we'd be staying in. We listened for voices as we approached. Had they come yet? But no—no brigadistas. The valley lay shrouded and still. By 8:15 I was stretched head-to-foot with Estela on our *tijera*; by 8:30 the noises of the other members of the household settling down for the night were far, far off. I lay like a rock in the vast silence.

There was another day of walking, and yet another before us. On that first day we had cut a swath down the length of the zone and circled through the more densely populated area to the east, where the Wapá River cuts off from the Old Matagalpa. On the second day we headed toward the hilly western extreme, step by painful step, under the same sun, through the same baking landscape. The path became more mountainous, until we came at last to a small settlement of houses and fields scattered across several cleared slopes.

"Where are we?" I asked Estela.

"Still Wapá," she said, "but another part. I don't know it very well, to tell the truth. All this will be your area." My head was swimming and I felt sick. Looking up, I could just make out the figure of Migdonio, a tantalizing black dot, far, far, ahead. He was approaching a genuine oasis, orchards of green trees rising from the dry slope.

"Oh, I know where we are now," Estela mused. "This is where Doña María Elsa lives."

She came running out of the house to greet us as we approached, a large woman with light complexion and clear, bright eyes. Her smile was broad and delighted as she herded us into the house, talking a mile a minute. Inside were the usual bare boards and dirt floor, but there was also a treadle sewing machine, and bright magazine clippings were pasted to the walls for decoration. There seemed to be hundreds of children, more children than I'd seen anywhere. One was sent to pick some oranges and make a drink; another was dispatched to help make candy; another to look for eggs; yet another to check on the baby, who was crying. During all this, two little girls of about two or three maintained a vigil from behind their mother's skirt, giggling loudly as they peered out at us.

Here there was no need to launch into our prepared speech. María Elsa knew exactly why we'd come and set out to give us a royal welcome. She directed the candy-making; dug us up pieces of *quisquique*, a kind of wild parsnip; pressed out cheese from the container of curdled milk; made tortillas; showed off the dishes she had carved from gourds—all the while keeping the chickens out of the house and rocking any of the six or seven small children. She'd had seventeen, she told us; twelve were living, five dead.

The orchards of mango, orange, lime, and lemon trees were all her doing, as was the yuca root planted in puddles by the stream where they'd also rigged a shower out of an old hose. There was an outhouse, too, on the property, the first I'd seen. She and her husband actually owned their own land, unlike the campesinos we'd met yesterday, and they'd taken advantage of it. In addition, she told us, she sewed and made candy to sell, knew the medicinal plants and delivered babies. "People who know how to work," she quoted proudly, "never lack the necessities."

After a huge lunch, she offered to guide us around the immediate area. We set off alone, despite outraged howls from the children left behind. More burnt pastures, more hills and sunlight, more shacks of sticks and dirt. The houses were closer together here, but because of the hills the walking was difficult. More dark faces, some welcoming, some cautious. A grizzled older man greeted us on the porch of his tiny hillside hut. "Cuál es la nota que se trae?" he demanded to know, using a slang remark that the rest found hilarious. (Roughly, "What's the scoop here?") Nevertheless, he was the first campesino to rebuff us directly.

"Nope, not interested," he said firmly. "Too old. For the kids it's fine, but it's no use to people like me." Estela pressed the matter further, insisting that she was going to send him a beautiful young girl to take him in hand. He wouldn't budge. "Nope, it's not for me."

"Old Agapito Cruz..." Doña María Elsa shook her head as we walked away. "He's a fine person, but he sure is stubborn."

On the third day, we crossed the Old Matagalpa River behind the school to visit the crumbling hacienda El Esquirín, then crossed back down to canvass the more affluent houses along the dirt road from the highway. It was early for once as we headed homeward to total our scrawled figures.

All told, we had counted approximately 182 illiterates over ten years old, a good-sized task for the fifteen to twenty brigadistas we were expecting. But, for now, it was time to sit back and take a breath. Pooling the data, the sketches, and the shifting impressions of the last several days, I was able, at last, to compile a rough picture of my new community.

The territory of El Jícaro could be divided into three more or less separate areas, including Wapá. The area around the highway—the part historically known as El Jícaro—was the oldest and most prosperous. This was the section we had covered during the morning. Here were eight or ten good-sized family farms and, along the gravel highway itself, the more extensive properties—perhaps up to a thousand acres each—belonging to Pancho Martínez and Rito Gonzales. Martínez, like many Nicaraguan landowners, had parcels in neighboring communities, so it was impossible to tell how prosperous he was, but he was certainly one of the larger fish in this little pond, with several *mozo* families dependent on him. The community of El Jícaro had been able to raise enough money for the school, thus bringing primary education to the area for the first time. And, being nearer the road, it also had access to transport, and to the things transport could carry. Here Doña Mencha Meruillo, Migdonio's great-aunt, sold her bread and warm Coca-Cola—unthinkable luxuries further back. And here, too, was the cantina where ancient Don Valerio maintained his stocks of alluring Ron Plata, the cheaper of the two well-known brands of Nicaraguan rum.

An hour's gentle climb from El Jícaro brought one to the sloping hills where Doña María Elsa lived, surrounded by perhaps fifteen other *parcelarios*, or small-plot owners. Here the farms ranged in size from eight to about fifteen acres. Not a good living, and not much spare cash, to be sure, but with a few cows and chickens, enough to

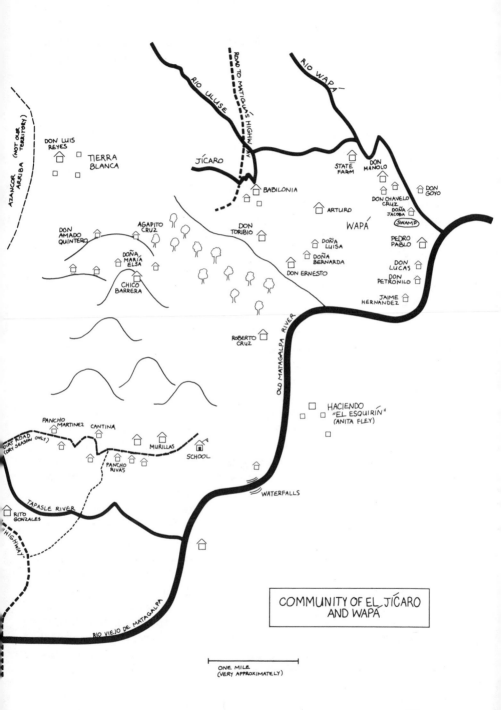

COMMUNITY OF EL JÍCARO
AND WAPÁ

ONE MILE
(VERY APPROXIMATELY)

provide a healthy diet for the children. Given a bit of luck and a good harvest, one got by without having to go out and work for wages, perhaps by selling surplus corn or a slaughtered pig to the neighbors. Those slightly wealthier hired workers themselves during harvest time. This was the economic sector that needed the most persuasion about the value of the revolution. Shaken by wild tales of "communism" and rumors of confiscation, they trembled in fear of losing the little they had.

The flat, rich plain of Wapá, demarcated on three sides by rivers, comprised pure feudal fiefdoms—an utterly obvious economic chessboard. There were six big landowners, four of them absentee. First was Anita Fley, who lived in Muy Muy. She owned the hacienda El Esquirín on the rambling cattle land that fronted the eastern banks of the "Old River." She also owned the miserable shacks of Roberto Cruz and Toño Ortega, as well as those of the ten or so farmhand families resident on the hacienda itself. Her sister-in-law, Cloris, had a series of parcels in the river section that I would later call the "back corridor," which she rented out to tenant farmers. She, too, lived outside the community, and seemed to have other properties elsewhere. The remote hacienda Babilonia, on the other side of the plain, included several networks of resident families amid acres and acres of fertile bottomland. The luxurious cement house of the owner was boarded and closed—"FSLN" was scrawled across one wall—but the land itself continued to belong to its old owner, now in Matagalpa. Similarly, the opulent house of Ramón Arrancibia stood half empty, ownership unchanged. These ranches were run by hired administrators. One large cattle spread along the Uluse River had been taken over by the government, but its pastures and workers were on the other side of the river, and hence not in our territory.

Then there were the two resident ranchers. The miserable wooden mausoleum of Ernesto Membreño, from which he and his four sons ran their small, three-hundred-acre empire of perhaps a hundred cattle, a few horses, and an oxcart team, stood as the southern sentinel of the valley. At the north end, near the state farm, was the equivalent spread of Ramón Arrancibia's uncle, Don Manolo—old Sí-sí-cómono. Each commanded half of the pastureland in the middle, and each had a sizable cornfield as well. Between them, and on all sides, huddled the various *mozos* who worked the lands of these six, perhaps forty families in all, in their monotonously similar shacks. The *mozos'* existence consisted of trying to scratch enough food from their one-acre plots to supplement the scant daily wages—when they were paid daily wages, when there was work.

The entire community, along with most of the Nicaraguan countryside, had nothing in the way of running water, motor transport, electricity, or medical care. The haciendas themselves were distinguishable only by their relative size and their wooden floors, not by any modern conveniences. Even an outhouse was a sign of unusual industriousness.

Lack of effective irrigation equipment limited them all to one harvest a year, despite the proximity of good-sized rivers. Movement within the area was on foot or horseback, along paths known only to the residents themselves. To reach Muy Muy or Matagalpa meant several hours' travel along these paths just to get to the highway. In the rainy season, which would commence in May, the rivers would rise on all sides and movement within and beyond the community would virtually stop. A few basic items—cigarettes, sugar, aspirin—were brought in from time to time by ambitious residents and resold to their neighbors. The rest was done without. On a minimum wage of $2.50 a day, there wasn't much you could buy anyway.

This was the over-all picture that our brigadistas, and all the others, would be seeing for the first time. This world—silent, scattered, primitive—was as unfamiliar to these teenagers from the urban centers as it would be to teenagers from another country. And my fatigue, my amazement, as I walked around it for the first time would be little different from theirs. In many ways, we were all foreigners.

CHAPTER 3
The Troops Arrive

Where were the brigadistas? Five days had gone by, now six, and still no word. For the first few days, the radio carried special reports of brigadistas' departures, but now these bulletins, too, had ceased. We were left alone with our data sheets, our provisional placements, and our worries. Could we have been forgotten somehow? And, worse yet, the next day, Sunday, was the start of Easter week, the holiest week in all of Latin America. Nobody would move after Sunday, unless it was to go to Muy Muy to see the big procession.

There was nothing to be done. Estela left early Saturday to spend the holiday weekend with her family. I sat alone, studying and restudying the prospective class groupings, while my memory of their locations grew dimmer. How many households could we squeeze into one class? What about the family of four whose yard became a small island when the river rose? What about the isolated hilltop where there were three illiterates and nowhere to house a brigadista? How could we reach everybody? It was like trying to do a jigsaw puzzle without knowing what the finished picture was supposed to look like.

What if they gave a literacy crusade and nobody came?

Sunday arrived—March 30, Palm Sunday. *Rosquillas* everywhere—fragrant biscuits of corn and cheese topped with burnt sugar. I was chewing one by the river when Don Chavelo, the thin, eager man with all the children, burst out of the coffee grove behind me.

"They're coming! I saw them in town today, *maestra*! All boys. They'll be here by afternoon. Yes, absolutely for sure. Late today, they said, or tomorrow at the latest. Remember, we're at your service in anything you might need."

A few hours later they were piling off the truck, pushing and shouting—an uncountable mass of teenage boys.

"Is this it?" "Yay! We're here at last!"

*"Profe,** we spent five *days* at our school waiting for our placements! How come it took so long?"

"Profe, they didn't give me a hammock."

"Profe, we don't have any pencils, only the other group got them."

"What happened to my brother? He got on the other truck by mistake."

"Profe, can we go now?"

"I'm in charge of this group," I was brusquely informed by a handsome, dark-skinned boy of about sixteen who introduced himself as Miguel, "and we all need to go to Bonifacio Quintero's. Is it far?"

"Huh?" Sure enough, they were all happily waving their placement papers from Managua—six for one shack, seven for another, and five for a poor peasant who had been told that the brigadistas were all atheists and didn't want to house even one.

"Where is it, *profe*? Can we go now?"

"Wait a minute. I have other locations for you. Just let me get your names." I began frantically looking for my notebook. "How many are you, anyway?"

"Dunno, *profe.*" Nobody seemed to know. "About fifteen, I think. Our squadron was thirty, but they split us up in Muy Muy and then they put this other group in with us. Ramiro, how many with you?"

"Uh, six. No, seven, I think."

By the time I had rounded up my notebook and the census sheets, there were all of two brigadistas left by the school.

"They went to the river to bathe," Ramiro, the one in charge of the second group, explained hesitantly. I preferred not to think about the brigadista reported drowned on Friday, the second day of the crusade, deep in the eastern jungle zone.

And the militia members who had promised to act as guides? "They're off playing baseball."

"Don't worry, *profe,*" Miguel assured me. "We'll just spend the night here in the school."

"No, no. I've got your placements organized, I really do," I said, waving my sheets of names and locations, and trying to give an impression of calm control. Never mind, I comforted myself, it's a confusing time for the whole country.

---

*Profe, pronounced *pro-fay* and short for *profesora*, is considered somewhat more polite than the equivalent "teach," but not as formal as *maestra*.

The kids were coaxed up from the river at last, and the militia decided to call off the game. We began the work of distributing the brigadistas. An older boy for the cantina—there'd be drinking there. Some younger kids for the hacienda El Esquirín—they could house four. Who wants Bernarda Ocampa? How about Chavelo Cruz? It was a bizarre sort of lottery, but it worked. Before the sun had sunk too low, the last groups were walking up the hill, their makeshift dufflebags bobbing on their backs. "Oh, it's just around the bend," their campesino guides were telling them. I didn't have the heart to tell them that the "bend" was some three hours away. A few of the boys gazed longingly back at the little schoolhouse, a last tie with civilization, with the city. Then they were over the hill and gone. I was alone again.

Toward evening I found Ramiro and we walked down the road toward the hacienda to check on his group. He was a tall, quiet, serious boy with a mop of dark hair that flopped in his face as he walked. He was new as a squadron leader, he told me, and a little concerned about his group.

"Well, what I'm worried about is deserters," I confessed. "I wonder if all these kids will really go through with it."

"Yeah," he answered quietly, "I guess everyone feels a little over-whelmed tonight." Something in his tone made me turn to look at him.

"You're not going to leave us, are you?"

He laughed briefly. "Of course not! But I don't know about these others."

One young brigadista was already asleep on a bench, his new mother watching him proudly. The kids from the hacienda were splashing in the river, and another brigadista, Mario, with his nearly shaven head and round child's face, was running out to join them. I was startled to see him; he couldn't be more than twelve.

We found the last member of Ramiro's group busily moving pots of plants around a spacious yard. He'd be teaching the hired hands while living in the boss's house with all the comforts of home. "It's nice," he said, but his smile was thin. Although he looked as young as Mario, he was obviously trying hard to maintain an air of maturity. Ramiro patted him gently on the back as we left, and as he stood there, alone in the empty yard, I realized that he was trying hard not to cry. Five months suddenly seemed like a very long time.

But there was no point pondering that now. I had some moving to do, too. The taciturn family Estela and I had been staying with now had a brigadista as well, and I happily seized the excuse to move into the house of Doña Chenta Murillo across the way. Migdonio's grandmother's house, it was classic—sprawling rooms full of children and grandchildren; pigs, dogs, chickens, cows; a grapefruit tree in the yard; and something always cooking in the kitchen. Everyone here already knew how to read, but they had proudly agreed to house *la profesora*—"because we've always cooperated," and because it would bring them prestige in the community.

Bidding goodnight to Ramiro, I dropped gratefully onto the outside bench of my new lodging. Red-summer twilight over the pasture; I watched it deepen, smiling smugly to myself. Twenty-two brigadistas—I could finally count their names. They were really here, and lodged! We were ready to go.

Unfortunately, despite Sunday's euphoria, the placement wrangles were far from over. Monday there was an early morning news flash, brought again by good old Don Chavelo, who had heralded the arrival of the brigadistas. The news was that a splinter group of seven boys from yet another squadron had arrived by the back road into Wapá the night before. They were now encamped at Don Ernesto's spread, awaiting placement. Where should they go?

All our scheduled lodgings were now occupied. Off to check the new arrivals—a very mixed group, led by Narciso, a pudgy, pale brigadista who appeared to be in his mid-twenties.

"We're the Red and Black Squadron 'Armando Bonilla' from Managua," Narciso informed me, "and we have to stay together."

More censusing then, rechecking some who'd said "maybe," and a survey of our farthest base. By nightfall, all but two of the new arrivals had a home. Once again, order had been restored, for the moment.

Two more days in the field, sweating breathless behind Doña María Elsa. Working out the last lodgings, she led me farther afield yet, to places we had missed in the census. I could hardly keep up with this super-woman. On she marched under the blazing sun, hatless and tireless, all the while delivering a nonstop discourse on the plants, animals, customs, geology, and history of everything and everybody.

We stopped for a short while at a wake. A child had died during the night, and, as is the custom, the body was laid out amid flowers so the neighbors could come by and pay their respects. I was surprised at how cheerful everyone was. Apparently it was a common enough event.

I discovered yet another corner of our territory, the foot of the steep hill that sloped down from Agapito Cruz's shack. A lush, beautiful pocket dotted with fruit trees of every kind; four little shacks, reasonably close together. Don Luis Reyes, a white-bearded patriarch who looked more like a retired philosophy professor than a campesino, was eager to fill his empty house with a brigadista. "Then me and my wife could practice some, too, even if we don't see so well anymore." I decided to dispatch Raúl from the Red and Black Squadron out there.

Then there was Fernando. A strangely sullen boy, he abruptly informed me that he wouldn't stay with Juan Polanco, where he had been assigned, and that if I tried to make him, he would just leave. I was left with my mouth agape until, a few minutes later, Doña María Elsa drew me aside.

"We had to tell him!" she stage-whispered. "There was a terrible murder committed here. The man and his two sons were cut up and left to die! Imagine that! My sons found old Don Miguel while he was still alive and he told them all right. 'It was Juan Polanco that did it,' he told them."

"But that's unbelievable! Couldn't you take him to court?"

"No, no, it wasn't like that, but we know it was him all right."

Looking over the peaceful hills, I found the story incredible, but it was obvious I couldn't put Fernando with the Polancos. Instead, he would have to stay with a generous neighbor and walk over to the other house when it was time for classes. He was amenable but ominously quiet about the whole deal.

When I got back to the school to fill Estela in on my day, I learned that hers hadn't been exactly uneventful. One of the other kids had reportedly changed his lodgings, I wasn't sure where or why, and Miguel had spent the night in Muy Muy without permission, so now everyone else wanted to go, too, and there were at least ten brigadistas at the school during the day, Estela said, with ten different problems, and we had three pencils per brigadista and half the campesinos were gone anyway for Holy Week, and...

DIARIO DEL CAMPO

Tuesday, April 1

There was a moment today, a sight that stopped me dead in my frenzied race behind Doña María Elsa. Late afternoon, sun just getting low—and there in back of the dilapidated shack near the gate, the first class beginning. On a bench against the wall, five or six campesinos sit intently, books open on their laps. The tiniest children crawl about a piece of plastic that has been set out for them, while other children, still too young to study, pull impatiently at their mothers' skirts. With equal impatience they are brushed away. "Be good now, mother's studying." The brigadista standing before them all with extraordinary naturalness— explaining, helping, guiding the work-roughened hands. Dark faces squinting in the lowering sun, dark fingers tracing the letters.

It's one of the houses that doesn't have a table, and they're sharing the few pencils there are and it's the holiest week in the country—some of the peasants don't even milk their cows during this week, I've heard. But, there they are, starting. Infinite patience in the gestures, a kind of transcendance. Eternal postures of teacher and student formed against that vast sweep of pasture, those far-off hills.

After the first step, we won't ever stop walking.

RICARDO MORALES AVILES,
REVOLUTIONARY LEADER
CAPTURED AND ASSASSINATED,
SEPTEMBER 18, 1973

BOOK TWO

APRIL
Digging In

In April, in Nicaragua, the fields are dry.
It's the month of field-burning.
Of heat, and pastures covered with embers
And the hills which are carbon-covered;
Of the hot wind and the air that smells of burning
And of the fields blue-tinted by the smoke
And the dust-clouds of the tractors clearing;
Of river beds dry as roads
And the branches of trees bare as roots.
Of the suns blurred and red as blood
And the moons, huge and red as suns,
And, at night, the far-off burning, like stars.

ERNESTO CARDENAL, *HORA 0*

Profe, do you really think they can learn to read in five months?

MIGUEL, APRIL 2, 1980

The first month was a month of discovery. The ambitious structures and channels of the crusade, mounted on a base of enthusiasm and improvisation, were now to be put to the test. The mobilization had been a huge success, the objectives were neatly laid out, the methods had been thoroughly explained, and most of the materials were on their way. On paper it looked terrific; in practice we were to learn the meaning of the term "field expediency."

April brought problems that no one could have anticipated. It exposed all the gaps in the system—difficulties in communications, the sketchiness of the original training, the immaturity of the brigadistas, problems with health. We scratched for immediate solutions and clamored for supplies that had been overlooked. And all with a sense of urgency, for May would bring the rains, and what was now merely difficult would then become virtually impossible.

Yet this first month was also a time of joy. We had taken the first step—and we were still walking. All the campesinos would learn to write their names; every brigadista would learn to hold a machete. Nothing short of that would do.

The Brigadista's Manual
I. Objectives of the National Literacy Crusade
a. Eradicate once and for all the social phenomenon of illiteracy in Nicaragua.
b. Promote a process of awareness at the national level, so that our formerly marginated masses can integrate freely and effectively in the democratization process and take an active part in national development and reconstruction.
c. Contribute to national unity, integrating the country with the city, the worker with the student, the Atlantic with the rest of the country, etc.
d. Continue, immediately after wiping out illiteracy, with the education of adults, creating the Vice Ministry of Adult Eduction.
e. Facilitate the development of the New Nicaraguan Society, eliminating the evils that derive from illiteracy.
f. Contribute to the awakening of the newly literate through their closer contact with national events.
g. Carry out complementary investigations which will help us appreciate more than cultural and natural richness of our country.

CHAPTER 4
Uncertain Start

On Wednesday I learned that Rafael had gone. I followed his squad leader, Ramiro, across the long flat field to the small farm where he'd been placed. There the señora wordlessly showed us into the bare room with the primers and pencils neatly lined up, reminding me somehow of the wake I'd been to the week before. There wasn't much to the story, but she told it anxiously, as if we might accuse her of somehow driving the boy away. "...and in the morning he was gone. There were two or three of them, I think."

Hurriedly, I assured her that we in no way held the family responsible and that we'd send another brigadista as soon as possible. Then I hustled Ramiro out and back toward the school, quizzing him closely. Two or three of them?

Well, Orlando was Rafael's cousin and wanted to go home. Maybe he was the other one. Mario, the twelve-year-old who had bounced off to the river the first afternoon, and Guillermo were still at the hacienda, but they were talking flight, too.

Stopping briefly by my house for my notebook, I learned that Doña Chenta had heard the news, too. "Poor little fella. My grandson Ricardo saw him sitting on the bridge early this morning, crying his eyes out. These little boys just get desperate to see their mamas, that's what." We headed off to the hacienda.

"No, *profe*, honest, I wouldn't take off." Mario's high voice was just a little too reassuring. Mounted gleefully on his horse, he looked like a ten-year-old playing cowboy. "And if I did go, I'd come back. I even told Doña Luisa that I'll come back in August to see them after the crusade's over and we go home. Is that all you wanted?" And with a yell, he was off in pursuit of his new brother, giggling as he bounced in the saddle.

"I just wanted to go for a few days, that's all." Guillermo's eyes gleamed oddly from under the plastic visor he wore. "I don't have anything to do anyway until Monday, and I got some stuff at home I want to bring. Who told you I wanted to take off?" A slightly abashed grin, half confession, half denial.

It was Orlando, though, who was hurting the most—such a tiny boy, with wide serious eyes. "Rafael's my cousin. Yeah, I knew he was going to go. He wanted me to go, too, but I said no. You remember I told you how we were talking about going to El Salvador? Well, I thought, how could I go to El Salvador if I can't even stay here? Anyway, it's our duty as revolutionaries to help the oppressed here. Are you a Catholic? Well, Jesus said to love our brothers, and that means I have to sacrifice myself even if sometimes I want to go home. Have you ever read about Che Guevara, *profe*? He was an internationalist. That's what I want to be. I could lend you the book if you want."

It was almost night when Orlando's bravado broke down, and his smooth delicate face twisted with conflict. "Sometimes I think I just can't take it. Only at night. But I know how important it is and no matter how much it hurts I'm going to try and stay." Che and revolution and God, a dedication he wasn't quite big enough for yet. He'd asked too much of himself. I had to contain the impulse to hug him and tell him to go on home and be a child for another year or two. Instead, I reminded him how much we needed him, how important it was that he stay.

"I know," he said, and as I walked away, I found myself thinking of all the Nicaraguan children who had left their childhoods behind for the revolution, and how many never came back to finish them.

Meanwhile, Estela's trip to Muy Muy brought less than reassuring news. No materials had arrived, no other help, and classes were to be suspended for the rest of Easter week. How were we going to keep the brigadistas from running if there was no immediate reason to stay?

"Stay in your places." The order came over the radio, in the newspapers, through the official bulletins. "Brigadistas, remain in your battle trenches." The Minister of Education issued a patriotic call to all the teachers of Nicaragua not to leave the kids alone in the days of Holy Week. Well, I had nowhere to go. But the kids?

The answer wasn't long in coming. One by one they began slipping off. The news reached me as a steady stream of rumors.

"Raúl and Elvis took off."

"Roberto was seen drunk in Muy Muy."

"Jorge's father came and took him away. Only for the weekend, I think..."

Indeed, the visits I made were notable for the absence of brigadistas. We were faced with a flight—permanent or temporary, it was hard to say. If only Easter hadn't been the first week of the crusade...if only we had known each other better...if only we had had better communications.

But there it was. Four days under our belts and a major desertion. While I recognized that the trouble lay in a combination of bad timing and tempting placement—after all, the trip to Managua just wasn't that difficult—it was hard not to feel discouraged. If the kids couldn't discipline themselves after only four days, how were we going to control this thing? And if we *started* this way, what would the next months bring?

And, most important of all, how many would come back?

But for the moment, there was nothing to do but wait and see. Once again I found myself alone by the river, as if the events of the past week had been a dream. But it was easier now. I knew where I was, and I could use the time getting to know my new family.

The Murillos. It was always Migdonio who was up first, turning on his radio long before dawn; but by the time I straggled out of bed to meet the sunrise, they were all up. The three women—the recently widowed Doña Chenta, her daughter Guillermina, and plump Gloria, married to Doña Chenta's son Chico—would all be clustered in the ample kitchen, milling the corn and patting out the tortillas, helped by the three little girls, whom I still couldn't tell apart. Ricardo would be milking and the littlest boys busily chasing the pigs into the forested back yard. Despite the early hour, the neighbors would soon be stopping by, and the house must be made decent to receive them. Movement to and from the house was almost continuous. This was the first family to settle in the valley and the closest thing to community leaders that there was.

Despite the abundance of life in the house, the chief figure here was a ghost. It was Don Chico senior, Doña Chenta's husband, who had died just three weeks earlier. His figure and legend pervaded the household, from the scrawled words he left on the blackboard to the nightly reminiscenses. "Eighty-eight years old when he died and just as strong as he could be, right up to the end. He went fast, he did, at the last. 'My time's come,' he said, and within three days he was dead. Ah, you should have known him, though. He taught us all to read. He knew a little about everything. Put this map up here and these words on the blackboard. Used to change them every week or so. He wrote books, too, books and books, but just gave them all away. Now we don't even know who has them."

He was a living figure to them, but to me he was history. It was Doña Chenta who fascinated me, there in her black dress, looking out past the road to the distant pastures and beyond to the hills near the highway. She appeared to see other things as she sat and watched the dry blue sky.

"Yep, winter's coming. They're hard, the winters here. We can't even leave the house sometimes, that path there gets so muddy and slippery. But wait till you see how beautiful it is when the corn starts and the tender beans—the *camaguas*. You can look out here and the whole field is little green shoots. Don Chico used to love it. If you'd only heard how he used to talk about it when the first seeds started to grow." Her parched face would soften as she spoke and her eyes would light, trying to communicate the love of almost fifty seasons of watching the land.

"I was about seventeen when I married and him already well seasoned. When we came out here, there was nothing. You couldn't hear a neighbor's cock crow from here. Now it's practically a town. But I remember when my first was just a *cipote*—younger than this one here—and I was big with my second. He'd be out there working all day and me here by myself, drawing water from that river and listening to the Congo monkeys howling. Pure jungle it was. You think I didn't get desperate?

"Ah, but it's all over now. When you lose your life's companion...And my children—fourteen I had, and eight living—now only these two here with me. That's the worst for a mother, when your sons leave you. That's what really hurts."

At this, the light in her eyes would die, leaving two dark pools in a sagging face. It was then she would turn away to swat at the little boys. "Have some manners, Jairo! Go play out back." "Children weren't this insolent in my day," she would tell me, as grandmothers have said and will say till the end of time.

The five children belonged to Doña Guillermina, a robust, handsome woman in her mid-thirties. She was a widow, too. Her husband had been killed in an encounter of random violence, a violence all too common in the Nicaraguan countryside before the revolution.

"He left one day and then they told me he was shot. No, I never found out. I don't think he was with the Sandinista Front, he wasn't that kind. I was six months pregnant with Jairo when he died."

Doña Guillermina had a more cosmopolitan air than the women around her. "It's hard being without a man," she confided, "but finding a good man in the country isn't easy either." Maybe that's why she made such frequent visits to the city, she and the little girls, in their immaculate identical dresses of bright-colored cotton.

Don Chico, Jr., was the new head of the household, and apparently not quite sure that he was ready for the job. He was a quiet, meek man with an unusually high voice, quiet, that is, when he was sober. When drunk, as he was regularly, the words would come tumbling out. He was proud at these moments, and touchy. He wanted, I thought, to be who his father was and couldn't.

"Go to bed," Doña Chenta would order him curtly.

"No, Mama, I want you to know that I love you. I don't want you to be sad for my papa. I'll take care of you."

"You'd make me less sad if you'd just go lie down. Here, I'll fix you some beans and then you go to bed."

This, plus the constant procession of visitors and relatives, was the family unit. Though there were no luxuries here, the Murillos were considered enviably prosperous. Through several lifetimes of hard work, they had managed to acquire a good-sized fertile farm and a small herd of cattle. To them the revolution was just a better way of doing things. It had brought, or threatened, no great changes, but "It has made things more decent." They cooperated with it as they had always cooperated in community projects, holding fiestas to aid the school, and now housing me, the teacher. They were also helping organize the new local CDS—one of the neighborhood-based Sandinista Defense Committees spawned in the final stages of the war. The role of the CDS now was partly to protect the community from remnants of the National Guard and partly to be the people's link to the new government.

It was secure in their curiously ordered world. At night, after the family rosary, I lay on my cowhide bed, which used to be Don Chico's, falling peacefully asleep as I listened to Doña Chenta's quiet snoring.

As Easter week drew to its close, yet another problem became apparent. This most important holiday in the year had long ago been suggested as a time when concerned parents might visit their children in the countryside. It was to be a visit of reassurance for the doubtful, and of warm encounter between the brigadistas' real parents and their campesino surrogates. Unfortunately, no one had taken into consideration the last-minute confusions in the mobilization, the problems in getting the system organized, or the difficulties in communications and transport as a whole. As in El Jícaro, many thousands of brigadistas were relocated at the last minute. Their new locations were known to their advisors and supervisors in the field, but not, as yet, to the municipal offices. The telegraph system—free to brigadistas—clogged completely in the first week of the crusade. So did the telephones. Many, many messages never got through, and many more brigadistas were far too distant from a telegraph or telephone to send any message at all.

The result was nationwide confusion. All over Nicaragua, determined parents set forth to find their children. Crowding onto packed public vehicles or hitchhiking, they set off into the unknown countryside, clutching enormous packets of food and clothing. For all too many, it was the confirmation of their worst fears, for the addresses given them in Managua bore only the sketchiest relation to their son's or daughter's actual location, and no one could be found to tell them exactly where they were. Their children, for all intents and purposes, were lost.

A parade of tearful, disgusted, desperate, hysterical, footsore parents filed through El Jícaro over Holy Week. José Ramón's mother arrived on Thursday and snatched him from our first weekly meeting, as if from the jaws of Somoza himself. "Come on, Ramoncito, we're going home!" A few hours later, calmed and rested, she was all for us. It turned out that no one in Muy Muy had had the slightest idea where her son was or the least interest in helping her find out. She had already visited two communities before she finally found him in the school with us. Fernando's mother, who arrived late, set out over the hills to Wapá with Estela and a lantern at ten o'clock at night. Another plump señora insisted on setting off immediately to find her son—she wouldn't wait for us to send for him or for someone to guide her. Wonder if she ever got there. Most pitiable was the man who got to the house after walking eight hours from Matagalpa! Worst of all, I had to tell him I'd never heard of his son.

The best scene could have been right out of a television situation comedy:

About four o'clock one afternoon, the hour when the sun begins to cool, I set out up the hill a little way to watch the river. About half a kilometer from the house I came upon a lone woman sitting by the side of the road, heavily made up, wearing tight pants that screamed "Managua." It turned out she was the mother of one of the boys in the hacienda.

Their car was stuck in the river, she told me, and the grandmother, with the baby, was waiting by the school. She had been on her way back to get the baby bottle she'd left in the car, but couldn't stand the walk in her high-heeled shoes. Sure enough, she was barefoot, thin sandals lying in the dirt. So off we went, she in my huaraches and me barefoot, over the hill and down to the river. There, indeed, was a Toyota station wagon, like a half-beached white whale, nosing out of the river. The brigadista and several younger brothers and sisters were watching their father, who was bent over pondering the intricacies under the hood. His immaculate white pants were coated with wet mud.

"He shouldn't be doing this," the mother stage-whispered. "He has asthma. Dear, why don't you wait for the man to come help you?"

"Don't bother me. I've got it!" He poked a red face out in time to slap at the little boy poking around the jack. "Don't touch that!" His outburst ended in an alarming gasp for air.

The grandmother arrived on this cue, screaming baby in tow, and, after I was introduced all around, implored me to intervene and per- suade her son to let little Julio go home. I glanced in surprise at the brigadista, leaning expressionless against the hood.

"I told you to shut up about that!" The man was up now, and glowering, first at the grandmother then at the boy. "We didn't want to give you permission in the first place, but, oh, no, you begged and begged until she"—the finger swung to the mother—"talked me into it. One week later and you want to go home. Well, you made your decision and I'll be damned if you'll back out now."

Now the grandmother was crying and hugging Julio, while the mother sat in the front seat of the car, studiously adjusting her makeup, as if in that action a solution might be found.

"It's your fault!" the man gasped at the grandmother. "You're the one who spoiled him all these years. Whatever he wants, you have to give it to him."

My attempts to talk to Julio were lost in the roar of battle. "I'm going," he muttered at me.

"No, you're not! Look at this young lady. She comes all the way from another country to be here, and here we are acting like a bunch of goddam Indians. I tell you he's not going in my car!"

"I'm going!" insisted Julio. "I'll walk to Managua if I have to!"

"Carlos, let him come. Look how it is here. Look what they're giving him to eat in that place."

"He's not going!"

The night shadows were fast closing in when a campesino finally appeared with his team of oxen. In a few minutes the wooden yoke had been hooked to the chrome, and the oxen were plodding slowly up the hill, utterly uncurious about the metal cargo they were towing out of the muck. The campesino guided them with his stick, gazing wonderingly at the fifty córdobas—two days' wages—the woman had just passed him.

I took this as my cue to leave. From the distance, I could hear the motor at last taking hold, and sure enough, just as I reached the school, the parade caught up with me. There was Julio, suitcase on head, marching grimly alongside the car. The father, equally grim behind the wheel, would neither speed up nor slow down. Keeping pace at a respectful distance behind came the campesino, now more quizzical than before, leading his oxen home.

As the car crawled past, I heard the wailing from within. "Carlos, open the door for god's sake and let the boy in—" Curtain falls as receding image fades into darkness.

The brigadistas began trickling back on Saturday, with sheepish faces and flawless excuses. "I wanted to bring some pencils from home." "My brother came and I wanted to see him, since they're separating us." "I was in Muy Muy waiting for my dad to show up." The entire Armando Bonilla squadron showed up together on Saturday morning; they'd held a "group meeting" in town. On Sunday afternoon, Estela returned from another trip to Muy Muy with new orders and a description of "one of ours" who'd spent the weekend drinking in town. But at least they were back—or most of them were. It was now March 30. Holy Week was ending, and it was time at last to get down to work.

Time to take a count of who was with us and who wasn't. (To my surprise, all had returned except little Rafael, who had left the second day, and Julio, who, to the best of my knowledge, was still walking, suitcase on head, beside his father's car.) It was time to gather the scattered classes and put them back in order. It was time to quiz the brigadistas and, if they didn't remember the teaching techniques they had learned in the workshops, to set up some intensive cramming sessions. It was time because, all over Nicaragua, we were opening the primers to Lesson 1.

CHAPTER 5
Beginning Again

The literacy process is an act of creation in which people offer each other their thoughts, words, and deeds. It is cultural action of transformation and growth.

NATIONAL LITERACY CRUSADE, *Cuadernos de Orientaciones*

The methodology developed for the literacy crusade was a blend of libertarian pedagogy and immediate pragmatism. Drawing heavily on the ideas of Brazilian educator Paolo Freire, the technical team had struggled to accommodate these complex theories to an inexperienced teaching force and to the need for rapid political education in the countryside. Aided also by the Cuban experience, the team eventually succeeded in developing a method and a primer that would prove remarkably effective in the months to come.

The idea underlying the crusade is that the process of learning to read should embrace far more than just an intellectual advance. As the process develops, the campesino, previously powerless in the face of the unknown world outside, begins to take control over "the word." Through this mental transformation comes the realization that one is the actor, not just the recipient of another's actions. Thus, in learning to control the alphabet and printed word, the campesino also learns to step away from the old order, internal and external, and to begin to effect change. It is a real revolution from within.

The true Freierian method begins with the exposition of evocative slides, and an open dialogue. During this conversation the teacher is supposed to take note of certain key words, the words most central to the life of the community. These words are then used to teach the phonetic skills and, simultaneously, to reinforce the student's maturing perception of his or her own reality. This use of dialogue and analysis is central throughout Freire's process of literacy training. The method has apparently been effective enough to cause his expulsion from Brazil, Chile, and Argentina and to make literacy work a highly suspect profession in the eyes of more than one Latin American dictator.

In Nicaragua, though, the limitations were completely different. To do true Freirian literacy work, educators must be highly skilled and sensitive, as well as schooled in political philosophy. This, needless to say, was out of the question when 60,000 youths of varying backgrounds had to be trained in two weeks for a campaign of barely five months. As a compromise, the pedagogical team developed a ten-step formula:

1. The presentation of an evocative photo from the primer to stimulate dialogue within the class, leading to the conclusion expressed by the short sentence that followed;

2. Focus on the key word culled from this opening phrase;

3. The separation of this word into syllables, and the selection of one specific syllable as the lesson's objective;

4. The presentation of the consonant sound of this syllable together with the five possible vowel combinations (for example, *la le li lo lu*);

5. The copying and later writing of these syllables, with small and capital letters;

6. The formation of new words by combining the new syllables with others learned in previous lessons;

7. The presentation of all possible variations of these syllables—for example, inverted (*al el il ol ul*) or with an ending consonant sound (*las les lis los lus*);

8. The reading of words and sentences that contain the known syllables;

9. A dictation to test the student's mastery;

10. The *muestra*, or demonstration—a phrase or motto to be copied in the student's best handwriting.

Because Spanish is such a highly regular language phonetically—one letter, one sound—a method based on syllable recognition will eventually permit the student to read virtually any word in the language. Thus, it was hoped that this simple formula, combined with an open dialogue, would both create competent readers and open some of the doors to inner transformation.

The first lesson of the primer then, following an introductory chapter of readiness exercises and the teaching of the student's own name, presents five vowel sounds. It begins, as does every subsequent lesson of the primer, with a photograph.

EL AMANECER DEL PUEBLO

Cuaderno de Educación Sandinista de Lecto-Escritura

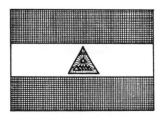

Cruzada Nacional de Alfabetización
Héroes y Mártires
por la liberación de Nicaragua.
Ministerio de Educación
República de Nicaragua.
1980.

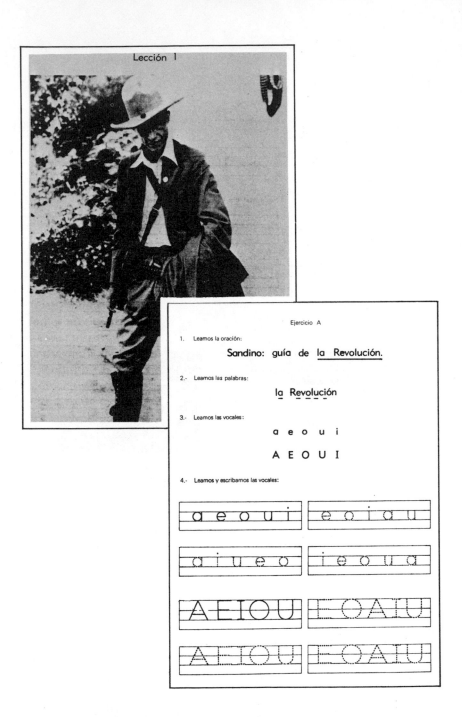

Lección 1

Ejercicio A

1. Leamos la oración:

Sandino: guía de la Revolución.

2.- Leamos las palabras:

la Revolución

3.- Leamos las vocales:

a e o u i

A E O U I

4.- Leamos y escribamos las vocales:

a e o u i   e o i a u

a i u e o   i e o u a

A E I O U   E O A I U

A E I O U   E O A I U

"Let's look, then, at this picture. Do any of you know who it is? That's right, it's Sandino. How do you know? Oh, you saw his picture in Muy Muy. Well, look at him here. What's he wearing? What kind of a man does he appear to be? Is he fat or short? Does he look rich or poor? Yeah, that's a big hat he's got. Well, why are we hearing so much about Sandino all of a sudden? What did he do that was so special? That's right, you got it. He fought against the Yankees when they invaded Nicaragua. But why did he fight? What did he want? Yes, he was a patriot and a soldier who wanted Nicaragua to be led by Nicaraguans, not by the Americans. But besides that, he had lots of good ideas about what Nicaragua could be like. Let's talk about some of them . . .

"So we've come to a sort of conclusion here. You've said that it was Sandino that really began the revolution. Well, here, to begin the lesson, is one way of putting the idea. I'll write it on the blackboard and then let's read the phrase."

Sandino—Guide of the Revolution

"Repeat it with me . . .

"Now this last part, where it says 'the Revolution,' that's really an important word in our lives. Let's read it over several times. *La Re-vo-lu-ción*.

"There are five basic sounds here, sounds we call vowels. Instead of just learning the alphabet letter by letter as some of you are expecting, we're going to begin with these five sounds because they're so much more important. Later we'll see how they combine to form syllables—pieces of words—and then words themselves. But for now, let's read the vowels—

"*a e i o u.*

"And in letters we call capitals, the sounds are the same. We use the capital letters for names of people or places—

"*A E I O U.*

"Now, where you see these lines, we're going to practice writing these letters. First we'll be just tracing them, but shortly you'll be writing them yourselves. Now in your books, let's write. Hey, that's good . . ."

Later, after introducing the first syllables, the students are taught how they combine to form words and are encouraged to make words of their own: *sa se si so su*; *esa* (that), *sesos* (brains), *seis* (six). This step is pivotal. Once the learner can begin forming words, he or she has grasped the fundamental process—the rest is merely a process of memorization. By Step 7 all the syllables are listed: direct—*sa se si so su*; indirect—*as es is os us*; and triple—*sas ses sis sos sus*. In Step 8, words appear, to be read in one solid breath; here also are the first simple sentences, read first by the brigadista and then by the students. Though these beginning sentences are limited in vocabulary, the context is specifically adult: Manuel goes to the mines. When do they cultivate cacao?

Step 9 is a dictation, the test of a student's mastery. Here, the brigadista reads six or seven words from the lesson while the learner, without looking, writes them in the notebook. If the learner is incapable of writing the words, the brigadista needs to do more reviewing before going on. The tenth and final step is a sample phrase for the learner to copy over to develop handwriting skills: We have little, we'll cultivate more.

The first real reading appears with Lesson 10:

Austerity

The country has many debts. We have no money.
Many citizens are unemployed.
We have small harvests.
This is all the fault of Somoza's system.
In spite of these conditions, we can improve the economy.
With more dedication, we'll increase the country's resources.
We are sharing the little that was left by the Somocistas.
Austerity is necessary.

Though each of the twenty-three lessons introduces only one key phrase, each lesson has two or more sections, concentrating on different words and syllables from this phrase. For example, accompanying a picture of craftsmen at work, Lesson 7 has the phrase, "Spending little, saving resources and producing a lot is making revolution." Exercise A follows the ten steps with the word *poco* (little) and the syllable *po* (*pa   pe*...). Section B takes up *mucho* and the syllable *cho*. Still a third part of the lesson treats *hacer* (to make) and the syllable *ha*.

Lesson 14 ends the direct syllables, and subsequent lessons take up consonant clusters: *tra pra   bra*, etc., always presenting them with all the different vowels and within the standard ten-step lesson plan.

At last, after four readings similar to the one in Lesson 10, there are some photographs with blank lines for the students to write their impressions. By this time, it is assumed, the students will not only be reading and writing fluently but will also be able to formulate and record their own original commentary.

Accompanying the primer was a newsprint notebook and pencil for each student, and a manual and calendar for each brigadista. The latter had the months of the crusade divided up into blocks, with a lesson to be covered within each allotted period. Anywhere from three to seven days were suggested per lesson, with a postscript emphasizing that the orientation was flexible and that individual differences had to be considered. The calendar had us ending on August 7, with a week left for organization and consolidation.

Finally, there were three tests—initial, middle, and final exams. As well as being individual progress checks, these were intended to provide hard statistical confirmation of the crusade's results.

So this was our arsenal. A week late, with few pencils, fewer notebooks, and no initial tests, which were still missing, we dug in for the long struggle. The same way the revolutionary war had begun, I mused—much enthusiasm, half-trained soldiers, and most of the arms still to be recovered.

CHAPTER 6
New Routines

As the March moon was fading, Celestino of the Grange
With hopes held high was waiting, to kill ignorance and bring on
    change.
And after a few short weeks, he was showing his cousin Lou
How he could trace a slogan there in his primer on page number two.

Chorus:
With the A, the B, and the C
Soon a-reading we're all gonna be
And with all the letters together,
The more we'll be seeing, the more we'll be free.

"WITH THE A...", CRUSADE SONG
BY CARLOS MEJÍA GODOY

Back on the trail after Holy Week, following whoever was willing to guide me, I managed to find most of the brigadistas' new homesites. I began to work out a routine for my days—one that could continue for most of the five months. The mornings were for visits, the continual check on progress and morale.

"*Buenos días*, Doña. Is the *muchacho* here? No, he's not...well, is he out working? Oh, at the river. Well, how are you all coming along? Is he doing his share? And the classes?" These first visits were far less difficult for me than the census had been. But the families, not knowing exactly what was expected of their brigadista, tended to be protective of him in questioning. Later, we'd all know each other better. But for now the silent questioning had at least been replaced by smiles and grapefruit *frescos*. Everyone was eager to tell me about the classes they were starting, about their brigadista's special merits.

In the late afternoons, I'd watch the classes. Crouched unobtrusively in the background, I'd scribble my observations, criticisms, suggestions. Later, these would be written up on a formal observation sheet and passed along to the brigadista, sometimes with the recommendation of a personal conference or, if necessary, a reorientation session.

Between these two basic activities, there were statistics to collect, supplies to distribute, orientations to be passed along, health problems to attend to, group meetings to call and coordinate, conferences with Estela and the team from Muy Muy, and the constant problems of substitutions and relocations. On top of these the first weeks brought a steady stream of unforeseen crises.

The main difficulty was the distance between brigadistas, making regular communication close to impossible. Three or four visits and a class observation was a day's accomplishment; only by dint of ceaseless walking could I catch everyone in his home at least once a week. The longest route took me over the hills to Don Roberto's shack at the halfway point, across the creek to Don Ernesto's barnlike house, then in rapid succession to Doña Luisa's, Doña Bernarda's, and Arturo's tiny shacks in the plain of Wapá and, finally, across the uninhabited prairie to Don Manolo's large brick house, which fronted the river and marked our far boundary. Then, if there had been no delays, I would swing wide on my return route to visit the shacks of Don Manolo's two nearest *mozos*, Don Chavelo and Don Juan. If all went flawlessly, which it seldom did, from there I would cross an arid scrub plateau to yet another lineup of shacks where three more brigadistas were placed. This was the dawn-to-dusk circle that we'd covered on the first day of censusing, only now I seldom had the luxury of stopping to check on families without brigadistas to see how they were finding the classes.

The second circuit began with a climb to the small farms that dotted the hillsides west of Wapá. Here Chico Barrera maintained an expanse of good pastureland, and another twelve or so families shared the rest of the arable land. With the small houses relatively close together, this part of the community was easily covered by the five resident brigadistas. After checking the two who lived with Don Chico Barrera, I would descend the hill to Doña María Elsa's , where one was housed. Up the next hill for two more visits, and finally down a steep, switchback path and along the stream that fronted Don Luis Reyes's, the boundary of our territory. Then back along the stream to where the ancient Don Toribio maintained his family and brigadista and finally past Don Ernesto's again with a wave, and over the hills toward home.

The last cycle of visits would be to the squadron of younger boys spread out along the direct road that led from the highway and petered out at the river fronting Anita Fley's hacienda El Esquirín. There were four—now three, minus Julio—at the hacienda, one at the cantina, another at the house that becomes marooned during the rains and, maybe someday soon, a replacement for Rafael, the brigadista who had abandoned the prosperous farm of Don Rito on the other side of Tapasle River.

There were still more shacks and brigadistas to cover, on paths that fit no possible circuit. With luck, I'd meet them at the rivers—favorite gathering points—or in the shacks of their more accessible neighbors. If not, I had to depend on the group meetings, or on Estela's trusted network, for news of problems.

Estela and I were coordinating closely during this first month—I on the trail and she between the school and Muy Muy. We'd meet over lantern light at the school, compare notes, and try to compile a picture of the progress. Surprisingly, despite our inability to really control anything, the situation seemed to be coming along all right. The brigadistas, after the first week of chaos and second thoughts, were beginning to do the job they had come to do.

No rain in sight. Every day the sky gleamed blue, and at night we watched the orange teeth of far-off field burnings in preparation for the new season of plowing and seeding. I slept uncovered on my hide bed with the soft snores of the grandmother in my ear and dreamed I was looking for water. "April brings only thirst," the campesinos would say.

My first act each morning was to pull some grapefruits down from the tree in our front yard. At noon I would eat several, sitting under a tree out there somewhere. At night I chased the heavy supper of beans with grapefruit pulp, pitching the rinds off down the slope.

Hanging dignity of the trees they call *guanacaste*. I stopped under them when I could to rest, looking at the cows and wondering if we would make it. Orlando was gone now, left Sunday without saying anything. Jorge was in bad shape, too, the kids told me, and José Ramón had been crying at night.

I spent a few nights at María Elsa's while her son and husband patrolled with the militia. Everyone in the house slept fitfully until, toward morning one day, they returned. Chickens climb trees, I learned there, and pigs substitute for latrines. I was also learning to mill corn, to haul water, to live surrounded by others, to get around. Yes, you can sleep in a plastic hammock, if you're tired enough.

Carrying water. Twice a day—once at sunup and again at sundown—Doña Guillermina, the three little girls, and I would descend the hills with our buckets. Across the road, across the pasture, and down the last steep clay bank. There a deep hole lined with sand formed the Murillo's "well"—fed by the muddy stream that ran beside it. It was a good well, I was assured, always cool and fresh, never dry.

A family's source of water, the distance to it and its quality, affects their entire lives. Arturo and Daysi's waterhole is foul. so they are always sick. Doña Bernarda, in her fifties, must walk almost a mile to hers; so keeping everyone clean is nearly impossible. Don Manolo, on the other hand, is right by the river and, what's more, he has horses for hauling water.

Once we had skimmed the bugs off and filled the buckets, we ceremoniously placed them on each others' heads; Doña Guillermina was the only one who could lift a full bucket to her head without spilling anything. What a stately procession we made, five women marching slowly back across the pasture, heads upright, posture stern. I cut the least imposing figure. Sweat trickled down my back and muscles began to tremble before I even topped the first clay bank. At first I had to stop for rest two or three times, shamefaced, while the others waited patiently for me. Day by day, though, I could feel myself getting stronger.

The official rest stop was the barbed wire fence beside the road. There we would all lower the buckets, one helping another, then duck under the fence and resume the last lap. The fifty yards from the road to the house were straight uphill, with a low-hanging clothes-line waiting for us at the top. With luck, Migdonio or Ricardo would meet us at that point and take the buckets down. Hauling water was women's work, but the men were permitted to help a little.

The most incredible turn of events was the relodging of dark little Luis with the family of Agapito Cruz—the old man who had all but chased us off. I had to make Doña María Elsa repeat the news, sure I'd heard wrong.

"Old Agapito's not bad; his gruffness is mostly bluff," she assured me. "When they heard that Bonifacio wouldn't take the boy and that he had nowhere to stay, they felt sorry for him and brought him over there. Now you should see how happy he looks. They've got a boy the same age and they're already running all over the valley together."

Neither Luis nor Don Agapito was there when I stopped by, but the señora greeted me with a resplendent smile and a big glass of *pinolillo.** Sure the boy was there. He was having a great time and they'd all started studying. "Don Agapito, too?" Now I was really dumbfounded. "Well, why not? But, ooh, if you knew what a time we're having with it. I can't get those letters right, my old hands are just too stiff." But in spite of her words, her face glowed as I examined her work: M A R I A, the crude forms of first letters, the R backward, the M swallowing the A, and yet "absolutely clear," as I assured her, anyone could read it. Delight radiated from her stocky figure as she carried off my glass.

The shack was only one room, and the plastic hammock supplied by the crusade filled the middle of it. How many slept there? "Oh, there's only four of us now, plus him. It's good having another boy around the house. We were getting lonely."

DIARIO DEL CAMPO

Tuesday, April 8

The magic hour of four o'clock—the time almost everyone has arranged for their two-hour classes.

Walking into Alejandro's class at Don Chico Barrera's is like entering a crude country church. Silence in the bare room, blending with the hush of evening just beginning. There are twelve, arranged around two tables in a spacious front room. Scratch of pencils and heavy breathing as they laboriously form the letters. Those at the table near the door are working on their names while at the second table the more advanced students forge ahead with the syllables of Lesson 3: *Liberación—li la le lo lu.* The brigadista and I creep around, causing barely a stir in the intense concentration as we look over shoulders at the newly learned names and syllables, Alejandro guiding without interrupting. Letters crude but clear, set with patient care between the guiding lines.

The sinking sun sends an orange glow through the open door, enhancing still more the impression that we are in a hallowed place. And with three days' classes under his belt, Alejandro is a marvel. Soft-spoken, solemn, patient—where is the skinny hipster who'd seemed so flippant when he got off the truck? There are no words to describe his complete transformation, his dark face now softened and reddened by the fading sunlight, his air of confidence, of seriousness.

As I make my silent exit, he follows me out the door. "How'm I doing?" he half whispers.

"It's fine; you're doing fine." I wish I could tell him the whole thing—

---

*A traditional Nicaraguan drink made of finely ground cornmeal, cacao, cinnamon, sugar, and water.

the crimson light, the glow of his presence in the rude hall. But trapped by shyness before someone I barely know, I confine it to a few words of encouragement, and the news that I'll be back the next day to pass along the full report on the official observation sheet.

CHAPTER 7
First Skirmishes

Anyone who harms a hair on the head of any brigadista will rue the day he was born.

TOMÁS BORGE, MINISTER OF THE INTERIOR

The literacy crusade had been basically conceived as a dialectic—a meeting of opposites: city kids with country people, intellectual with manual work, independence with discipline, traditional thought patterns with revolutionary new ideas. Before any resolution could emerge, there were bound to be clashes. These would take many forms, from direct struggles with recalcitrant landlords to quarrels within the kids' own groups, from clashes within the rural community to those between elements of our own organizational structure. It was all an integral part of the growth process.

With such volatile elements, the first ripples of turbulence weren't long in coming. Right on the heels of our initial actions would come the reactions. While not lethal in themselves, the inevitable series of small explosions were enough to shake us up. More than that, they served as a reminder that we were dealing with serious issues. It wasn't a picnic, it was a war on ignorance.

With all the confusion of the first weeks, I was always behind on the news. I hadn't learned how to plug into the community rumor mill that had perfected itself over the centuries. Thus, I was not prepared when Don Petronilo popped out of Arturo's shack and motioned me over. "Can I talk to you a minute?"

A tall peasant with a wiry athletic physique, he cut an imposing figure. I'd met him only briefly, but knew that he was considered a hard worker and "real active." Now it was obvious from his manner that something serious was up. I followed him back into the corn-filled room and waited for the obligatory polite preamble to end.

I didn't have to wait long. "Listen, I've got a problem," he began in his low, hoarse voice. Then it began to come in a rush. "This woman, my *patrona*, my boss Doña Cloris, she wants to get rid of me for having a brigadista in the house. First she comes in the middle of class and dumps everything off the table—the books and everything. Then she begins yelling at everyone: 'Let the counterrevolution come,' she screams, 'so all these damned brigadistas will be hung!' Can you imagine that? Now she wants to get rid of me 'cause she says it's her house and she hasn't given any kind of permission to put a brigadista there."

"What? When did this happen?" Both he and Don Arturo watched me intently from the shadows of the shack, gauging my reaction. My tongue was tripping and I was beginning to sweat. What should I tell him?

I could picture her—Doña Cloris Fley, a naturalized American, now well advanced in age—*la viejita*, the old lady, they called her. Owner of approximately one fifth of Wapá, forcing her big car over the barely discernable back road into the community to make her monthly inspection, and now she'd seen the face of changes she didn't like. "Let the counterrevolution come!" What did we do now?

"Well, she can't really evict you; it's against the law now." Of this much, anyway, I was sure.

"Naw, I think I'm going to get out of there anyway. She's been trying to nail me for a long time. She doesn't like it that I'm with the farmworkers' union, that I complain when things aren't right. First she was after me about some pigs I had, and now this. And she says she won't rent me the land to work this year. And, anyway, she's not paying me right. The last time, she gives me the money and I says, 'Wait a minute, let's look at this sum.' 'Oh, no, it's fine,' she says. But sure enough, I figure it up and she owes me fifty córdobas more. She gets all upset and everything, but of course I'm right, and she has to pay up. That's 'cause I learned math. With someone else she would have got away with it."

"You're right. It sounds like all she wants is someone less active so she can take more advantage." No wonder she wanted all the brigadistas hanged. Can't have these peasants learning math! "But look," I implored Petronilo, "don't just take off and leave. You should claim your rights in town. I'll ask Estela exactly how we put the complaint. I think someone should go to the literacy office. Threatening brigadistas is definitely against the law. And the other part, about not renting land and such, should be taken to the farmworkers' office, or maybe the Ministry of Labor. Let me get these details and I'll get back to you in a day or so. Okay?"

We'd been more than an hour in the close, hot room and "I'll ask Estela" was all I'd come up with. Eyes staring from leathery faces, serious nods, but I felt like I'd been a disappointment to them.

A short while later, I caught up with Matías, the brigadista living at Petronilo's house. A short, intense youth, he had all but escaped my notice before. Now he nodded at me solemnly as he spoke. "It looks like we'll be moving. I told Don Petronilo I'd go with them if they go. Nah, she doesn't scare me. I don't mind dying, *profe*. That's what this revolution's all about."

By the time I got home, I realized the story had already made the rounds, the subject of twilight conversations all up and down the valley. Was Petronila wrong to go? Should Doña Cloris be arrested? Was anyone really in danger?

Estela had the ultimate answer, in the way of small town politics everywhere. "Don't worry, I know her niece's husband. He works for the government junta in town. We'll get him to reason with the old bag."

Next on the list of problems was Raúl, head rebel of the Red and Black Squadron. Twenty-two years old and set on forging his own path through the literacy crusade—a path considerably to one side of the official EPA guidelines—he'd caught my attention in the first days, mainly because we'd had to send him to three different placements before he found a permanent home. There was something noteworthy in the exaggerated good humor with which he had endured the moves, and in his crooked, mischievous grin.

Now comfortably installed in Don Luis Reyes's house out at the west end of the zone, he was rapidly making his mark. An ex-combatant, short and comic, he did have plenty of *conciencia*, but it was not partner to discipline. Chronically late for meetings, gone for Holy Week, butt of endless unprovable rumors. Just when we'd be getting ready to "seriously consider the problem," there he'd be, sauntering up on Don Luis's bony old mare, airtight excuse all ready, and that impossibly cocky grin plastered across his face.

Now Don Luis had called me aside. Erect and serious in his patrician style, he asked, "What exactly is our responsibility with these boys?

This one's been seeing a woman, a real no-gooder named Blanca. I warned him, but he just thinks I'm an old fogey. What else can I do?"

It was hard not to smile at the image of them together, Don Luis so much the patriarch and Raúl, *enfant terrible* with primer and roving eye. "I don't suppose there's much you can do," I told him frankly. "Raúl's all grown up."

A few days later, I made my next round to Don Luis Reyes's, this time to catch Raúl's class. The sun was hotter than ever, and there was Raúl waving his machete in the middle of the path. Alas, my joy at seeing him at work was short-lived; the peasant who had lent him the machete five minutes before soon arrived to reclaim it.

His students were beginning to trickle in as we arrived at the house. There were sixteen, more than a full house, and the vast majority were young girls. They sat giggling around two large tables while Raúl conducted his class. It was exactly the style I would have expected—full of energy, jokes, good humor, and completely disorganized. I don't think anyone had the faintest idea what was going on, but they were having a wonderful time. A new variation—giving out Chiclets as rewards for correct answers on the board. B. F. Skinner 1, Paolo Freire 0.

In the middle of the class session a strikingly beautiful woman with long black hair appeared at the door. The class stopped still, the giggling turned to whispers. This, I presumed, was the famous Blanca. "What can I do?" I heard the echo of Don Luis's plea and my own dry answer, "Not much." Now, looking at the girl, bewitching in her simple white dress, I was sure it was true. After all, Raúl was twenty-two. Not an age to heed warnings from surrogate fathers—or *gringa* surrogate teachers.

By the time the class was half over, it was impossible to fit another word onto my observation sheet. Suggestions, criticisms, pointers, reorientations. How would we ever mold this court jester into a pillar of the crusade? And how serious an issue could his peccadillos really represent? Inwardly I shrugged and dismissed the thought—a dismissal I would soon regret.

Deserted women—I began to think about the subject when I met Nubia, one of Doña María Elsa's daughters. A plump, bubbly girl of about sixteen, her pretty face marred by already decaying front teeth, she had served me up a warm Coca-Cola and bubbled on unreservedly about her new life. She'd gone off four months earlier to live with her boy friend, in a part of El Jícaro I barely knew, and this was her first visit back to see her mother.

"Have you met Salvador yet?" she had asked, and in fact I realized I had. He was a thin, strikingly handsome youth who had given me a quick lift on his horse several days before. Nubia's face had glowed as I praised his good looks. Despite her clothes and surroundings, she looked like any teenage girl with a crush on the Most Popular Boy.

Now her aspect had changed completely. Her mother warned me about it first, in the stage whisper she used for tragedies such as the Polanco murders, looking up only occasionally from her mountain of laundry. "Imagine," she said, "two weeks ago this Salvador brings Nubia home after four months, so she can visit us. Now last week without saying a word he sends back her suitcase and the message that she shouldn't bother to come back. Poor baby, she's been crying for two days straight, won't eat, doesn't sleep. Can you figure how he could do a thing like that? And you should see how good she was to him."

Sure enough, Nubia's face in the kitchen was swollen and unhappy. She turned away as I came in, unspeaking. "See?" her mother said. "Now do you think that's right? It's like it was a dishpan we lent him and now that he's done with it he says, 'Here, now, have it back and thank you very much.' And she's—you know—too. Well, I don't care. What's another baby around the house? We always have enough for one more, but it's the idea. You think as a mother I don't feel it?"

I thought about the houses I'd been visiting, how many lone women there were. Doña Chenta, of course, was a widow, as was Doña Guillermina, but the household next door was also without a man, except the half-grown sons. Doña Bernarda had been deserted long ago. Doña Luisa lived alone with a six-year-old girl. There was one man for three women in the rickety shack of Doña Santa. And I'd passed at least three households, including that of Don Manolo, where there was an extra woman with a child or two.

To my cautious, overly polite questioning, Doña Luisa responded with the directness I had begun to value greatly in her. "Good men are mighty scarce here," she explained. "Mine was a good one. Lord, that man loved his children. But the rest? Hah! The men work a little when they can, but when they get a little money in their pockets, right away it's off to buy liquor. *Guaro**—that's been the ruination of

---

*Cheap rum.

this country. The only thing we've got going for us here in Wapá is that they don't bring it in to sell. If they want liquor, they have to go look elsewhere for it."

It made sense. In the all-too-short harvest season, when there were wages, the men had a little money in their pockets. They were the mobile ones, the ones who could drink, the ones who went to town when there was something to be done there. How many of them who had put in a week's work with a machete for 150 córdobas—$15— would gladly watch it all disappear in two pairs of cheap children's shoes, or a secondhand dress for the woman and a gallon tin of frying oil? How many could forego the temptation to spend a day's wages on rum to share with one's sweaty companions of the harvest?

More wrenching yet, men often migrated during harvest season. When the coffee was picked clean in Matagalpa, it was usually about time for the cotton to be ready in León and Chinandega. It was not uncommon for a man to have families in two or three different areas of the country. Since most had shied away from the expense and the intimidating paperwork of marriage, the women had no legal recourse before the revolution even if the government cared about the problem, which it didn't.

So the women grew old fast after the brief flush of teenage beauty— burdened with children, bad teeth, chronic headaches, and eyes that failed at twenty-five from constant exposure to smoke from the wood cooking fires. And the men, equally frustrated with wages that were too low, and work that was too short, would simply leave when the responsibilities became too burdensome.

Chapter 19 of the primer has the key phrase, "The woman has always been exploited. The revolution makes possible her liberation." But we were only on chapter two or three of the primer, and of the revolution. Nubia, convinced that the world had ended, was barely opening the introduction.

CHAPTER 8
Enforcements and Reinforcements

Work Plan for the First Weeks—Bulletin from the Municipal Office, Muy Muy

1. Confirm the class group size, with at least one brigadista for each ten students;
2. Check the census;
3. Arrange meetings between the technical assistants, brigadistas and community supervisors in the course of the week;
4. Carry out a survey for families who will need food supplies to feed their brigadistas;
5. Construct skits and wall posters with available materials;
6. Hold study groups at all levels, related to the political themes;
7. Structure a health plan for the brigadistas as well as for the community as a whole;
8. Arrange a sharing of the brigadistas' field diaries and draw general conclusions;
9. At the level of technical assistant, hold at least one meeting weekly with the brigadistas;
10. Arrange for assistants for community supervisors and technical advisers;
11. Arrange weekly programs between brigadistas, technical advisers, and community supervisors to make class plans;
12. Inform brigadistas of the emulation plans.

Third week in April. Temperature going up outside and in. Unforeseeable problems of initiation now replaced by the predictable ones of adjustment. Sixty thousand teenagers and subteens from the cities with a crash course in teaching were now learning how well they could adapt to a rural setting in which, for five months, they had to adopt the persona of worker-teacher-adult. Childhood without responsibilities is a luxury afforded few youth in third world countries, and fewer still in Somoza's Nicaragua. So these kids were, on the whole, far readier than their U.S. counterparts would be to shoulder such a task. But we weren't without our problems.

There were the inevitable teaching problems. Miguel, one of the squadron leaders, was frightening his students with too strict a manner; José Ramón conducted his sessions with an air of utter boredom; Geraldo was ignoring the slower students to concentrate on the most advanced; Roberto was requiring his students to write out the entire key phrase from memory. Then there was soft-spoken Pablo, not on the regular routes, who kept begging me to come and see his classes; and Fernando, whom I could never find.

There were also discipline problems. Mario went "on vacation" and Guillermo followed. And aside from one or two, I had yet to see any brigadistas actually out in the fields working. "I have allergies," they swore, or, "The sun gives me a headache," or, most unanswerable of all, "My family hasn't got any land and I'm not gonna donate my time to the *patrón*."

But how would they ever understand life in the countryside if they didn't fully share it? Or if they wouldn't stay put day after quiet day, week after changeless week, to let it all sink in?

On the other hand, what could we really do to enforce the rules? Tie them to trees? Lecture them on discipline and obedience, on their responsibility to the revolution? Not even I could always keep a straight face as I tried to fix on their children's countenances and ignore their furtive glances toward the cool river.

The squadron leaders were little help, though they were supposed to be handling the disciplinary problems, leaving me free to deal with the strictly pedagogical aspects. That didn't happen, for reasons both structural and personal. According to plan, there should have been one leader and an assistant for the whole squad of thirty, with no other role than to supervise the general deportment of their briga-distas, their health, keep track of their location at all times and provide periodic reports to their superiors in the zone. But we had ended up with fragments of three squads, each with its own late-appointed leader. And because we were short of brigadistas, the leaders doubled as teachers.

Ramiro, a model of responsibility in his own behavior, didn't know his group well, nor was he outgoing enough to take charge. Narciso, older and more confident, had his boys in tow, but in *his* tow. His ideas on what they could or could not do, I had already learned, didn't always coincide with the official guidelines. And finally there was Miguel. With his handsome boyish face, he reminded me of high school student council presidents I had known. Just a little too eager to please when Teacher was around, but when the working hours came—"I can't, *profe*, I have allergies. Honest, I break out in a rash in that dried grass." So far, the two meetings of his group had resulted in near mayhem, with him threatening to quit as leader and everyone shouting at once. All was smoothed over each time, but he wasn't the candidate to bring order to the ranks.

Estela's trips to the town office were now less frequent, and the scarcity of radios in the community made the daily crusade program, *Puño en Alto* ("Fists on High"), a rare treat. I began to lose touch with the national movement of the crusade. More and more, we were a world apart in our little valley, grappling with our problems and fighting off the sense that we were the only ones experiencing them.

Just as these problems were beginning to arise, we got a reprieve from the conviction that they were ours alone. The first month's evaluation was getting under way. Official visitors came and went. Questions were asked and forms filled out. Among the comings and goings in our valley, there were two new elements which would become a permanent fixture—the Saturday workshops and the zone leader. The first offered a forum in which to tackle our difficulties, and the second lent moral and political authority to the effort.

The first of these to arrive was Francisco ("Chico"), the overseer for our zone, one of four in the Muy Muy region. All zone leaders had to be members of the *Juventud Sandinista 19 de Julio*, the youth organization named in honor of the July triumph over Somoza. That meant they were likely to be the most politically developed. They were also selected from the cream of the squad leaders, which meant they showed particular aptitude for this task. Their responsibility, in coordination with the zonal teaching advisers, was to regularly visit the four or five squadrons of their district to be sure directives were being implemented and that serious problems were reported back up the chain for reevaluation. In part a disciplinary function, it was even more a creative political one; they were the power train of this machine called a literacy crusade. Transmitting the energy that was being cranked up in Managua, the zone leaders kept the wheels turning out in the field.

Francisco was sitting in the school when I arrived one afternoon, listening noncommitally to Estela. Quiet, with long black hair and small, deep-set eyes, he projected an indefinable sense of self-possession—one that drew me to watch him curiously. The bag at his side was stamped "National University," leading me to accept his air of responsibility as the maturity of a university student. Only later did I learn that it was a borrowed bag; he was still in high school.

He stayed over at our house that night, and the two Chicos—he and Doña Chenta's son—sat up late talking. In the morning over breakfast he announced, "My congratulations, compañera."

"For what?" I asked. They were startling words at six a.m.

"Your tortillas," he said, flashing a grin. Sure enough, he had noticed that I'd been in there patting the dough that morning, one of my early attempts that ended with the edges ragged and the middle torn. I turned red with pleasure and embarrassment and grinned back while the little girls giggled.

I should have had a clue in that show of sensitivity, uncommon in a *macho* society. But I had little intimation of what a capable and dedicated leader he was, or how important he would become to us when the rains closed in. In time, he would even become a role model for the brigadistas. But with summer still baking the land dry, he was just another visitor.

Then there was the Saturday workshop. Although we had been passed an agenda, I'd assumed it to be a brainstorm of the Muy Muy office. No one had told me that it was a nationwide organizing effort. What we had thought was our problem, it seems, was a national problem.

The very first feedback from the crusade confirmed the fears of the national planners. If two-week training sessions hadn't molded instant teachers, then individual visits and controls were gong to be insufficient to correct the deficit. The sessions would have to be on-going. Every Saturday, according to the new plan, the groups of brigadistas should gather to evaluate the week's work and plan the next lessons. In organization there is strength and in leadership there is direction. The structure of the workshops was explicit.

The first part would run about an hour. This was to be criticism and self-criticism, reports of student attendance and of advances during the week, of victories and setbacks, and the reading aloud of our diaries. At the end of this period, we would summarize the gains and then recess for fifteen minutes.

The second part would be political discussion and preparation of the week's dialogue, using the teacher's manual as our guide. Each chapter of the primer, as mentioned, was headed by a photo and a key phrase. In the accompanying manual, the political themes were taken up in greater detail. Two short pages outlined the overall situation—be it the history of Carlos Fonseca, the mass organizations, the need to conserve resources—and presented the revolutionary solution. Six or seven questions then followed, departure points for discussion among the brigadistas. These discussions, and the insights gained from them, would serve as points of reference for the dialogues and discussions with the campesinos.

Part three was to be a class simulation. Each week one brigadista would go through the steps in the next lesson, while his peers watched, in the role of students. Keeping in mind the stumbling blocks we had identified in the evaluation session at the beginning, we would critique the presentation method from the receiving end: "The tone felt condescending"; "That was a particularly clear explanation of the difference between 'L' and 'LL' "; "You were very patient answering all the questions of the brigadista who pretended to be slow, but it would have been better to give the rest of us something to practice, because we began to feel fidgety."

The final part of the agenda was "methodological orientations and information." This was my big moment to pass along whatever tricks of the trade seemed called for—specific orientations for the lessons, hints on making supplementary materials, devices for improving the class groupings, or the overall results of the week's observations.

This agenda was to fill our Saturdays, or at least five hours of them. And, in fact, whatever the defects of the workshops—and we would encounter many—they did help round our weeks into a routine and keep us all in contact with each other and with the crusade as a national movement.

Comunicado from the Popular Alphabetization Army
To All Members of the EPA

The headquarters of EPA of the town of Muy Muy wishes to communicate the following to all their members who are presently located in the different communities of the municipal area:

1.   It is absolutely prohibited for members of the EPA to drink liquor;
2.   All permission to leave your respective placements is suspended;
3.   Due to the irresponsibility demonstrated by certain squadron leaders, we have agreed on the following measures:
      a.   The squadron leadership will be restructured where necessary;
      b.   In these cases, the comrades who have shown the greatest discipline and progress will be selected;
4.   It is the duty of all EPA members to practice mutual respect with all other comrades (campesinos, brigadistas, technical advisers and community supervisors);
5.   The following measures will be taken against those EPA members who do not follow these guidelines:
      a.   They will be publicly criticized through all channels (*comunicados*, newspaper and radio bulletins);

b.   All the material given to them will be taken away, followed by

c.   Dishonorable expulsion from the glorious EPA.

Fraternally,
Headquarters

"Constructive criticism and exemplary self-criticism shall be my disciplinary arm."

One last change blew in on the dry winds of April, a reflection of this period of reassessment and, perhaps, of Chico's visit: I was ordered to move. "You're walking around like a Wandering Jew and not getting anything to show for it," the municipal instructor brusquely informed me. In five minutes, he sketched our community on a piece of paper and outlined the solution. Estela would stay put and cover the near half of the community; I would move to the other end of Wapá and oversee things from there. Though the idea of shifting homes was none too pleasant, I had to admit that his analysis had hit the mark. It was time for another pilgrimage.

But that could wait until next week. For now the meetings had ended, the Muy Muy visitors had gone home, and we were looking forward to a weekend fiesta—a fundraiser so we could buy a little cardboard for posters and maybe a few felt pens. The idea came from the El Jícaro local of the Sandinista Defense Committee. I'd known nothing about the event until Thursday, when Doña Guillermina passed me a carefully written invitation: "We hav the oner to envite you to a party in the school, Saterday, April 18. Pleas join us."

The idea of holding a fundraising party among such poor people seemed crazy, but everyone assured me that it wasn't. "People come from all over," they claimed proudly. "Wait'll you see them dance." There *was* a certain fever in the air now—the rains were coming soon. Though I still didn't understand the seasons here, I recognized the mood I associate with October: get your dancing in now, the days are getting shorter—the last frolic of the bears before hibernation.

By twilight Saturday, the school was immaculate, and the dirt floor—watered earlier—was drying to a solid clay surface. Passing by on my way to the house, I saw a beehive of gray tunics already buzzing around the door; the brigadistas were descending en masse from their scattered lodgings, lured by the honeyed promise of excitement.

By 7:30 the first rhythmic notes were wafting through the darkness as I left the house. It seemed scandalously late—I'd finally gotten used to the eight o'clock bedtime—but the school was packed, and the light from Estela's Coleman lantern was as dazzling to my unaccustomed eyes as the music from the battery-run phonograph was to my ears, now used only to hillside silence.

Midgonio was heading up the sale of *vigorón*—grilled meat, grated raw cabbage, and slices of steamed yuca root on banana leaves—while Doña Guillermina, barely visible behind the crowd, was selling beer and *gaseosa*—soda pop—at the other table. Watching some of the farmers knocking down their brew at six córdobas a bottle—a quarter of their daily wage, I felt a twinge of guilt. But, I consoled myself, it wasn't my idea, and the money was going to a good cause. My boys, too, I noted with even more concern, were keeping the beer dispatchers hopping. Out came all the bills tucked into pockets by loving mothers "for an emergency." Estela seemed quite unperturbed. She was waltzing with a tall rancher, cigarette dangling from her lipsticked mouth.

The scarcity of women was pronounced, more so with the presence of our twenty-six young boys. In addition to Estela and me, there were only three giggling young girls and several older women, including the famous Doña Eudomilia, "the best hopper in El Jícaro." But it didn't matter. Everyone danced with everyone, and all got their turn on the floor. I watched in fascination as Miguel and Doña Eudomilia rounded the room with a traditional bolero—she, demonstrating the technique that had won her acclaim, and he no slouch either at the quick, light steps. They were a great pair, this dark laughing boy, glowing with the energy of youth (and, I suspected, with a bit of the malt as well) and the tiny señora with her face wreathed in a toothless smile and her long lank hair swinging behind her.

"Let's you and me dance, Mario," I suggested, sending him over the banister and into the bushes amid hoots from the older brigadistas. Roberto was inspired at this to try out his English. "Dence? You want dence?" Raúl, waving his fourth beer, imitated my accent, "Booeno, booeno." The rest of the brigadistas stood in the corners, watching, occasionally daring each other to step out on the floor with one of the local *muchachas*.

For the fiesta, the brigadistas had scripted a sociodrama, a kind of guerrilla theater. Nelson, skinny Nelson, the absolute picture of teenage rebellion, begins by pantomiming the clandestine dissemination of literature to fellow students. It is clearly a representation of the way things were "before," and the other players look nervously around before grabbing the proffered scraps of paper. Bam! the door opens. Enter the Guardia Nacional in the persons of Raúl, Goyo and Rolando, all suitably ferocious in helmets and borrowed rifles. Nelson is grabbed. "You communist son-of-a-bitch!" "Take him away, the Sandinista bastard!" A kick sends him sprawling. "Get up! Who's your father?" "Sandino," Nelson answers softly. Another push and a blow from the rifle butt. "Somoza, Somoza's your papa!" "Sandino!" Nelson responds, louder now. Another blow, and Nelson yells in mock pain. "How do you like that, you little bastard? Now say it! Say it or we'll kill you—Viva Somoza!" Nelson spits defiantly and shouts "Viva Sandino!" as the vibrating broom-handle machine guns cut him down.

I looked at the dark faces around me, all convulsed with laughter. The brigadistas, too, were doubled up. To look at them, you'd think it was pure fiction, the greatest joke in the world, instead of the reenactment of a scene that was part of their nightmares and, for many of them, part of their lives. Fifty thousand dead, 90 percent under the age of twenty-five. I looked around at the kids, the campesinos, those wonderful bright faces, eyes full of sparks, and I saw also the dead. Because they're still dying, the defiant spirits of Latin American youth, in Argentina, in El Salvador, in Guatemala. Tears came to my eyes. For them it was a statement of triumph, a necessary psychological confrontation with what was now behind. But I hadn't had their experience; for me it was different—sadness, anger, a powerless feeling that my government was always on the wrong side. On a few faces there were shadows, too, the unspoken awareness that it was not really over yet.

By ten o'clock, things were getting rowdier, and the men who had been fortifying themselves with stronger drink than beer at Don Valerio's nearby cantina were staggering more than dancing. Taking advantage of a pause in the music, I slipped back up to the house. There was Doña Chenta, sitting silent on the outside bench, watching.

"Aren't you asleep yet?" I asked, surprised.

"No, we're listening to the music. They're happy tonight, the muchachos?"

"For sure. The CDS has really done a good job."

"*Alegre la música*—it's happy music. I can't go, since I'm still in mourning, but it's good for these kiddies; it makes them miss the city less. My Don Chico used to love fiestas." Her square face was outlined in candlelight. Jairo, the youngest boy, was sleeping on her lap while Lucía leaned on her shoulder, his eleven-year-old face turned wistfully toward the lights and music.

"Happy music," Doña Chenta repeated, and sighed softly in the hot night.

CHAPTER 9
In the Trenches

Lesson 3
"The FSLN leads the people to liberation"

Li be ra ción

I was seeing the page turned to this lesson more often now, the joyous smile on the face of the victorious *compa** in the photo. Occasionally I was even seeing lesson four. White chalk letters bloomed like flowers in all the houses. *A E I O U, F S L N, E P A.*

We were pretty much in for the long haul now; rumors of desertion had stopped. The disconsolate longing for home had begun to melt under the warm appreciation and nurturing the brigadistas were finding in their new homes.

I was beginning to know them all better, too—the brigadistas, their families, the community as a whole. There was Nelson, with his nervous restlessness and sharp wit, lodged with the inscrutable Jaime Hernández and his equally silent wife. Tall, choleric Roberto, who had his "mother" convinced he was the saints' own gift to her. At any rate, each time I passed the house, there was Doña Bernarda popping out to tick off the virtues of "her boy." Humble Pablo, leaning over his family's table in clothes as ragged as theirs, his low patient voice in the classes repeating, repeating, repeating. And Jairo, our second youngest brigadista, in the bosom of the Ernesto Membreño clan, whose cobwebbed house reminded me increasingly of the Addams Family mansion.

Matías had indeed moved with Don Petronilo to temporary lodging on the state farm back by Don Monolo's. Their cottage was quickly reoccupied by a Don Justo, together with his various family members. They were Protestant evangelists—considered somewhat suspect in Catholic Nicaragua—but young and active, and eager to house a brigadista. I was all ready to move one there to take Matías's class, with

---

*Short for *compañero* or *compañera*, it is a blend of comrade and friend. Always used for those who share the revolutionary sentiment, its diminuitive form is particularly reserved for those who fought or, after the victory, joined the Sandinista Popular Army or other branches of military service.

or without Doña Cloris's approval, but Estela was firmly opposed, seconded by Chico, the zone leader, who now made weekly visits. "We don't really know what *la vieja* might be capable of," was his explanation. The menace, the threat of right-wing violence, was something that they had seen made real too many times. I was again reminded that our experiences had been different, that there were things I was still far from understanding.

So Miguel was ripped from his comfort at the house of Arturo and Daysi, Doña María Elsa's daughter, where his class had shrunk to three, and sent to squeeze in with Don Luis's family, just up river from the new arrivals. "Just as I was going to get a new brother," Miguel lamented, referring to Daysi's very advanced state of pregnancy.

It was now time for me to consider my own move, something I had busily put off. A quick census of possible lodgings revealed that I had little choice: the only possibility was to ask Don Manolo, with the largest house in the neighborhood, to take me on as an extra.

I hadn't seen the old man since I met him on horseback, a long month ago. But his image remained vivid in my mind, particularly since he had become a favorite target for the brigadistas' imitations. "Sí-sí-cómo-no," they'd grunt in simulated bass voices during the group meetings, followed by a simulated spit on the floor, much to the delight of the others. On a more serious note, Jorge, the brigadista at Manolo's farm, had approached me at the last Saturday workshop, a worried frown on his elfin, fourteen-year-old face. "Listen, I've got a problem with Don Manolo," he confessed. "He comes to class all right, but after about twenty minutes he just gets up and walks out, and I can't get him to come back. And another thing, he's been working on his name for the whole three weeks and he still hasn't got it."

"Well, have you talked to him about it?"

"I asked him if he wanted to study, but he just said, 'Sure, sure, why not?' and walked off." Jorge's innocent face was so solemn, I resisted the urge to smile, though the thought of the two of them together—little Jorge holding the primer and pleading as the grizzled old farmer stalked away—was priceless. I promised him that I'd make a special visit to his class. Little did either of us know then that I would come to stay.

Now there on my new mission, I had ample time to look around as I consulted with a tall, stately, unusually self-possessed woman whom I assumed to be the cook. The cement floor in the kitchen, the ample sideboard of planed wood, saddles on the wall of the shed, and the big brick house beyond—a month ago, all this had barely attracted my attention. Now, though, I recognized what wealth these things signified in remote Wapá.

The idea of becoming part of one of the bosses' families had me worried. I wondered how it might change my relation to the community. And how much of an exploiter of his workers was the old man? I'd been able to catch nothing definite from my contacts in El Jícaro.

It was done, though. I'd laid out my case, and Doña Leopoldina, the cook, was smiling warmly. "I think we can make room for you."

Not forty-five minutes later, on the other side of the prairie, Doña Bernarda popped out of her hut to greet me as I went by. "We hear you're moving to Don Manolo's," she blurted out. "Well, don't worry. If he won't let you stay there you can always come and stay here."

But how did she find out?

The traditional fiesta days of Muy Muy at the end of April were almost upon us. Still no rain, no clouds, only the stifling sun. The campesinos were beginning to be concerned. "Last year we were ready to plant by fiesta time." I, too, now scanned the sky, waiting for the long, dry days to end.

Goyo was carted off by relatives on "urgent family business," steady, serious Goyo, the best teacher in the group. He would leave a hole—for how long? Then came the dropping of Raúl's other shoe.

Racing back over the hills from my rounds, I was thinking of nothing but a plunge into the cold twilight river. But there on the porch of my house were two strange figures. Drawing closer, I could see that it was Estela, with Raúl. Drawing closer still, I made out the look on the latter's face—a look of deep, practiced penitence that I had already come to know all too well. Ay, Raúl, what is it this time?

Between the two of them, the story came out. It seemed that Blanca—the infamous Blanca—had a boyfriend, and that boyfriend was a *compa*, and had a pistol, and was a verrrry jealous type.

And it seemed that the day before, our Raúl heard a knock on the door of Don Luis's shack, where he was staying, and upon opening it found himself looking down the barrel of that pistol. A good scare for all concerned, and a warning to us about respecting the norms of the community. Fortunately, Don Luis was a respected figure in the vicinity, and a good talker. Even more fortunately, he was home at the time.

So now Raúl had to be moved again, this time under a threat to his life. He would go to Don Rito's ranch—the place little Rafael deserted way over on the other side of the highway, where, hopefully, he could mend his ways.

Yet, despite Estela's grim face and the long, sad story, I glanced at Raúl's downcast eyes and broke into un-advisorly giggles. I just *must* get my reactions more in line with Nicaraguan reality, but it seemed such a wonderful scene for Hollywood, pistol and all:

"You Raúl?"

"Yup."

"You the alphabetizer here?"

"That's me."

"Well, you ain't alphabetizing, you're womanizing, and with my woman! Take that!"

Bang!

That was it, then. More than a month gone by. April ending, the dry season ending, my time in El Jícaro coming to an end. Four months to go, and almost twenty lessons still unopened.

I learned we would get time off for the fiesta. "You have *me* to thank for this," Estela announced. "I fought for these days off."

"And the brigadistas?" I asked. She shrugged. Things could go along for three days without us.

So on Friday, morning-fresh and strange in my good trousers and shoes, I walked toward the highway, humming "Avancemos, Brigadistas..." Behind me, Wapá and El Jícaro shrank into themselves.

BOOK THREE

MAY
The Larger Reality

In May the first rains come,
The tender grass is reborn from the ashes,
The muddy tractors turn the earth,
The roads fill with butterflies and with
        puddles.
And the nights are fresh and charged with
Insects; and it rains all night long . . .

HORA ERNESTO CARDENAL, *HORA 0*

*Any education that merits the name must prepare people for freedom—
to have opinions, to be critical, to transform their world.*

                    FATHER FERNANDO CARDENAL

The literacy crusade had been choreographed to the rhythm of national unity. But already, less than a year after the overthrow, the anti-Somoza alliance was starting to falter. Disagreements over the political or economic direction of the revolution were forcing redefinitions, which were in turn often met with new dissent. The community of El Jícaro was too isolated to readily grasp the meaning of events in Managua, but it felt the discordant reverberations in its own way. The tensions hummed, too, among the brigadistas, particularly those who were beginning to define themselves within the new political process. As the dazzling novelty of our arrival wore off and our intuitive eye became used to the surroundings, we began to discern the shape of local conflicts, traditionally there but now brought into clearer focus by that social upheaval called revolution.

CHAPTER 10
Beyond Literacy

The Literacy Crusade is indoctrination. It's an attempt to domesticate the minds of the poor.

ALFONSO ROBELO, MAY 1980

During the previous weeks, it had been all too easy to forget about everything but the crusade. Monitoring classes and watching the smoky skies for signs of the promised rains, I hadn't noticed that clouds of confrontation had been gathering over Managua, casting a shadow on the euphoria of victory. But now it was inescapable; the growing polarization had brought its first thunderstorm. The newspaper *La Prensa*, formerly the printed embodiment of anti-Somoza sentiment, was on strike, and the two "moderate" members of the government junta had just resigned.

We hadn't heard much about all this in our little valley, but I had used my brief vacation to visit friends in Matagalpa, and there the city was abuzz with the events. Some had seen it coming, had been watching the signs of weather-change as they approached.

In the first five months after victory, everyone had been a Sandinista. The final push to victory had involved all sectors of Nicaraguan society, even some of the industrialists, financiers, and business owners. Theirs wasn't so much a dispute with Nicaragua's economic system—basically, agricultural exports made competitive by extremely low wages. It wasn't even the abusive National Guard, whose role was to assure that the situation wouldn't produce rebellion. No, for them, "Tacho" Somozo went too far only after the 1972 earthquake, when he encroached on the only turf left to non-Somocista capitalists—banking and the suddenly important construction industry. But Somoza had maintained himself in power partly by keeping these opposition groups divided among themselves. Having decided that Somoza had to go, his opponents were unable to agree on how to get him out, or on how a post-Somoza program could be shaped or what it should look like. In the eyes of Somoza, Pedro Juaquín Chamorro, the courageous editor of *La Prensa*, was the glue that threatened to hold a significant portion of these groups together. So, on January 1978, Chamorro was gunned down on his way to work. It was impossible to find anywhere a Nicaraguan who didn't believe Somoza had ordered the murder.

The business opposition immediately called for a general strike, and even went so far as to pay their workers for its duration. But without Chamorro, this unity was short-lived. While they wrangled through 1978, the FSLN was demonstrating that it had the leadership and the strategy to beat Somoza, to say nothing of the determination and support of the people. The handwriting was on the wall. While some wealthy Nicaraguans supported United States efforts to negotiate the preservation of the old system without its figurehead—a solution derided locally as "Somocismo without Somoza"—others were footing the bill for black market purchases of weapons for the Sandinistas, and some were doing both simultaneously. By the end, business leaders, the press, and world opinion were throwing in their lot with students, clergy, and the masses of workers and peasants, with the Sandinista commanders clearly at their head.

Then suddenly Somoza was gone, and everyone had different ideas of what this miraculous victory was going to bring. Peasants expected land, the unemployed wanted jobs, the middle class and some businessmen hoped for a "system like Costa Rica's." Many were sure that their last-minute valor would be rewarded with patronage. And everyone wanted a raise. These ideas were not necessarily compatible with each other or with the programs developed by the FSLN during long years of study in the mountains—or with reality.

After the flags, the slogans, and the mass celebrations came the sobering economic assessment, and the new government's program for recovery. It was all packed into a 140-page booklet called *Plan 80*, published together with a shorter, popularized version for discussion and debate in workplaces and communities.

The plan focused on increased production in all areas, organization of the Somocista properties that had come under state control, strict wage and price controls, and a slow reorganization of the economy to benefit the poor majority of the population. At the same time, the private business interests were given ample incentives, economic guarantees, and encouragement to play a role in the new economic order.

Most business leaders intially gave lip service at least to the idea of responsibility toward those who had suffered most under Somoza, but one could often detect an undertone of *noblesse oblige* that faded as the intended "recipients" of this benevolence suddenly began organizing in their own interests. Activism had not been written into the private sector's script.

It was the organizations of the far left, though, which first began to mutiny. Seeing an opportunity to increase their own small political bases, they demanded the confiscation of all large properties by those who worked them and the doubling of wages for all workers. Their call, in short, was for the immediate creation of a workers' state. These demands resonated among the more combative and impoverished, setting off a rash of small strikes and spontaneous land seizures.

The FSLN, or "Frente" as it was popularly called, moved quickly. Frente leaders fanned out to the trouble spots and listened sympathetically as groups of workers and peasants demanded to know why the Frente was not backing this expression of the rights they had won in battle. It was an awkward task to explain that, given the economic crisis, planting the crops and getting the factories running again had to take precedence over the right to strike; that massive wage increases would only fuel inflation; that there were not enough skilled people to run the properties inherited from Somoza; in sum, that precipitous action would be against the workers' long-term interests. How do you persuade people who have just accomplished the unimaginable that the fruits of victory will not come overnight?

In many cases the prestige of the FSLN and the patient efforts to present the facts to the workers prevailed. But the far left persisted. When discussions failed to persuade the left, the Frente reacted, or, as some would argue, overreacted. In January 1980, leaders of the small Workers' Front were briefly jailed, arms caches were seized, and their newspaper was shut down. And two months later, zealous members of the Sandinista Defense Committees painted another organization advocating land seizures "an arm of the CIA," then sacked and burned its offices.

While these moves established the Sandinistas' determination to defend the economically pluralist reactivation plan, they did little to bolster the confidence of the business community. Businessmen had other reasons to be nervous. It had been a foregone conclusion that the Somoza family's private wealth would fall to the state sector. When all was tallied, this amounted to 15 percent of coffee-producing lands, 18 percent of cotton, 30 percent of sugar, and whole or partial ownership of some 150 business and commercial enterprises. It did come as a bit of a surprise when the government announced the immediate nationalization of all the commercial banks, giving it power over financial decisions. But even then the business groups were not too worried; after all, this would be a pluralist government, and who had the expertise to run the banks and make the credit decisions if not their people? Alfonso Robelo himself was the one who broke the news of the government decision.

But the government didn't stop there. Now it was taking increasing control over foreign and domestic commerce. Early on, it had formed ENCAFE, the only approved intermediary for the processing and exporting of coffee. And now there was ENABAS as well, the National Company of Basic Grains. The idea was to buy the grains consumed internally—chiefly corn, beans, and rice—at an assured price, and sell it at government-set prices, thus countering the damages caused by speculation.

While the progressive business sectors reluctantly accepted these nationalizations—a few of their more visionary members had even played a role in the grand design—it was predictably proving divisive. The conservatives reacted. If the revolutionary government was going to play a strong role in the economy, they concluded, their own people would have to be assured of a strong voice in government. They would not be assuaged with promises of a mixed economy; political power was the only security they could comprehend. It was their birthright, after all, so long denied them by the Somozas. Now, they feared, that birthright was about to be usurped by a bunch of ragtag guerrillas who knew nothing about running a government—certainly not running one in their interest.

This struggle, of course, is the essence of revolution. In the power vacuum that results from the overthrow of an old system, what will take its place? Who will hold the reins of power, and in whose interest? Will the sovereign power respond to the masses and move to build a new system that incorporates their participation and serves their needs? Or will it serve the wealthy, settling for a few social benefits amid a lot of rhetoric?

The business organizations moved to halt or frustrate the slow advance toward socialism, and to discredit the FSLN. Ostensibly aimed at preserving "liberty, international independence and efficiency in the marketplace," their platform was actually built around halting price controls of the basic goods, slowing the enforcement of mini- mum wage and social security laws, and sabotaging plans by the government to institute ENABAS. Some particularly sophisticated business owners even started paying workers much more than the minimum wage. It was all part of the scramble to erode in peacetime the political base the FSLN had gained in war.

That was at the overt level. Under the surface, deliberate subversion was intensifying the government's initial problems in organizing the new distribution plans. Truckloads of basic grains disappeared; cattle were smuggled across the border to Honduras; private buyers arrived in the countryside to promise the peasants more money for their crops than ENABAS would pay. Price controls were defied on all sides, and inexplicable shortages in basic consumer items developed. Meat became scarce, then eggs, then salt, then oil. While the shortages had not yet reached the levels seen in Chile, the people became nervous, and thus supersensitive to the "ruinations of communism" message preached incessantly by the opposition factions.

The newspapers not only reported the conflict, they became a major battlefield. Prior to the revolutionary triumph, there had been two major dailies in Nicaragua, the Somoza-owned *Novedades* and the opposition paper *La Prensa*. Under Pedro Joaquín Chamorro, the latter had become a symbol of the broader struggle. Closed by Somoza, allowed to open, reclosed, its editor assassinated, its plant bombed, *La Prensa* nevertheless continued as a tenacious and unsilenceable voice of opposition. After the war, the presses of *Novedades* were seized to become *Barricada*, official voice of the Frente Sandinista. *La Prensa* continued, as before, independent.

Now, though, a split had emerged within the paper itself, between those was supported the revolution and those who were—more and more openly—against it. In the last weeks of February 1980, articles began to appear with disclaimers at the end, written by the very linotypers who had cast them. The editorial page became contradictory; articles exploring different conceptions of socialism confronted rabidly anticommunist columns. In March a bitter strike broke out, centering on the decision of the board of directors to replace acting editor Xavier Chamorro with his far more conservative nephew, Pedro Joaquín, Jr. The strike ended more than a month later as 75 percent of the workers, headed by Xavier Chamorro, left to form their own paper, *El Nuevo Diario*—simply, The New Daily. *La Prensa* resumed printing, now unequivocally the voice of the reactionary business community and its adherents. The paper continued to exploit its old image as the voice of courageous opposition to evil forces, a source of no little confusion to readers who believed in the Sandinistas, yet still trusted *La Prensa.*

A similar process was taking place in the political arena. The five members of the government junta selected in the weeks before the victory had reached an impasse over a number of issues. The break surfaced when Violeta Chamorro, widow of the slain editor, resigned, ostensibly for reasons of health. She was immediately followed by colleague Alfonso Robelo, who was far more vociferous about his reasons. The final catalyst for his departure was the reapportionment of the Council of State, the legislative body whose composition had been established while the provisional government was still in Costa Rica.

The Council was not based either on geographic representation or on participation exclusively through political parties. Rather, it embodied a corporatist notion of sectoral interests, and its thirty-three seats were apportioned among political parties, unions, and business and professional associations. In the original allotment, approximately half the seats went to traditional political parties and other organizations dominated by business interests.

In the period between victory and the scheduled inauguration of the Council on May 4, 1980, however, some significant changes had occurred in the political configuration of the country. Pro-Sandinista mass organizations such as the women's association, the youth organization, the neighborhood defense committees and others had blossomed as if in a hothouse. Boasting tens of thousands of members each, they demanded that their interests, too, should be represented on the Council. This more articulated notion of interest groups led to a joint announcement on April 22 by the FSLN and the executive branch of the new government that fourteen additional seats would be created. Most would go to the mass organizations, including Misurasata, the Indian grouping on the Atlantic Coast. There would also be a seat for the Sandinista Popular Army. The conservative opposition bellowed its outrage. While their seats were not reduced in number (save for a couple of small parties that had collapsed), their political clout was nearly halved. Two days after the announcement, Robelo labeled the move a "totalitarian scheme" and promptly resigned.

A youthful millionaire businessman, Robelo had helped fund the Sandinista struggle, although he hadn't participated in actual armed combat. Now he had political plans of his own. His party, the Nicaraguan Democratic Movement (MDN), was breaking off from the national unity effort. He was now busily persuading the other opposition political parties, business organizations and the two pro-business union confederations to join MDN in a boycott of the Council's activities. It was an inauspicious beginning for the new legislative body.

Branded a traitor and opportunist on the one side, hailed as a hero on the other, Robelo immediately became a magnet for all the forces that wanted the revolution to stop where it was or, better yet, make an about-face. Even when the vacancies on the junta were immediately filled by two moderate and well-respected leaders—Rafael Córdoba Rivas and Arturo Cruz—the voices of the right, with Robelo at the lead, cried "betrayal." It was a shot that they made sure was heard round the world.

When I returned from Matagalpa bursting with all this news, initial discussions with the more politically aware residents of the valley revealed concern and confusion. Spying my favorite *guanacaste* tree just over the next rise, I decided to stop for lunch and ponder the significance of these events for our community. Sprawled in the tree's protective shade, I began peeling a grapefruit I had thrown into my pack.

In Matagalpa I had found several students of this new political scene who recognized the source of the opposition's anger for what it was. The issue wasn't about betrayal of principles or totalitarian schemes, they had explained. The simple fact was that in the revolutionary realignment, the opposition had lost much of its political base, and that was now being reflected in the Council of State. Pluralism was not dead; it just didn't look as appealing when the other side had the plurality.

But those who understood this were the exceptions. The people of Wapá, still distant from the reality beyond their valley, were not the only ones confused. It was happening all over the country. One doesn't move from alienation and cynicism to clarity and political sophistication overnight. Nonetheless, the polarization was already beginning to filter down, attracting the business opposition to one side, the politically aware workers and peasants to the other, and dividing the students. Small farmers and those who owned the tiny market stalls or ran a little shop in their house were caught in the middle. Often without sufficient education to grasp the process that was developing, they were distrustful of the changes, frightened of losing the little they had garnered over the years.

I began to understand better what this literacy project was all about. It wasn't going to be enough that the dispossessed looked up to the Sandinistas, revered them. There was certainly no dearth of that kind of support: in the impoverished countryside, a paper or plastic Sandinista flag to hang above the doorway was one of the few items as highly coveted as the image of a saint. Nor was it enough that they wanted a change in the miserable conditions of their lives.

Part of the problem was the campesinos' traditional sense of powerlessness and lack of self-esteem, the feeling that "we're just brutes here." The usual result of this was passive acquiescence to anyone they perceived as exuding power. It was a tried-and-true survival technique, one they would not abandon overnight. The other part of the problem was that while there were few disagreements about where forward was, no one was too clear about how to get there. This meant that a slick talker like Robelo had real room for maneuver. The shedding of passivity would have to be accompanied by greater understanding of the complexities, the likely consequences of a particular course of action. The forums for exploration that the crusade provided were designed to embolden the peasants to begin to think, to speak out. This was eventually bound to produce rich, even heated debate, but we had a long way to go and we could expect it to happen faster for some than for others.

Meanwhile here we were, with Nicaragua's brand-new legislature about to be inaugurated amid both hostility and great fanfare. And here I was, ringed by grapefruit rinds curling in the hot afternoon sun. Though the peasants here in Wapá couldn't read the papers, or understand all the words of the speeches on the radio, at least a few demonstrated that the gist of it was not lost on them. "It's a rare rich guy that has anything to offer a poor bugger," Doña Luisa snorted. Arturo, her son, said the same thing in more sophisticated terms: "This Robelo is just out for himself, and he wants to use us the way Somoza used to. Won't catch me helping a rich bastard get richer."

CHAPTER 11
What Is to Be Done?

The function of knowledge is but one—to transform reality. . . .

BAYARDO ARCE, MEMBER OF THE
FSLN NATIONAL DIRECTORATE*

Moving day. I had been with the Murillos a month, and they had been my center of gravity through those crazy first weeks. Lucy, Doña Guillermina's eleven-year-old, had tears in her eyes as she waved me goodbye. Everyone wished me *buena suerte*—good luck—as heartily as if I were going off to Miami.

Indeed, I was entering a new order of things. My new lodging was at the farthest end of the feudal plain of Wapá, and the long prairie stretched before me—an ocean bobbing with cows. The stability of old El Jícaro's modestly prosperous farm families had been replaced by a set of rural class relations that put me on guard. I had read about the skewed and politically eruptive land-distribution patterns in Latin America, and had seen their manifestations in my travels. Now I was living in the middle of a scale model of one—six big landowners and forty impoverished, dependent families. Here I would be drawn into much closer contact with the problems of the area, and the real meaning of the literacy crusade. I would be forced to grapple with some of the campesino's realities, and with those of the country as a whole. I, like the brigadistas, was finding this all very new. Now, at five weeks and counting, it was time for us—for me—to take a look beyond the primers.

It was the visit to Jairo that first made me realize I hadn't been paying sufficient attention to my surroundings. Little Jairo, with his delicate face and soft voice, for weeks had been living uncomplainingly amid the filth and neglect of Don Ernesto's. That unswept barn of a house, the air of misery, and the sour smell of the kitchen—I'd refused to believe the people in the valley who assured me that the family had money.

---

*Quoted in Valerie Miller, "The Nicaraguan Literacy Campaign," in Thomas W. Walker, *Nicaragua in Revolution* (New York: Praeger, 1982).

"No, really, he has all that land over by the river and back as far as the gate at Don Roberto's. And there's another farm, too, in some other community. I don't exactly know where."

"Then how come they live that way?"

Shrugs, cryptic smiles. "The señora's just that way—strangelike. Or maybe it's the son they lost—killed by the *guardia*, they say. They were after the old man, too."

I did like lame Don Ernesto, with his forlorn smile. The really sinister one was the señora—cold and stiff as the iron-gray hair perpetually wound in disarray around her head.

Now, for the first time, Jairo registered a complaint.

"She made me buy my food to take for lunch to the Saturday meeting. They're supposed to *give* us food, aren't they?" A problem easily resolved with a few orientations on either side. But it wasn't the only one.

"*Profe*, did you know that they only pay Don Jaime thirteen córdobas a day? Doesn't the law say that twenty-five is the minimum now? And they're supposed to be giving him lunch, but some days it's only *pozol** with salt—bitter, just like the coffee they give me. Now what do you say about that? I call it exploitation, that's what." The word hung awkwardly in his thirteen-year-old mouth, but he meant it, and he was right.

"Where did you hear all that?"

"I heard them talking in the kitchen," he said, solemn with concern. "And the brigadista who lives with Don Jaime, Nelson, he told me the same thing. Nelson's trying to get him to go to court, but Jaime's scared he might lose his job."

As I became more familiar with and to the campesinos in Wapá, I began to realize that Don Jaime's problem was far from atypical. None of this was new, except the workers' glimpse that there might now be something they could do about it. On the *pátrons'* side, there was the growing insecurity that came with the realization that they were no longer protected by the government. Thus there were strains on all sides—movement, fear, challenge, confrontation, confusion about how to interpret and therefore how to act. Silence had led me to believe there was conformity. Now I was learning that all was not so peaceful as it seemed in the valley.

---

*Boiled corn, served with salt as a dish for the very poor, or sugared, as a substantial drink.

A few mornings later I awoke to the sound of voices on the front porch. Don Chavelo's was among them, his voice low and suppliant, but insistent. I strained to hear his words, but they evaporated into the dawn. Then Don Manolo, in his unmistakable bass, said, "No one's denying you work, Chavelo. It's just that there *is* no work right now." More voices, Chavelo's and that of Doña Angela, the señora of the house, then Carlos, the awkwardly overgrown son: "My father said there's no work. There's no work." I could hear the tension in everybody's voice, but I couldn't piece together the snippets that I was catching. "No one's working. . ." ". . .but the children. . .?"

The kitchen was quiet as I entered, too quiet. Something was going on, that was obvious. I resolved to get to the bottom of it.

"I'm out of work right now," was one of the first things Don Chavelo had told me the day I met him. What I now learned through subtle questioning over kitchen and schoolroom tables was that "right now" had lasted months and months. Don Chavelo claimed that it was an act of vengeance, an attempt to get rid of him. "The law says you can't evict a *mozo*, but it doesn't say you can't starve him out." Without work there was nothing more than an acre of corn and a few chickens. No one could endure long under such conditions.

"But why do they want to get rid of you?"

"Because I'm active. . .the señor has it in for me."

We talked for a while in subdued tones. "Why don't you report it to the ATC, the farmworkers' union?"

"Ah, I've tried," he said, "but the representatives here won't back me up."

"Who, Don Goyo and Don Petronilo? I can't believe it."

"Yes, they're just out to save their own skins. Afraid the same thing will happen to them."

I walked around indignant until evening when, there in Daysi's little shack, more sordid details emerged. "It's the señora. She's jealous, and that's not something the ATC can deal with."

"Jealous?"

"Well, because of Don Manolo and Chavelo's daughter. . ."

Tale of a gothic romance. Elderly lord of manor takes a fancy to pretty eldest daughter of one of his serfs, promises her presents and promises to marry her. Lady of manor (whom lord has never married) finds out. Slightly simple son lines up with mother, who flies into a rage. Girl's father—poor but proud—gets wind of infatuation and emphatically repulses his liege. Romance over, lord redeems dignity and honors serf's "property." But lady remains threatened by presence of pretty peasant daughter and, joined by son, conspires to banish peasant family from the castle grounds by whatever means necessary—handicapped only slightly by revolutionary laws, something most Gothic romances don't have to deal with.

Was all this true? Daysi said it was. Don Petronilo said it was. "Well, the old guy's always treated me fair. This thing with Chavelo, I see it as a woman's fight." Don Chavelo mentioned none of it, attributing his problem to activism. Doña Angela, I was not about to ask, let alone Don Manolo.

Whatever the real story, the result was one unemployed peasant, eight children and a brigadista, no food, no land, no savings, only the slim support that Don Chavelo's father provided from his little plot in El Jícaro. And, seemingly, no recourse.

Was there anything we in the literacy crusade could do? To come out directly against the landlords, openly challenging them, would turn the crusade into an advocacy force. It would exacerbate the landlord-peasant tensions in that it would be easier to get back at the crusade through the peasants than the other way around. And we would sacrifice any chance we had to make inroads, if not with the old landlords themselves, then at least with their children. After all, the revolution had much to offer them, too; part of our job here was to make them see it. "Keep a low profile," I cautioned myself. "We'll get 'em little by little."

Yet a side of me was unconvinced by my own arguments. Was I being influenced by the tortillas and cheese at the boss-man's table? I felt over my head, awkward in the face of cultural traditions that were not my own, and full of questions about the new laws and the government's ability to enforce them. I wished I could sit down with Estela, who, after all, knew the community and was sympathetic to the needs of its residents. But I never found the right moment or the right words.

Mario shot! "What? Say that again!" I demanded, voice rising. Estela, perched calmly behind her desk in the school, cigarette dangling from one hand, nodded in affirmation. "Well, we really don't know too much. He went to the fiesta with Doña Julia and the family, and was sitting in the bleachers at the bullring when a bullet hit him, in the flesh of the thigh. He'll be all right. They have him in Matagalpa now, but they'll be moving him to Managua in a few days so his mother can come see him."

"Was it an accident or what?" I still couldn't seem to absorb it.

"We don't know. No one seems to have seen who did it. I'll tell you one thing, though. I told those kids not to wear their uniforms if they go to Muy Muy. That gray *cotona* with the six-sided badge sewn on over your heart. . . Whooh! It's like a target for trouble from people who are convinced this is all just some sort of brainwashing project. But, oh, no, he didn't want to listen, so there he was in his *cotona*, right up toward the top where everyone could see him. Who knows, Sheyla, times being what they are, anyone could have done it."

Muy Muy was a classic cowboy town, but who could have guessed that little Mario with his crew cut and bright smile—and neat trick of being in the river when it was time for classes—would catch a stray bullet. Or as Estela suggested, maybe it wasn't a stray. "Poor little Baldy," remarked the brigadistas, opting for the first explanation. "Guess we won't be seeing him back here."

Maybe it was my preoccupation with the state of the world in general, but suddenly the face of misery seemed to be staring at me from all sides. This time it was Narciso, who drew my attention to the condition of the Santa Cruz family where he gave classes.

"They all have measles there, and they're going to die, *profe*," he announced. There was a serious look on his face that I recognized as genuine, for once. "Eight kids dying, no kidding! What'll we do?"

"Let's go," I said. "I need to see." I hadn't been to their shack since the day we censused, when the lineup of vacant-eyed children with distended bellies was as clear as a billboard: "No brigadistas here, please." Though they couldn't afford to house anyone, three young women and the ten-year-old boy had been studying—and advancing, according to Narciso, who made the daily walk to give them their classes. Now, though, there was good reason for his concern. Measles is a killer in Latin America, most of all among malnourished children. Classes had been suspended, while the women helplessly watched the dread illness spread through the household.

We could smell it as we came in, a fetid odor of diarrhea and fever. Narciso was wrong; there were only five sick children, but it seemed like a dozen, crowded onto two planks that served as beds for the whole family. Some lay sleeping while others moaned weakly. The house was the most miserable of any I'd seen so far, not so much for the obvious poverty as for the air of neglect, of hopelessness. The oldest woman responded impassively as I questioned her gently. No, they hadn't been vaccinated. No, she hadn't taken them into town— no money. Yes, they'd been sick for about a week now. Yesterday they thought the little girl was going to die, but today she seemed a little better. I looked over as she pointed at a painfully thin child of about three of four, covered with rags. Dirt-crusted scabs pocked her face and body. She appeared lifeless, a filthy doll tossed aside.

She's got a workings that just won't quit,'' her mother was saying. "And the baby, too. That's what's making them so weak."

I looked over at Narciso. "Workings?"

His face reddened. "Uh, that's like—uh—defecation."

Feeling incredibly helpless, I explained what I could remember of the training discussions about how to treat diarrhea. I had been horrified to learn that diarrhea was a common cause of infant death in Nicaragua. Billboards in all the cities, using drawings rather than words, showed what to do: boil any water before letting the children drink it, clean them frequently with clean rags, regulate their diet, and take them to the new, free clinics that were being set up, for medicines and vitamin replenishment. But out here, if anyone had even seen or understood the instructions, these simple steps were all so hard. The only rags were those they wore; there was no choice of diet for families as poor as this one; and transportation to the clinic was beyond their means, even if the clinic itself was not.

"There's little you can do once a child has measles," I explained somewhat lamely to the mother. Her unblinking eyes told me she did not find that news. "But when the health brigadistas come again to the school to vaccinate, you should be sure to take the children. That way you can protect them against other diseases."

She continued to watch me expressionlessly. I felt I was expected to do something. After all, I was from a country where children almost never die of measles, much less diarrhea. I sighed and signaled to Narciso that we should leave, promising to return with medicine if I could find any that was effective, promising to help her get the children to a clinic if they should get any worse, promising, promising.

Gulping the gloriously fresh air outdoors, we walked back toward Doña Luisa's. But those pockmarked faces, already scarred by more than just measles, did not vanish from my mind as easily as the gagging odor left my lungs.

The national political sideshow was coming to town! The kickoff meeting of Alfonso Robelo's opposition party was to be held in the prosperous nearby town of Matiguás, less than an hour by bus or car from the back entrance to Wapá. Chico, a frequent visitor these days, sounded the alarm. "Look, they're inviting the campesinos to come in, and they're offering them free transportation. Of course they'll go! It's a free ride to town! And then they'll be billed as the great grassroots supporters of Robelo, and it'll be the old *'bolis y nacatamales'* all over again."

My questioning stare brought a wink and an exchange of smiles between Chico and Estela, "When Tacho Somoza had 'elections,' " Estela explained, "his party, the so-called Liberals, would bring all the campesinos into town and give them popsicles made of frozen rum and sugar and Nicaraguan-style tamales. Then they'd all get roaring drunk, put their mark on the ballot where they were told to put it, and be hauled off yelling 'Viva Somoza!' just before they fell down."

"So now," Chico chimed in, in his low, decisive voice, "there are campesinos who can't believe that the junta is really in power. 'Who's this guy, Tomás Borge,' they say. 'I haven't tasted *guaro* or a *nacatamale* since he got in.' " Don Chavelo and the group of other listeners who had gathered laughed unselfconsciously. "But now we've got to explain to people who this guy Robelo is and what he stands for. Not that they shouldn't go if they want to, but they should be clear about what's happening before they go—not let themselves be deceived yet again. We want to have our own meeting before the Matiguás thing, and we need the help of the brigadistas and the CDS, fast."

Everyone was nodding like mad now. Chico had such a natural way of putting things, friendly but completely forthright. And he was right, too. The people in my house had been interested in going to Matiguás because they'd never seen a member of the governing junta. They didn't even know that Robelo had resigned some weeks ago.

So we would hold Wapá's first political meeting in the schoolhouse on Friday. Chico would talk, together with a brigadista and maybe someone from the community. Then, with luck, people would feel encouraged to talk or ask questions. It was nearly dark before we got the plans made and hurried off to our separate shelters.

I sat silently that night on the porch at Don Manolo's, thinking about Robelo, and wondering how much of a following he could attract, between unhappy property owners in the country and all the outside forces who would be happy to see this Sandinista experiment undermined. What he wanted and represented was completely clear to me: a turning away from real change and a return to a liberal facsimile of the past. A turning away from the harsh necessities of independent development and back to the familiar old traps: new international debts secured just to pay off old ones; Nicaraguan workers assembling blue jeans from American cloth made from Nicaraguan cotton to sell in America; selling sugar at low prices because there was no other choice in order to buy tractors at high prices because there was no other choice; white faces with portfolios in the bar of the Hotel Intercontinental; the right to put one of two names on a piece of paper every four years, if you could read, if you could get to town, if you thought it mattered And, for a while, the absence of overt repression, just quiet oppression—until you started organizing to try for real change once again.

I knew it all, like a movie I'd seen several times. But could it be stopped by meetings like ours? Would the awakenings of the literacy crusade be enough to sustain the revolution in the countryside? Would *consciencia* come in time?

Friday morning. Meeting planned for the afternoon; Roberto looking for me with the news that he was supposed to give a speech and didn't know what to say. Now, why him? I wondered. Certainly, we had agreed that Miguel, the squadron leader, had been overexposed, and that Roberto, at nineteen, was an ex-combatant and a reasonably good talker, when he was in the mood. But he was so indifferent, and with a growing reputation for eccentricity. But the decision seemed to have been made. Together we went over the folders he'd been given by the Juventud Sandinista, which was co-sponsoring the talk with the CDS, and worked the elegant phraseology into a simpler form. It still didn't exactly sound off the cuff, but it was the best we could do in three hours.

When I dashed back to the house for lunch, I found everybody getting ready to go, excited and curious. I was surprised by the enthusiasm; perhaps I had underestimated the community's hunger to know about the world outside. "We've never had anything like this before," explained Leopoldina, who it had turned out was the cook. There she was, preparing her two boys for the hike. It was the first time I'd seen her leave the house since I'd moved in.

In the end we were a small army mounting the final hill to the schoolhouse. Most of the brigadistas were already there, and so, I noted with relief, were Chico and a young woman from the Muy

Muy office. The school was soon filled to overflowing, even with the children left outside to peer in through the windows. Doña María Elsa suspended her sale of sugar candies and we prepared to start.

As Chico got up to speak, the room fell suddenly quiet; the only sound was the respectful shh-ing sound the women directed to the fussing babies they rocked on their laps. In his most natural manner, sincere and direct, Chico explained Robelo's background and the party he was forming. Without sounding the least imperious, he urged them not to make clowns of themselves Sunday. "You're worth more than that; the revolution's worth more. We're not saying don't go, or don't listen—nothing like that. Only, brothers and sisters, let's be very clear that what this man wants isn't what you here want and need. And if you go, go for the experience. Don't let yourselves be deceived as you were so many times in the past."

People were listening, really listening. Now, why hadn't we prepared something like that? After a few minutes, he paused, calling on others to participate. It was Roberto's turn. Blinking nervously, he read through our carefully prepared discourse at breakneck speed— it was perfectly incomprehensible to all. Miguel put in a few words, flowery but not inappropriate, then silence fell in the packed schoolhouse.

Now Chico was pleading for someone from the community to talk. This was really new: campesinos raised for centuries to keep silent were being begged to rise and speak.

Arturo, the bravest, got up to say he still wasn't clear, but he did want to ask some questions. "So, what exactly is Robelo's position in the government?" "Why did Doña Violeta resign from the junta, then?" With the help of these, Chico clarified things still further.

Don Chico Murillo, Doña Chenta's son, was the one from the community who at last was willing to speak. He spoke mostly in generalities, about his pleasure at seeing everyone gathered and his willingness to help the community in any way necessary; but he spoke! I knew from living there that much of it came from the burning desire to live up to his father's memory, and so, probably, did everyone else. But that didn't seem to matter—or, perhaps the fact that he didn't quite fit his father's shoes was what bridged the gap with the poorer peasants. In any case, he was cheered as a living example that campesinos, too, could get up in public.

Just as the meeting came to an end, there was a stir in the room; Rito González's white truck had pulled up to the door. Smelling

Departure Day for a brigadista. She's only a little nervous. "In the mountains we swear to smother / The ignorance that we uncover. E.P.A.!"

"March 23, 1980—the day of fists on high and books open...the day to say 'basta ya' to ignorance."

Doña Amelia, who housed Estela and gave me my first breakfast in El Jícaro.

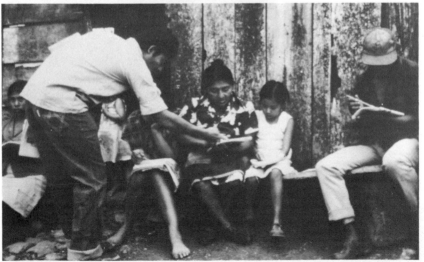

Goyo's class. "It's the holiest week in the year, but there they are—beginning—even though they don't have a table, and they're sharing the few pencils there are..."

"Lesson 2. The FSLN led the people to liberation."

Doña María Elsa with the youngest of her twelve children, enjoying the only shower in Wapá, which they contrived through their own ingenuity.

A class in progress. "Sandino vive: vi, vo va ve vu."

David, Roberto, and Matias at a Saturday workshop.

Don Toribio, the old Sandinista veteran with his brood and brigadista.

And Doña Bernarda with hers.

"Campesino aprenda a leer."

Arturo looks worried as he stares out from Don Manolo's kitchen, during the disappearance of the owner.'

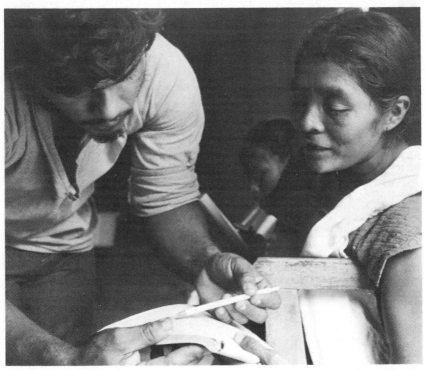

Phlegmatic Fredy, so patient with his students, so impatient with his advisors. "For me, it's a great honor to be able to teach here."

We salute the first anniversary of the revolution, alphabetizing. Back row, left to right: *Goyo, Elvis, Pablo, Narciso, Roberto, Jairo, David, and the technical advisor squeezed into the middle.* Front: *Jorge, Silvio, Miguel, Geraldo, Matias.*

Doña Poldina. She earned two hundred córdobas for cooking, doing laun-
dry, and making cheese from five in the morning till dusk.

Then Don Manolo was back, thin as a rail and drugged to the teeth, a ghost of the gruff landlord I'd met that first day.

Doña Luisa. *"The accumulated wisdom of seventy-odd years. You didn't learn more than your name, but you taught us a great deal."*

"We're going home! Territorio victorioso *and goodbye."*

Victory rally in Matagalpa. Jairo, Carlos, Pablo, Ramiro. "We DID *it!"*

Homecoming parade in Matagalpa. "We became a hundred, two hundred, a thousand, two thousand...sixty thousand."

slightly of liquor, he stalked into the room and ostentatiously took a seat near the front. Those who had already walked out crowded around the door. I'd had only passing contacts with him, but everyone else seemed to know what to expect. Assuming a bellicose air, he pulled himself to his feet and launched into a diatribe. "And why have these people resigned?" he demanded rhetorically. "What is the Frente doing telling people they shouldn't go to Matiguás? Is it a free country or isn't it? And people are now with the Frente who just two years ago were screaming 'Viva Somoza' in Muy Muy. Tomás Borge calling for austerity from his Mercedes Benz. . ." On he went with his insinuations and half-truths. People were whispering and looking toward Chico to see how he'd react. Certainly no one else was prepared to take Don Rito on. With his big farm over by the highway, he was a force in the community. Those who had just tried out their public voice for the first time were suddenly mute and defenseless again. But Chico just listened, face inscrutable.

"Is Tomás Borge a communist?" Don Rito challenged the room. Here Nelson, bless his clear head, broke in to beg a clarification of the term. Nothing could have tripped up Don Rito better. Before he could figure out how to regain control of the situation, Chico quietly took the floor.

"Listen, brothers and sisters, communism is a perfect system, like perfect Christianity. It is something so perfect that you don't have to worry about it because it'll never get here in a hundred years. Despite what you hear, there's no country that has it. Not Cuba, not Russia. Under communism, if I have land and you don't, now that's going to be your land, too. And if I have tools, they're as much yours as mine. It's where everyone shares everything, like in the Bible—you know, 'Love thy neighbor as thyself.'

"At the same time, it's where everybody works, not because they're paid, but because they understand all by themselves that the work has to get done or nobody eats. Now, do you think we're ready for that here?" Smiles and shaking of heads. "Like I say, it's a system so advanced that we're not going to see it on this earth in a hurry. Meanwhile, though, what we do want is socialism. So that everything that Somoza and his cronies robbed now belongs to everyone in Nicaragua. And the money that comes from that is going to pay for this crusade, and fix up the clinic in Muy Muy, and maybe help build a school in Wapá. And we want all the money that we Nicaraguans make to stay here and benefit us, the people who work—especially you, the campesinos, who produce all the food we eat—instead of going outside the country like it did before. But this means that we have to keep working and produce more, because we already owe so much money that I can't even tell you about it. And like I say, you have to be careful about people like this Robelo who use a lot of fancy words like communism, liberty, pluralism. There's a reason he's using words you can't understand. It's not convenient for him that you, the campesinos, really understand what he wants. Why do you think he was so upset when your workers' confederation and the CDS and all won seats on the Council of State?"

Arturo, the world's most genuine straight man: "So let me get this straight. All this time we've been thinking that communism is like slavery and killing off the old people when they can't work, and now you say it's really just like the Bible—everybody sharing everything."

"That's right," Chico grinned, shrugging.

Arturo whistled incredulously. "What a bunch of *babosos* we are." The meeting broke up in laughter. Only Don Rito remained, arguing with a small circle of campesinos and brigadistas.

Doña Guillermina went off with the girls and a handful of other people from El Jícaro to see the Robelo meeting. They returned in the late afternoon, the children clutching red-and-white flags that had been passed out to them. Doña Guillermina wore a visored cap that said MDN, and was clutching the colorful folders of the meeting. "How was it?" I asked.

"Hot," she said, "and crowded. But kind of fun. There sure were mobs of people there."

"And what did he say?"

She smiled, a little abashed. "Well, to tell the truth, *maestra*, there were delays and more delays, and finally we got so hot we couldn't stand it, so we went looking for something to drink. By the time we got back, it was over."

Pancho Rivas hung the flags over his doorway where they slowly rotted in the sun and the rain. I never stopped to ask him if he really liked the party, or merely appreciated the free adornment.

CHAPTER 12
Dialogue Is the Key

It's difficult sometimes. Tomasita is smart and wants to study but her baby cries a lot and she can't put him down. I visit her three times a day just on the chance she'll be free but. . .she's only on lesson 4. . . . Camilo doesn't seem to assimilate his sounds very well. Of course he does need glasses. He's 67. . . . Socorro and Joaquina are way ahead on lesson 14 but Julio left to pick coffee and Catalina's in bed with malaria. . . . Vicente has improved incredibly since he fell off his mule. He was really a lazy bum before. But now, with his broken arm, he's quite serious and dedicated, even though he's had to learn to write all over again with his left hand.

GUADALUPE, 16, BRIGADA ENOC ORTEZ, MAY 1980*

The first National Literacy Congress was scheduled for June, and information was now being requested to augment and correct the hurried census that had been taken last October: How many illiterates were there in the community, how many studying, how many per brigadista, how many without a teacher, how many incapable of studying, how many plain uninterested? At the Congress the data would be analyzed and correctives would be suggested where necessary, before it was too late.

The distinction between those who were incapable and those who were reluctant was difficult to make. Already it had become clear that a very large proportion of the older women were dropping the class. "I don't see well," they would say; or "I get headaches when I study." Many of these complaints were real. You don't live your life amid constant smoke, work, and pregnancy without feeling the effects before you're out of your twenties.

An additional factor was that the women had little contact with the outside world. Many of them rarely left the house, sending their man or oldest son to town when it was necessary. The constant isolation left them with little need for a skill as alien as learning to read, and

---

*Quoted in Valerie Miller, *op. cit.*

thus little desire to attempt it. Sad, but with the older generation there was little to be done. Their development had been stunted. After persuading them to attend the first few classes, in hopes that their interest would be caught, we didn't press the issue further. Many of the women continued to hover proudly around the classes, but ceased to participate. Occasionally, though, I would catch a glimpse of one of them secretly practicing, copying half a name on a piece of paper tucked stealthily into a corner of the kitchen.

Doña Bernarda, on the other hand, was one of our most enthusiastic students. "She just doesn't have any memory," moaned Ricardo. "I give her classes at short intervals all day long, but nothing stays. Everyone else is on Lesson 5 or 6 and she's only on Lesson 2. Then yesterday I reviewed Lesson 1 with her and she doesn't even remember the vowels."

"It doesn't matter," I urged him. "Go back to Lesson 1 if you have to, but don't give up on her. There's more at stake in all this than just learning the letters. She'll get something. And keep her participating in the dialogue."

"The Dialogue." It was Step 1 in every lesson, and by far the most difficult to conduct. The brigadistas found it a frustrating and confusing assignment. What was it for? Certainly *they'd* never been taught that way. In all too many of the classes it was done badly, or ignored altogether.

Saturday after Saturday we spent trying to make them see its importance and master the subtleties of conducting it: "It has to be a conversation, not a lecture. And it has to come from the campesinos themselves, from their experiences. It has to be their thoughts. Look, everyone likes to talk about their experiences if they think the other person is interested. With the photo and your encouragement, they will get over their feeling of intimidation. But you have to think of questions which will unlock their experiences, then get them thinking about them.

"When you get to the actual key phrase in the book, it can't just be something out of the air, but the actual summary of what you've talked about. It really won't be that hard once you all get the hang of it. The phrases in the book aren't any different from the things almost everybody here already says, in one way or another. You just have to keep your ears open, and study the chapter beforehand, to get your questions ready."

"But what's it got to do with anything, *profe*? I try to do it right, but students say, 'We don't want to talk politics; just get on to the syllables.' "

"May I speak, *profe*? Listen, *compa*. If your students say that, it's because you've made them feel that it isn't important. If we just come and teach reading, we aren't doing anything. This crusade was planned so that the workers and peasants could really understand the national reality, and if you just teach letters and syllables, you're not even fulfilling your duty as a brigadista."

"That's right, Miguel, but you have to be careful about the opposite danger, too, which is that the exercise itself becomes more important than letting the students know you are really interested in what they have to say. When I saw your class, you started really well, but when people remained shy, you ended up giving a speech. That's when people get the idea it's some kind of political indoctrination."

"But I ask questions, and my class just giggles," Jorge objected.

"Try starting with concrete questions, questions anyone can answer."

"I did. I showed the picture of the *compas* winning, you know on page 14, and they told me it was the *guardia*."

"Okay, try not to get frustrated. Just keep going, and get them to think about what you're saying. For example, ask them how they could tell. What does the guy look like? Is he smiling or frowning? Young or old? Does he have a helmet? Does he look kind or cruel?

"Look, here's the official guide they've given us. There are five types of questions, ranging from basically concrete to abstract. This is what they give us for Lesson 6."

Los Comités de Defensa Sandinista Defienden la Revolución

1. Description	Who's in the photo? What are they doing? Where are they?
2. Analysis of the photo	Why are they meeting? What do they want?

3. The relation between the situation in the photo and the actual reality of the learner	How long has the CDS existed? Why didn't they exist before? What are the goals of the CDS within the revolution? What work has the CDS done here? What are the problems? What are the causes of the problems?
4. A search for solutions	How could we solve these problems?
5. The group commitment to transformation	What can we do as a group to solve these problems? What will we commit ourselves to do?

Number five was the key to the whole thing: the transformation of the peasants into activists who can analyze and then move; the transformation of the brigadistas from students to committed revolutionaries; the transformation of the whole damned society from passive to active. And it has to come from within or it will never be real. Most important, it has to come or the revolution won't thrive. The Sandinista goal is to make the revolution by the people, not for them. The peasants know that this magic gift of letters has something to do with the whole dream—work, good health, hope for the children—but they don't see the link between "learning" and thinking, the dialectic between outside and inside.

"But I still don't understand how I can get them to talk..."

The other brigadistas, who probably didn't understand either, copied my words diligently into their notebooks, as they had always been taught to do. Change doesn't come easy for anyone.

And so our own dialogue went on and on. We made a strange chemistry, these twenty-five Nicaraguan boys and I. There was one, as there always is, who stood out from the beginning, a cut apart. Had it not been for an essential shyness around groups, Matías would have been an inspiration to the others, as Chico was becoming. As it was, he was respected, but from a distance. While Chico spoke earnestly and passionately in meetings about the goals of the literacy crusade or the alliance of workers, peasants, and students in the march toward socialism, Matías sat quietly, his calloused hands taut on his lap and his brain spinning from "trying to get them to see."

What first caught my atttention was a look that I couldn't quite define. It radiated from every fiber of his slight, dark body—the look of someone with a dream and a decision. It had something to do with a tightness always within him—body erect, military style—and an intensity, almost overintensity of concentration. Little by little I plumbed the depths of his quiet intensity and of his dream.

Matías was nineteen and had just finished his first year of high school. He came from a poor family just outside Managua. His mother and migrant father were now both dead, leaving two other sons and a daughter. The scars on Matías's face were from a childhood bout with chicken pox. "In these countries," he told me with an ironic smile, "poor children get sick. It's rare to find one who doesn't have scars of some kind."

We'd walk all over the hills when I came to visit, talking about everything in the world. He believed in the revolution, in the rights of the workers and peasants to the fruits they created, in short, in Marxism-Leninism. He said so proudly, right out loud.

"How did you come to understand these things?"

"I thought it out, looking at everything around me. And my father, when he'd come home from work, would talk to me about how it was, how he'd worked all his life and had nothing."

"Was he a union member then?" The smile again, just slightly amused. "No, my parents weren't people like that. The only unions in Somoza's day were yellow unions. But he understood things and he talked to me about them."

We talked about religion, too, which he had given up, and about families, and about the hills and the legends and the histories of the whole world. He had Arturo's quality of eager interest and the gift of asking questions. During our long walks each week, I felt I could stop being the *profe* for a few hours, and just share.

It was raining when I awoke. So it really is going to come, then. But not this day. This day the sky swept clear again, and I went off to check the troops.

Fernando and Alejandro were out plowing. Fernando accepted my praise pleasantly for three whole minutes before he began to beg favors. "*Profe*, I need a new pair of pants. Can't you get some for me? How about my points [for good conduct]? Are they going up now? Why can't you let me have permission to go to Managua next week?"

Up the hill, I found Marvin in the mango tree. Marvin, with his low voice and torn pants, was a brigadista so steadily reliable that I sometimes forgot all about him. We talked of the war, the whole time chewing the hard, green mangoes, so acidic they made our tongues pucker. The *guardia*, he told me, came looking for him one day—they knew he'd been involved as a *correo*, or messenger, for the Frente. Fortunately, a cousin got word to him in time and he escaped, hiding in a neighbor's back room until they'd gone. He was another of those with stars in his eyes when he talked of the revolution. And very much a man, though he had just turned seventeen.

I stopped by to see Luis, but he wasn't home, so I talked for a while with Doña María. She'd written her name in chalk all over the kitchen, together with Don Agapito's and the syllables *sa se si so su*, "so I can learn something while I work."

Elvis, the brigadista living with Don Chavelo, had taken another unauthorized trip to Managua, so I stopped by to talk to him about it. "Look," he said, "do you think I just go for fun? Every time I go, it's to bring back food. I get my supplies from ENABAS,* sure, but how'm I supposed to sit and eat my beans and rice when the family hasn't got a damn thing but corn? So I share it out and my month's supply lasts about a week. What am I supposed to do? The señor can't find work. And they're all sick, Sheyla, it's one solid cough in the night." Skinny Elvis, distant and and unknowable. Was he telling the truth about his motives? "And Alva Rosa?" the boys razzed him. Seems he took Don Chavelo's pretty sixteen-year-old daughter with him when he went. Not the first time I'd noticed them together. I made a mental note to watch that relationship more closely.

Pablo's class, there in Don Goyo's hut of thatch and sticks overlooking the juncture of two rivers, looked like a scene from *Jungle Diary*. Don Goyo himself, mustached dark face immobile, sat erect on his simple chair directly in front of the blackboard, as if posed for an old-fashioned daguerreotype. The rest of the class—women and assorted children—perched in a straight line on the edge of the boards which formed the family bed. Poor Pablo, visibly nervous with me watching, darted back and forth, teaching the children the alphabet

---

*Monthly allotments of food for all brigadistas contained powdered milk and cereal; those living with the eight poorest families in each community were also provided a personal ration of corn, beans, cooking oil, sugar, and soap.

and giving the normal lesson to the adults. The chanting of syllables joined with the chirp of cicadas, the smell of the river weeds, the hot breeze of evening. *"Me-sa ma-sa mo-li-na mi-na."* And in the tree, one chicken. Evening in the jungle, branches forming black lines against the sky. Pablo's features began to fade in the gathering dusk, and the crusade, like the river, ran slowly on.

I was beginning to understand the human landscape of my new community better, too, its little peaks and valleys, the paths that cut through bramble patches, the areas of unsolid ground that might give way under too much weight. Doña Luisa, along with most of the Ocampo clan, for example, did not get along well with Doña María Elsa. This, unfortunately, divided Wapá loosely into two camps, making the work of organizing somewhat delicate. While one was identified with community gatherings, the other usually cooked for fiestas. It was important to remember which was which. Arturo and Daysi, as the Romeo and Juliet of this small feud, held a vital position as mediators. Moreovers, the people on the plain were jealous of those on the mountain, most of whom owned small parcels; and everyone from Wapá, for some reason, considered the Esquirín hacienda to be a den of vice and iniquity.

With familiarity, my bonds to the campesinos were growing stronger. They were no longer a category of people, new and culturally strange to me; they had become dozens of distinct personalities. Some were so timid that it was a challenge to wring a conversation from them. Others were more comfortable, easy with themselves and happy to share the world they lived in. Still others—Arturo and Daysi, Chavelo, María Elsa—were hungry to step outside their narrow confines, to learn, to grow. With these, the friendship was most genuine, the dialogue easiest. We were learning from each other, and here, too, we were becoming family.

Only with Estela was the dialogue growing sparser. With two hours distance between us and our zones of work clearly separated, it was increasingly hard to coordinate our efforts. We were beginning to cross orders and, worse, the brigadistas were learning to take advantage. "Estela already gave me permission," or "Sure, I already talked to Sheyla"—messages which, as they knew, couldn't be checked in a hurry. We would see each other at the Saturday workshop and, just occasionally, in passing. With never enough time, somehow, to really talk things out, small tensions were building.

Doña Leopoldina, the cook at the house of Manolo and Angela, where I lived, didn't know if her name was Deopoldina or Leopoldina. She'd been writing it with a D ever since childhood, but one day she asked me what I thought. "I'm not sure. I've never heard the name Deopoldina, but then I'm not from here." Arturo confirmed that it was Leopoldina, and she began to practice the new signature. In a world where everyone's always known everyone else, it doesn't really matter what your exact name is. Most called her Poldina, anyhow, or just Poldi. But now she had it right.

She was a tall woman, with an unconscious grace in her thin, agile figure. At thirty-five or thirty-six, she would have been extremely attractive still if it weren't for her teeth, all of which were decayed to the roots. Nevertheless, at moments, coming up from the river in the late afternoon with her long black hair swinging, for example, she was striking. She just laughed when I told her so. "No, Angela and Bernarda are the pretty sisters. Luísa and I are dark, the ugly ones."

The house we all shared had three bedrooms. One for Manolo and Angela, one for Carlos, and one for the rest of us. Before the brigadista invasion, Poldi and her two sons each had a *tijera* in their spartan 10′ × 15′ room. When Jorge came, thirteen-year-old Denis and nine-year-old Rolando had generously doubled up on one *tijera* to make room. With my arrival, a fourth cot was brought in. Clothes hung on a string between them, and any other possessions were kept in boxes underneath. The arrangement was close, if not exactly cozy.

Little by little—in conversations over the morning tortillas, or half-exhausted on the veranda in the hour between darkness and bedtime—I began to unravel Poldi's history, the family history of the Ocampos. She was the youngest of five—perhaps twenty-five years younger than her oldest sister, Doña Luisa—and the one who was left to take care of their mother. "I nursed her for the last year, in the house where Arturo and Daysi live now. Poor thing, she could hardly get around at the end. And the others were too busy to help half the time." When the old lady died almost two years ago, Leopoldina had to go out to work. "I worked for a while at Babilonia, the hacienda out by the road. But it was terrible, you can't imagine how bad, cooking for all those *mozos* from four in the morning to nine at night sometimes. Then we had to sleep in a room full of pesticide sacks that turned out to be poisonous. I didn't know what was happening, but the kids kept getting sicker and sicker until finally I got desperate enough to take them to Matagalpa where they told me that they'd been poisoned. They just escaped dying on me. Think the boss would help pay for their medicine? So then Angela said that I could come here and be the cook, so I figured 'What else can I do?' "

And the kids' father? "Well, they were two different fathers. Why lie? Neither of them was any good. Men here just aren't responsible, Sheyla. That's why I prefer to live like I am, in disgrace like this, rather than put up with another man." Her eyes burned for a minute as she spoke.

She was at home in the kitchen and, in her ceaseless activity, could be mistaken for the actual señora. Yet when Don Manolo came in, or Carlos, the son, there was a tightening, a hint that she felt her role of servant. Still, I thought her fairly content in her role, safe and protected under her sister Angela's wing.

Then one night it all poured out into the hot, still darkness hovering just beyond the kitchen lantern. Doña Angela was in Matagalpa. Jorge, the two boys, and I slouched over our little stools in the kitchen, joking, as we did almost every night now, while Leopoldina boiled the corn for the next day's tortillas, fed the dogs, cleaned the last of the plates, swept, and prepared to close up at last. This night, though, she worked without her usual animation; she seemed exhausted and depressed. They were paying her two hundred córdobas a month, she said at last (they didn't even pay this for the first five months, Estela told me later), and she was fed up. They'd hired her on to cook and do laundry, but now they had her making cheese as well, and that meant hours and hours of extra work. When Doña Angela was gone—as she was more and more frequently—Leopoldina couldn't even find time to go to classes and, though she could already read quite adequately, she wanted to advance. She wanted to go to Matagalpa and work, and was thinking of leaving right after the crusade.

"But life in the city as a servant!" I protested. "It's hardly any better there."

"No, Sheyla!" This in the strongest tones I'd ever heard her use. I realized I was picking at a dream. "In the city you can make four hundred or five hundred córdobas a month."

"Up to six hundred in Managua," Jorge put in.

"And here there's never a holiday or a day off. I've got the children to think of, too; Denis is going to be fourteen and ought to learn something so he won't always be just a *mozo*."

I thought about her possibilities that night, lying sleepless on my cot. She had absolutely none. Thirty-five, an age when campesino women are already considered old. No education, no capital, no real skills. Her kids, growing up the same. And Denis, let's face it, was smarter than Jorge, better behaved, more honest. In a few years, when Jorge was entering the university, where would Denis be? Where would they all be? In the city trying to live on sixty dollars a month? If she could get that much. I felt the utter rage that makes people pick up guns and overturn systems.

Yet this one had already been overturned. "Patience," I heard the new leaders counsel, "we can't change everything at once." But patience was a hollow word for the people in-between, the ones caught in the very gears of change.

She was back in the kitchen the next morning, smiling again, listening eagerly to the news, to find out what was happening on the outside. And when I was done palming my share of the tortillas, she put one on a plate for me, with a big slice of *cuajada*, the salty white cheese. Her thoughtfulness, together with a shy smile and wry jokes, touched me especially that morning. I realized I had made a friend.

In the absence of available medical care, every disease was a major concern for the campesinos, a major calculation. While it might be difficult to get a sick person to the highway, it was twenty times more difficult if the patient became critically ill.

Further, for a people with no education or knowledge of their own bodies, sickness was seen as something out of their control. It was an act of god, or of the devil. I had known all this intellectually, had seen it in the eyes of Leopoldina each time Denis ran a slight fever, heard it in the worried whisper, "He just escaped dying on me." Then suddenly I was cast into the same position, and the powerless feeling became my own.

I awoke Tuesday to hear Chanito in the kitchen, his clear child's voice high with importance. "My dad sent me to tell Sheyla that Ismael's much worse." Ismael? Sick? He *had* mentioned something about an earache. Now, like a tape being replayed I heard his soft, diffident voice trying to get my attention—at the fiesta, before the meeting he didn't want to go to, when the commission visited from Muy Muy. I hadn't paid much attention, so many were complaining of being sick.

"Chanito?" I called out, throwing on my clothes. "Hang on a minute, I'm coming."

Ismael was lying on a pallet in the corner of the hut. He had a high,

high fever, his face drawn and sad, his eyes unnaturally bright. When had he lost so much weight? How had he gotten so pale?

I turned to Doña Petrona, who was hovering nearby. "How long has he been this sick?"

"Well, for a few days now. One day better, one day worse, but then yesterday night his fever went way up and it hasn't gone down since."

"Ismael, you should have complained more!" I said, then immediately felt a fool.

Ismael smiled weakly. "I tried to tell you, but you just said I should report it to Muy Muy if I wasn't feeling good. I don't like it there."

"Well, we're going there now." It was clearly impossible to leave him any longer in the filthy shack, surrounded by other sick children. The only problem was how to get him out.

"We've got a mare," Juan, Jr., suggested. "If you can borrow a saddle from Don Manolo, Ismael can ride to the school and walk out from there. I'll come and get the horse later."

Within an hour I had gotten the saddle and was walking double time behind Ismael, who swayed half-asleep astride the plodding mare. "The motion gives me a headache," he whispered. I moistened the rag I'd brought and put it on his head, feeling the heat of the fever burning even hotter than the day.

In a little over an hour and a half we had reached the schoolhouse, closed and quiet in the morning heat. "We have to walk to the road from here," I explained, dubious. "Do you think you make it?" We moved slowly toward the gate in front of Don Valerio's. From there we could cut down to the river.

Damn! Why hadn't I paid more attention! And the others, too. I was sure they were goldbricking, but what if someone really did get critical, particularly once the rains started?

At the river we stopped while Ismael rested, half-fallen against the swelling roots of the *chilomate* tree. "One hundred percent guerrilla," I praised him. He'd been doing this walk as he'd done the crusade— uncomplaining, dogged, cheerful when possible, and conscientious.

Just before the last open stretch, he began to vomit. Once, twice, long rests between and weaker each time. We limped the last stretch to the road. It had to be about ten o'clock, I calculated; the busy hours of the morning had passed and it would likely be a long wait at the highway. "Just this curve, and over by where you see that pole."

Two cars zipped past, one after another, leaving us in the dust.

Ismael was dozing now, face turned up to the hot sun. Another car passed without stopping. Another endless wait. Finally I could hear the motor of another approaching car. This time I wasn't waiting for charity. I planted myself in the middle of the road, waving desperately.

So, okay, even if you're a rich *pendejo* bastard on your way to Matiguás, you can't refuse to stop for a foreign woman waving frantically in the middle of the road. Clearly, you *can* load her semiconscious companion into the back of your pickup and drive like crazy, jolting him still more, then drop them at the gas station, a good twenty minutes from town. After all, it isn't your problem, and you don't think much of this alphabetization business anyway, do you? You'll never know just what harsh thoughts this dusty young woman was thinking about you.

Slowly we plodded down the arroyo and up the other side to town. At last, with a sweaty sigh of relief I sat Ismael down in the cool waiting room of the Muy Muy health center. It was an old clinic, with one examination room, one doctor—usually absent—a nurse, and a nurse's aide. The health brigadistas based there doubled as auxiliary personnel when they weren't out on their rounds, dispensing pills and vaccinations to brigadistas and any campesinos who showed up. Now under the Ministry of Health, the clinic charged ten córdobas a visit to anyone who could pay it, and was on the list for upgrading. It was scheduled to get more personnel, and there were plans for a maternity system. But with the scarcity of medicine and lab equipment, it was not a place for operations or serious illness; such cases would be transferred immediately to Matagalpa. After a spot diagnosis of malaria topped by bronchitis, Ismael was bedded down. We could expect him back in about a week and a half, the nurse consoled me.

"From now on," I made a mental note, "brigadistas who fall sick have permission to leave the community—immediately.

Stopping in at the school on my way back, I found five or six brigadistas grouped around Estela, amid an air of festivity.

"What's up?" I asked, curious.

"Oh, we're going to dig for pottery fragments behind where Jarvin lives." We'd talked about this project before, but there was always the same obstacle.

"But that's old Doña Cloris's land, remember?"

"Yup." Mysterious smiles all around.

114

"So, what do we do when she complains?"

The grin on Estela's face grew more mischievous. "No problem. Doña Cloris is a good friend of ours. Listen to the latest. Miguel was just telling us about it. The other day she comes driving up in her big car and walks into the house. "Where's the brigadista?" Doña Carmen gets all flustered, of course, and says, 'We don't have a brigadista here.' 'Oh, what a shame,' Doña Cloris says. 'Here I've brought this box of food for him. Well, maybe you can give it to someone else.' "

"You're kidding!" I exclaimed to Estela. "What did you do to her?"

"Well, we wrote up those complaints and all, but what did it was that I talked to Justo, on the municipal junta, who's married to one of her nieces. She seems to have gotten the message. 'What a shame there's no brigadista here,' she says, '¡Qué lástima! And there's so much room.' " At that, all the brigadistas broke into hoots of laughter.

Still waiting for rain. The campesinos had all finished plowing the burnt stubble under, days of walking back and forth behind lumbering oxen, those who had them. Now they had to wait until the first hard rain to plant the seed. "Won't be any corn this year until August," they were predicting. Animals were dying for lack of grass, their loss heralded by circling buzzards. As with illness, there was this sense of terrible weakness before the caprices of nature. "It doesn't want to rain," was the expression they used.

At night we lay panting in rooms that refused to cool, and each morning we arose looking for clouds. But always there was the glass sky glaring over the hard-baked ground. Sad as the thin cows, we held our breath and waited.

Classroom Observation: It is the heaviest, hottest part of the day. Inside the house the heat is more oppressive, despite the poorly chinked walls, the roof filled with holes. A crowd of filthy, naked children playing just inside the doorway, while on the platform that serves as a bed, a sick child whimpers faintly. Ignoring them completely, the brigadista sits by a small table while three women group around him. One other, shyer perhaps, and older, stands watching from a short distance away. Syllables on the plastic blackboard. "Repeat," and they chorus the sounds. *Na ne ni no nu.* In the heavy afternoon, it is as if the sounds are wearing blankets.

Two of the women are surprisingly young and pretty in their unhemmed skirts and clean jerseys. They've dressed up for the brigadista's visit. The other has a rip down the side of her cotton dress, a perpetual slot for nursing. The three women know the syllables well. Only the fourth continues to look on silently, face long ago bleached of any expression except resignation.

There's a stirring in the pile of rags, and it becomes clear that two children are sleeping on the boards, not just one. One flails and whimpers a while, its face covered with crusted sores, then falls silent. None of the women look up. "Now we're going to add a third letter to make yet another sound," the brigadista intones. Thin squeak of chalk in the breathless silence.

The eight-year-old comes in from outside, his beltless shorts drooping beneath a swollen stomach. He crosses through to the other room and returns, dangling the baby from his arms. Just outside, he places it on a fallen board, resting its head on a rag.

"Now the words." The brigadista's tranquil tones never vary. At last the fourth woman has brought out her book. She's on an earlier lesson and, as the others read their words, she drones her own assigned sounds.

Outside, the child has picked up the baby bottle and is carefully filling the baby's small ear with milk. The three-year-old watches intensely, his face a mirror of his mother's, already pockmarked. This child is repulsively fascinating, his arms and legs mere sticks, his belly enormous, his swollen scrotum looking hugely out of proportion behind the tiny penis, his eyes two black holes. The milk overflows the baby's ear and trickles down his neck. The women remain by the table, mesmerized, three of them frowning over phrases in their book and the fourth intoning the syllables louder and louder as if the chant could save them all.

The sick child has begun to cry in earnest. The mother picks her up, revealing a pool of diarrhea beneath. A faint stoic sigh. Glancing over, even the brigadista reflects a vague dismay. "She's never got over the measles," the mother murmurs. "We took her to the hospital twice, but it seems the medicine just didn't agree with her." She puts the child down again and goes out, returning with a handful of cornhusks to scrub the board. Another trip outside and she returns with a wet branch. With this she quietly finishes cleaning.

At the table, they're now writing in the newsprint notebooks, yellowed and wrinkled after a month of use. Three dogs come in, bumping each other and play-fighting like the children. One of them sports a bright strip of red cloth around his neck, the only sign of adornment in the entire household. Outside, the monkeylike toddler is peeing in the dust without moving or changing his expression. The water trickles yellow to the ground from beneath his swollen belly. The brigadista leans toward the women, patient, patient, as if luring the syllables from their lips. One small bead of sweat runs down his face and splashes unnoticed on the wooden table. The lesson goes on.

The old woman reaches out through a space in the stick wall that separates the kitchen area from the rest of the hut. "Take them," she says, and places in my hand two green peppers, vibrant green, shiny and sensual. I turn to thank her, but she has already faded into the shadows, obscured by the smoke of the fire. The lesson continues.

Technical Advisor's Bimonthly Report, Mid-May: El Jícaro and Wapá

Alphabetizing:	183	Deserters:	2
Drop-outs:	36	Illness:	0
Without brigadista:	20	Wounded:	1
Alphabetized:	0	Change of Residence:	1
Brigadistas:	26	Progress:	Slow

CHAPTER 13
The Rains Came Down

Eight ex-National Guardsmen crossed the border from Honduras yesterday and murdered the literacy teacher Georgino Andrade.

NEWS BROADCAST, MANAGUA, MAY 19, 1980

The last weeks of May brought the first rains and the first assassination of a brigadista. The rain fell in the night, waking us all. We lay in silence, listening to the unfamiliar drumming sound, loud on the zinc roof.

In the morning the world was entirely different. The morning glowed new-polished, an enormous rainbow stretching from beyond Don Petronilo's to the field way below. Already everything was muddy; Roberto and his brother arrived with their feet completely covered. The river had risen, brown water rushing in small whirlpools where before there was only a sluggish current. Out beyond the house was a maze of rushing streams where previously there were only baked clay troughs. It was a landscape altogether new.

I had planned a morning visit to Pablo at Don Goyo's house, across the shallow river. Not only was the river well over my head, but the sudden surge of current had carried off Don Goyo's canoe. Pablo was stuck on an island for a while. Off, then, to Don Ernesto's, my sneakers picking up a coat of muddy topsoil. Puddles and streams were everywhere, and in the silence of the prairie, I would swear I could hear the new grass growing.

We caught the news first over the morning tortillas, although it would be a few days before we knew all the details: "Brigadista murdered in the north." During the day the news spread from field to field. Georgino Andrade was his name. Little by little, we learned the circumstances of the murder.

He wasn't a teenager from the city, but a campesino living in one of the villages further north. Coordinator of the local CDS, chief of the militia, and a member of the alphabetization subcommission. This made him a target for the bands of embittered ex-Guardsmen who lived just across the nearby Honduran border.

At first, the only thing certain was the survivor's story. "It was around 7:30 at night, when we were reading a book by Che—Georgino and I. All of a sudden, several uniformed men appeared. They grabbed both of us and forced us to leave the house. They asked me if I was a brigadista. I told them no, but they were after Georgino anyway. They took him off. The face they wore as well as their style of talking was of Somoza's guard.

"That same night, we began to look for him. But it wasn't until the next day that we found his body. It had multiple perforations and all his teeth had been broken."*

Several weeks later, when the band was captured, the full story of his torture and death would be revealed. But it didn't really matter. The country was already exploding with indignation.

"No more indulgence!" was the cry. "Heavy hands on our enemies!"

The Sandinistas had shown an unprecedented generosity to their vanquished enemy. Despite the savagery of the National Guard in the war, no one had been officially executed, and many minor offenders had been pardoned. In fact, the death penalty itself had been abolished. Now, it seemed, some were repenting the soft stance that had let their rabid enemy live to attack again.

"Today is not a day of happiness," declared Tomás Borge in a speech the next day, "nor is it a day of sadness. . . .Today isn't a day of extended hands, but of closed fists to repel our enemies."

But if the Somocistas had expected to stop the crusade in any way, or even to slow its momentum, they had guessed wrong once again. Georgino Andrade was converted overnight into a symbol, a challenge to the nation to carry through with the literacy crusade whatever the consequences.

> *Por la sangre derramada / Terminaremos la cruzada*
> *Patria alfabetizada / O morir en la cruzada.*

> For the blood spilled / We'll dinish the crusade.
> A nation of literates / Or die in the crusade.

Georgino was the first martyr of the alphabetization; he was not to be the last.

---

*From the story related by José Ignacio Bustos in the May 23, 1980, edition of *Barricada*.

I waited for a reaction from the brigadistas or their parents. Fear? Desertion? None came. For one thing, we were far away from the embattled frontier, safely sealed in our valley. For another, they were used to martyrs, more than accustomed to the idea of death. "I wouldn't run away," Miguel said sincerely. "That's what they want us to do." And Matías asked me, half-smiling, "Aren't you scared, *profe*?" Without waiting, he answered the question himself, with words he'd used once before. "I'm not either. That's what the revolution's all about, isn't it?"

Planting time. I walked behind Don Chavelo, trying without success to imitate his practiced movements. Ahead of us were the plow and oxen, borrowed from Don Manolo. Juan Espinoza was teaching Jorge how to guide the team. With tin cans tied to our waists, we followed behind, each in one of the furrows. Drop the seed, kick the wet dirt, take a step, drop, kick. Chavelo was already far ahead, jigging lightly toward the retreating plow. "Hey, wait for me," I joked, while the others turned around to watch, laughing. "Well, these two rows are mine," I announced finally, turning my can over to the group. Reluctantly I walked away from the new-turned earth to begin my morning visits.

May crept along. "The masses of the people made the insurrection." *Ma me mi mo mu.* Wasn't anyone getting beyond Lesson 5? We needed paper and crayons to make syllables charts; where were we going to get them? Mosquitos were breeding in the puddles, and each day dawned hotter. Geraldo sneaked off to Managua, then Elvis, then Raúl. We set up a schedule of permissions, hoping to replace unauthorized visits with permitted ones, though the EPA guidelines still said no. The lamps finally came, tiny hurricane lanterns no better than the smoky tin ones that the campesinos already had. "We can't give night classes with these," the kids reported.

The news reached us that the United States had frozen the $75 million loan for Nicaragua while they examined the causes of the two junta resignations. *Us is es as os.*

Food supplies are reportedly on their way for everyone. The plan to provide more rations to brigadistas staying with the eight most destitute families in each community had proved problematic. In some areas the poorest families didn't need subsidies as much as others did. But now international aid had come through, and ENABAS was struggling toward the goal of equal distribution of these provisions to all, every two weeks. "They'll have to hurry," said Estela, worried. "If they try to send the food after the river rises, we won't have any way to get it here." She had been making daily trips to Muy Muy, trying to straighten out the supplies situation. She was irritable and distant, when I saw her. *Dis das des dos dus.*

The national agricultural survey we'd been scheduled to conduct was postponed by order of Father Cardenal; it was causing too many problems. There was a rumor afoot that the brigadistas were surveying the land in order to take it away. On the other hand, Sandino's birthday celebration, May 18, was a big success, with songs and sociodramas.

Rolando reported that three of his students, young girls who lived on the other side of the river, had been chased off by the hacienda's manager. Seemed he was angry about the syllables chalked on the doorways of "his" houses. Anity Fley, owner of the El Esquirín hacienda, hardly ever came around, preferring to leave the details in the hands of her administrator. Clearly, he had chosen the buttered side of his bread.

I paid the girls a visit, together with the brigadista. "This man has absolutely no right to interfere with your studying. If he creates any more problems, we'll talk to the commission about it. Meanwhile, you should come back to class. Really, he can't do anything to you." Eyes watched me soberly as I talked. "Will you come back to class?" I wondered. *Wo wos sow ow.*

Don Jaime was finally going to the Labor Ministry to complain about his inadequate salary at the Ernesto Membreño ranch. I pulled Arturo aside to talk about putting some pressure on Don Manolo as well. "Yeah," he nodded, "no one who's been active in anything since the revolution has had a day's work from the old man. Only Juan Espinoza, because he works like a dog and says nothing." The excuse that Don Chavelo's problem with his boss was unique—a women's fight, as some had claimed—had all but evaporated.

Ma me mi mo mu. Mother's Day coming up. "I need permission for Mother's Day," pleaded one brigadista after another. "*Profe,* you gotta let me go." Raúl dispatched to his doctor in Managua after the third week of continuous complaint. The lesson of Ismael was still with me. Raúl returned with an official appointment, for May 30, Mother's Day. *Pa pe pi po pu.*

By the week before Mother's Day—as sentimental a holiday in Nicaragua as it is anywhere else—the brigadistas' morale had sunk to zero. Trapped between their rebellion and their desire to fulfill their commitment, each was determined to wrest permission from Estela or me, rather than just leave and take the consequences. "Okay, they can't let everybody go home, but I'll just go alone and come back Monday without telling anyone. Well, WHY NOT?"

There came a moment when I couldn't sit through another class. Jumping up, I half-ran home, impelled by a restlessness I couldn't understand. I, who had spent day after day haranguing brigadistas about the necessity of giving the complete two hours of class.

A quote from Che Guevara popped up on the wall at Don Ernesto's, brought to us, I supposed, by Chico. "A man who tires has the right to rest, but he can't be called a man of the vanguard." *Va ve vi vo vu.*

DIARIO DEL CAMPO

Sunday, May 25

Tired and depressed. Sorry, Che, the kid is trying to be of the vanguard, but it ain't easy. Why do they keep pestering me, as if it were my personal idea that they not go home to see their mothers?

People issuing unrealistic orders from the central offices and everyone scared to protest, until I wonder if indeed Stalinism is creeping in under the brim of Sandino's hat. Or is it just me, tired with the loss of my free Sundays and the haggling over boots that never come? Raúl, with who knows how many missed classes, trips to Managua and drunken ambles through the valley, is allowed to stay on for lack of a replacement, thus destroying what little credibility we have in the disciplinary line.

Amid all this Chico comes up with the suggestion that we hold weekly meetings with the campesinos to discuss selected topics of historic and world-wide importance. Chico is wonderful, and all that, but why do none of us say to him what we say to each other: Look, a weekly political meeting is nonsense; to speak against Robelo to excess just gives him publicity. Or: I'm the only one in the whole valley, maybe in the whole municipality, who has the vaguest idea what on earth the Polisario Front, this week's selected topic, is. Estela is afraid of being called unwilling and I of being seen as a malintentioned foreigner.

So, any more complaints tonight? I think not. In the day, the plain covered with tender shoots lifts my spirits; tonight, all I can think of is the bugs. Maybe tomorrow will bring some good news.

The news that came was not particularly good, but it was certainly unexpected. Don Manolo had flipped out. Gothic Tale, Chapter 2.

"While you were at the Saturday workshop," Doña Leopoldina said, "he came in all of a sudden, walking stiff and swaying like drunk, only he wasn't drunk. 'I'm going,' he said. 'They've confiscated the farm and they want to take me prisoner.' Then he muttered some more things we couldn't understand, something about brigadistas and *nacatamales* at Doña Eudomilia's. Crazy talk. Finally he took off, still all stiff. 'We've got to get him!' Angela said, and she and Carlos took off after him. According to Don Estéban, they caught up with him at the highway and took him to Matagalpa."

It was perplexing. Putting it together, though, we remembered other events that should have warned us. There was his complete retreat from everyone. In more than month, I hadn't spoken with him more than three times. He left before dawn, came back at dusk, ate, and went to bed. "He wasn't like that before," Doña Poldi told me now. Then there was the paranoia about the organization of the valley, and a court battle with his widowed daughter-in-law over his nonsupport of the grandchildren, and the day he confused Doña Bernarda with his sister. "Just like that, and he's known Bernarda for years."

It wasn't a subject of overwhelming concern to me, but it certainly was to the neighbors. More than a few were directly dependent on him for what scanty support they had. The lord of the manor had gone mad and, like it or not, the serfs were worried that their future might become still bleaker.

In the last week of May, Estela and I received an unexpected summons to Muy Muy. Together with selected brigadistas we were to participate in the Municipal Alphabetization Congress. Parallel efforts in the other municipalities would produce data that would be passed to departmental congresses and from there to the National Congress, coming up in June. This would provide the national planners with the basis to recommend and effect needed changes in the original program. The flaws we were noting could yet be corrected, we were told; our ideas would really be heard.

The conference hall was the corridor of the Muy Muy school. We numbered about a hundred, including members of the municipal commission, community supervisors, technical advisors, brigadistas, representatives of ANDEN (the teachers' union) and the Sandinista Youth, together with auxiliary personnel in health, defense, and documentation, and visitors from Matagalpa. It was a healthy crowd for Muy Muy.

Following the opening speeches, we divided up according to our function. Each group was to look at all facets of the crusade, from the materials to the Saturday workshops, from logistics to security. In each category we were to list achievements, problems, causes of the problems, and possible solutions. It was all organized and neat, just like the dialogue suggested for use with the primer photos. The result was an exhaustive and exhausting sharing of information with at least the comfort of knowing that none of us was really out there all alone.

The most common complaint was of failure in the shipment of supplies. The lamps, as mentioned, were virtually useless, and, with the rainy season setting in, the scarcity of boots was becoming critical. Apparently, it wasn't only a problem of irregular delivery from Matalpa to Muy Muy, but also between Muy Muy and the communities. Complaints about the Logistics Committee abounded. There'd been abuses; there'd been favoritism. Immediate reforms were demanded.

Other problems were less straightforward. All of us were way behind the official calendar and no one had found a workable way to speed things up. There were some minor problems with the textbook—the sample words in some of the lessons were too complex; the use of the r and rr* was explained in a way that didn't correspond to their actual use in Nicaragua; the inverted syllables were causing difficulties. The problem I had experienced with discipline, with disappearing brigadistas, with the use of the dialogue, with inadequate use of the syllables chart, with the Saturday workshop, were all common. "What about Mother's Day?" another teacher whispered, from across the table. "Mine are all going to take off." "Mine, too, I think," We shrugged, exchanging wry smiles.

In the plenary session, each group presented its analysis, and we exchanged questions. There was a spirited give-and-take between a zonal youth representative and the members of the crusade about the lack of rifles for the militias. Not all the communities had been as calm as ours, apparently. Those closer to the highway had suffered both robberies and threats. With the death of Georgino Andrade still fresh in everyone's mind, the cry for adequate protection was strong.

Nelson, Miguel, and Goyo had come along to represent the bri-

---

*In Spanish the double r is rolled and constitutes a separate letter of the alphabet.

gadistas in our community. Yet they seemed unwilling to move beyond rhetoric and broach their real problems. "We're moving along excellently in El Jícaro... winning the battle of illiteracy. Our squadron leader visits us regularly as does not our advisor, and with their help we're going to be victorious."

What? "Listen," I leaned over to whisper. "You've been complaining to me for three solid weeks—about the plans, about the discipline—now's your chance to really be heard!" They looked at me blankly. "And you, Miguel? Don't you want to present the problems you've been having as squadron leader?"

An impatient shake of the head. "No, no, this isn't the place to discuss it." They were still unaccustomed to speaking up, to voicing their thoughts. The lessons they were giving daily to the campesinos had yet to be internalized by the brigadistas themselves, it appeared. No wonder the dialogue section wasn't catching on.

More elaborate speeches, final conclusions, a call to redouble efforts—and it was over. It had been a productive three days, we agreed, but for our own immediate problems there was no answer. Back we waded across the swollen river to El Jícaro.

The Mother's Day activity was sparsely attended, the few brigadistas who stayed behind obviously wishing they hadn't. Eventually Miguel spoke a few soothing words to the community members who had gathered at the school. "We have to ask your forgiveness. It's not that we don't care for you, but maybe we're still a little young—and on this day we're all missing our mothers."

Some of these mothers showed up in the late afternoon. They came from another world with unfathomably large bundles of food and gifts. Elvis's mother, thin and silent as he; Miguel's grandmother, who marched me double-time across the swamp to find her boy so she could give him a hug she had been saving up for a month; Geraldo and Jorge's parents overflowing with generosity—and rum.

Doña Poldi and I sat glumly in the kitchen, she worried to distraction about Doña Angela, who'd been in Matagalpa with Don Manolo for ten days without sending word, and I busy brooding about my statistics. Of the 140 still studying, 92 were not past Lesson 6. Then there were the sick brigadistas and the Mother's Day mass exodus. And El Jícaro was an even greater disaster, apparently.

In the middle of my musing, Leopoldina remarked abruptly, "He would have been a year old tomorrow."

"Who?"

"A baby I had last year, born the day after Mother's Day. But he was damaged, all twisted up. Fourteen days he lived." She turned to chase the persistent pig out of the kitchen, perhaps striking it a bit more harshly than usual with the rope whip.

I never heard her mention it again.

Technical Advisor's Bimonthly Report, End of May: Wapá

Alphabetizing: 136	Progress Control:	
Drop-outs: 36	Students in Lesson	1: 1
Alphabetized: 2		2: 7
Brigadistas reporting: 10		3: 5
Illness: 2		4: 11
Absent or deserted: 9		5: 40
Change of residence: 11		6: 28
		7: 13
		8: 5
		9: 3
		10: 11
		12: 0
		13: 0
		14: 0
		15: 5
		16: 3
		17: 1

BOOK FOUR

JUNE
The Coming of Winter

CHAPTER 14
The Slump

Dear Mom and Dad,
*   . . .the mosquitos are driving me crazy. Whenever I talk they fly*
into my mouth. They say the mosquito nets are coming soon. I hope
so. . . .I'm learning a lot. I now know how to milk a cow and plant
vegetables. . . .The rains are constant. The soles of my boots came un-
glued and I had to sew them with a needle used to make sacks
with. . . .

LOVE, DAVID*

Doldrums. From politics to personalities, from puddles to pedagogy, June would bring great difficulties. The thickening Nicaraguan mud, if it did not cause them all, came to symbolize them. There were the logistical difficulties of the national crusade in keeping supplies coming and communication lines open; there were the illnesses and other crises that were pushing us far behind the official calendar; there was even the sense that the campesinos were so mired in ignorance that they weren't moving. We did not realize then that progress in the middle stages of learning is often difficult to identify, so the seeming stagnation played havoc with our soggy morales. Enthusiasm plummeted on all sides, from the central offices to the kids to the campesinos themselves.

In El Jícaro, isolated by swollen rivers and washed-out roads, we lacked the perspective to recognize that this was all just a phase—natural and temporary. We were plagued by the question: "Could we fail?"

Geraldo stopped me on the path. "Listen, I've got a real problem. Pedro, Pablo, and the boys are all telling me that they won't be able to study any more now except for an hour here and there. What'll I do?"

Quoted in Valerie Miller, op.cit.

"That's your job, convincing. Convince them that it's important enough to make time for. Remind them that you won't be here all that much longer, and that they won't ever get another chance like this. If everything else fails, we'll have to move you somewhere else, though I'd hate to do it at this late date." I hoped that the implicit threat might be enough to shake Geraldo out of his perpetual cool, but his downcast face said clearly that he didn't hold much faith that the prescription would work.

And he was right. The problem wasn't confined just to the classes of the lethargic brigadistas. Attendance in the functioning classes was dropping off rapidly, too. The months of rain meant greatly increased working hours in the fields. The *mozos* had no choice but to miss the late afternoon classes; others, more financially independent, were tired when they came home now. Studying was easy to put off, till tomorrow, till Sunday. The brigadistas, with few exceptions, lacked the confidence to make demands of their reluctant students.

Finally, there was the problem of light. On cloudy or rainy days, the light in the huts began to fade before five-thirty. By six o'clock, pencil marks could no longer be distinguished on the newsprint, though one could continue a short while longer on the blackboard. Since it was almost impossible to begin classes any earlier, hours were being cut. Shortened classes, missed classes, missing brigadistas. It all added up to a virtual halt in visible progress. Was this happening elsewhere, too?

Monday night brought the disaster. Tuesday we woke to a clear dawn after a night of tremendous wind and thunderstorm. As usual the last one out of bed, I was puzzled by the strange silence as I crept outside. No one was working. Instead, the whole family and several of the neighbors were lined up beside the kitchen, gazing down the slope. "The river's overflowed into the cornfield," Leopoldina announced to me in solemn tones. Sure enough, the field that had sparkled with new seedlings just yesterday, was now awash in brown puddles. The growth nearest the house was still intact, but the far end, where Don Chavelo and Don Juan (and I) had been planting, was sliced through with a new branch of the river.

It was like a funeral. How much was ruined? "We won't know for a while, but it looks like half of the acres nearest the river. For Don Chavelo, Juan, and Guadalupe, it's a disaster; the rest've lost a small piece each."

Arturo, who'd come to look, shook his head. "They can try to set the corn back up when the river goes down, but it doesn't look good to me."

"Can't they just reseed?"

"Nope, it doesn't work that way."

I was flooded with anger at the injustice. So much hard work, then—bang—in one blow everything was wiped out. And, even here, the boss got off scot-free—the *mozos*, of course, had been lent the land near the low end of the field precisely because it was less desirable.

The brigadistas, already restless and frustrated, leaped on any small failure as justification for their growing discontent. Every small failure of the crusade administration became another rallying cry to resentment—and to rebellion. The chief scapegoat was the supplies problem.

A literacy crusade as extensive as the Nicaraguan model was an expensive proposition. The cost of the primers alone was $800,000; to this had to be added the cost of printing the teacher's manuals, the mathematics booklets, and the notebooks. The equipment designated for each of the 60,000 rural brigadistas was valued at $146, and the basic grains distributed to them over the five months were worth some $2.3 million, transportation aside. Although local resources were used whenever possible, most of the necessary materials and equipment could not be produced within the country. Even pencils had to be imported. And this required dollars, a commodity that was worse than scarce in ravaged Nicaragua. The first estimates of the crusade's cost was $20 million, almost the same as that of the Cuban literacy crusade, eighteen deflationary years earlier.

It was inconceivable that Nicaragua could borrow more money; it had inherited a foreign debt of $1.6 billion from Somoza. The only solution was to appeal to national and international solidarity. The plea for cash or direct shipments of materials went out to governments and private agencies all over the world.

As fast as materials arrived, they were dispensed to the municipalities for distribution. Under these conditions, some delayed and unbalanced shipments were inevitable. Despite the heroic efforts of the national and departmental logistical support teams, screams began to echo up and down the chain: "My boots!" "Our pants!" "More pencils!" The lots that arrived were completely irregular—at different times, from different countries—and not until the final months of the crusade was a standard system of inventories and receipts developed.

Some zones got Coleman lanterns of the best quality and some got tiny hurricane lamps that barely shed light. Some groups received three uniforms, and some barely got one. My blue jeans of heavy-weight denim would go through three crusades, while our brigadistas received jeans of a light cotton that wore through in two months.

Out in the field, the supplies problem had two faces, the physical and the psychological. To the first category belonged items that were crucial to our survival—educational materials, boots, lamps and, for many brigadistas, the uniform, too. With parents too poor to replace the clothing that was so quickly ruined in the country, they were dependent on the crusade to keep them clothed. Problems with the receipt of any of these items meant frustrating delays or forced changes of plans.

On another level, the quality and quantity of supplies took on an exaggerated importance. To many brigadistas, the equipment represented their pay. Failures and inequities in the supply line led to jealousies and tensions that had little to do with the article's actual value. The theft of three felt emblems was a major item of contention. Nelson and Rolando nearly came to blows over the distribution of two unlike mosquito nets. The failure of boots deliveries nearly caused a sitdown strike, even among those whose parents had been able to supply them.

And who was the immediate failure at championing their cause? The technical advisor, who else? In the eyes of the crusade, we may have been sent to improve teaching quality, maintain statistics, and keep order, but to the brigadistas we were there to Get Them Their Things. "How come the Amando Bonilla brigadistas have two pairs of pants and we don't?" "Why can't you get me another raincoat? Mine got ripped off." "How come you always favor Raúl (or Nelson, or Miguel, or Jorge)?"

The hardest task was trying to convince the kinds that this wasn't just a big giveaway, but a plan that was costing their government millions that it didn't have. "Your government *can't* give you every-thing you want!" I found myself yelling at them. They had been promised, and they eventually received, one of each item. But the notion that it was impossible to demand replacements, and dishonest to hoard extras, was beyond the grasp of many of them.

In short, the problem was in accepting the idea of austerity, and the brigadistas were by no means alone in their incomprehension. All over Nicaragua supplies were scarce, prices were high, and people were feeling the pinch of the war's destruction. The call had gone out through every possible medium to restrict imports, conserve resources, save more. Never a wildly popular slogan, the concept was diametrically counter to what people had expected a revolution to mean. Those who had long been involved in the liberation struggle understood it well, but for the other 90 percent of the population, the reorientation was difficult. For them, as for the brigadistas, scarce items became symbolic of other, less definable frustrations in their lives.

June brought no essential change to the landscape, inner or outer. After a heavy rain, all the rivers would rise, and for a few days there would be no certain contact with the outside world. The passage between Wapá and El Jícaro was rapidly dissolving: where there had been a direct clay trail across the lowland prairie, there was now a swamp pocked with thorn bushes. Visits among the campesinos were reduced to the utterly necessary, while the women, the elderly, and the sick were completely immobilized. Others continued to force their reluctant horses through the mud or, like me, splashed clumsily through it in their thick rubber boots.

Our Saturday workshops had to be split in two—one in the El Jícaro schoolhouse and one in Don Ernesto's big living room. The trek across the valley had become too long and difficult, especially for brigadistas without boots. For us in Wapá, there were no more visits from the commission staff, no more organizers from Muy Muy. Even Estela stopped coming, passing necessary communications via messenger. Only Chico remained loyal, arriving regularly every Thursday that the river was fordable, mud to his thighs and a handshake for everyone. And every other week we descended to receive our rations of grains, soap, and sugar. It was also the only time that we all saw each other.

We were ever damper, sicker, more uncomfortable, more isolated. Little holes developed all over the community—classes without teachers, teachers without students. There were no substitutes in this school, and each illness multiplied the lost time. It wasn't just the brigadistas; no house was without its *enfermo*—a child pale and coughing, a man or woman dragging painfully through the daily chores. Spirits fell and refused to pick up. It was, in a word, winter, and the black mood seemed determined to linger.

I'd discovered another problem in the classes, one closely tied to the slow pace of advance. I'd noticed it first while watching Jorge's class. In his anxiety to move the pupils along, he was doing the lesson for them. He read the model sentence, which they then repeated; same for the key word. Next they chorused the syllables one by one, then on they went to the next step. Racing in this way, they were through the entire lesson in under two hours.

Some of this was due to Jorge's particular carelessness, but the bulk of the problem stemmed simply from impatience and his understandable ignorance of good teaching technique. Without independent thought and practice, there would be no lasting learning. The ability to repeat words and syllables within a two-hour practice session was no guarantee that the skill had been mastered.

As a demonstration, I sat down beside the youngest boy and turned the pages of his primer back several lessons, pointing to the sample syllables. "What does this say?" He didn't know. I tried another. The same. Then I turned all the way back to Lesson 3. He'd forgotten. This was worse than I'd imagined. There had been almost no retention.

With a penitent Jorge, I worked out a specific emergency plan: daily review for all the students and a return all the way back to the beginning if necessary. Duly warned, I spent the rest of the week in similar observations of other brigadistas. In class after class I checked real progress by turning the learners back to earlier lessons and testing them. All too often it gave the same result; while learning one syllable, they had forgotten the previous ones.

"The key to the problem," I hammered home in the Saturday workshop, "is the syllables chart. Use the brown paper we gave you to write down all the syllables in the order in which they learned them. Hang it up in the house somewhere. This will let the learner pass his eyes over the syllables at odd hours during the day, hours when there isn't time to open a book. Also, you ought to use it for review. Go over all the syllables before beginning new ones. Better yet, review them all at the beginning of every class.

"And when you get to the words and phrases, make the reader sound them out alone. The work of putting known syllables together to form a whole word is the essence of reading. If you don't make them do it now, they'll never really learn."

June 8 marked the midpoint of the crusade. It was also, more notably, the first anniversary of the beginning of the insurrection that brought down the Somoza dictatorship. The radio was full of the chronology of the war: on this day the fall of such-and-such a garrison, on that day the liberation of an important city. At one and the same time reality was being translated into history, and this history, so different from what we were struggling with today, was being brought back into our reality. "Where were *you* this time last year?" A few of our brigadistas had participated in actual combat; others had helped put up barricades in their neighborhoods, or acted as messengers. Nelson had received some shrapnel in his face; what I'd taken for acne was actually scars. In the countryside it had been a time of uncertainty, refugees arriving from all over, and no one knowing when or if the *guardia* might sweep through with their planes or tanks.

Now, one year later, it was easy to get impatient; there were so many necessities lacking. Yet Don Jaime had won his judgment; Don Ernesto and his stingy wife had been ordered by the Ministry of Labor to make up the difference between what they had been paying him and the minimum wage, plus lunch and Sunday pay. The renovation of the clinic in Muy Muy was coming along. There was a state farm on either side of the valley that would someday act as model and magnet. Then, of course, there was the crusade itself. These changes seemed sweeping to the campesinos, who had known nothing of change for a hundred years. Basically, the process had gotten a strong start. With unity, strength, and a little luck, I concluded, we might make it. As for victory in the literacy war by August, I was not so philosophical.

Geraldo paid an unexpected visit early Thursday morning. Don Lucas and Doña Justina no longer wanted Miguel as a brigadista, he reported. He'd been frightening the children and she wanted him, Geraldo, to take over the class. His face betrayed a bit of pride at one-upping the squad leader, but he didn't seem to know much about what had happened.

Since we had decided not to place a brigadista in the house of Don Justo and Doña Carmen, the family now working for Doña Cloris, Miguel had worked out a special arrangement. He ate and gave classes there, but slept in the tiny bamboo hut that belonged to Don Lucas, somehow fitting in among him, Doña Justina, five small children, and two teenage daughters, most of whom were in his class. The arrangement had quickly stabilized, and up to now I had heard no complaints. I had observed his classes several times and seen no hint of trouble.

Around noon, I spied Don Lucas's wiry figure in front of Doña Luisa's, standing amid a group of men waiting for the representative of the Small Producers' Association to arrive.

"Hi." Handshakes all around. After the preliminary exchanges, I approached the matter directly. "Geraldo says you wanted to talk to me."

"Yes, yes," he nodded vigorously. "I won't be home for a while, but you should go talk to my woman. She can explain it." There was an urgency in his face, but it was also clear that he didn't want to broach the subject in public.

"Trouble with Miguel?" I persisted.

"Well, yes, I'll be along in a while, but like I say, these things are best arranged between women." He shifted from foot to foot, clearly uncomfortable.

I found Miguel at the ample brick house where Don Justo lived, asleep on an almost hidden cot in the far bedroom. He sat up groggily as I walked in.

"What've you got?" I touched his forehead, finding it cool.

"I don't know, but I feel terrible."

"He's been sleeping here all day," Doña Carmen confirmed.

"Sorry to wake you up, then, but I hear you've got some kind of problem."

He nodded, face dead serious. "Doña Justina says I've been hitting the kids and making them cry, and that now they don't want to go to class anymore. But it's not true, *profe*. Honest. You've seen my classes. She doesn't know her own kids—they're impossible in class. Then they go back and tell her things, all kinds of lies, and she believes them." That overly sincere student body president tone always struck me wrong.

Well, okay, official denial had been issued. Now it was time to check the witnesses. "I'll get back to you later," I told him. "It sounds like something we can work out. You should probably have held your classes in the house there, where Doña Justina could see you, instead of here." He nodded and fell back on his bed.

On to the stick house, which always reminded me of the house of the Second Little Pig. Doña Justina, sitting inside, was nursing the youngest baby. A plump, good-natured woman, she always had a wide smile and a bite of something ready for me, together with a standard battery of questions and the current Wapá gossip.

Now, though, she had something else on her mind. Poking at the little children clustered around her, she gave me her side of the story. "Now me, personally, I can't study. I get terrible headaches. But I wanted the children to learn. They were doing really good for a while with that other boy, but this Miguel has been just too strict. He kicked my little boy, the kids told me, and he was pulling Rosa's hair. That's just too much, I think, don't you? It's got so bad that they don't even want to go to class anymore. So I talked to Lucas and we both think that Geraldo should come and give classes here. He's real patient, Geraldo."

I could see the oldest daughters, at fourteen and fifteen the belles of Wapá, listening intently from behind the stick partition that separated the kitchen from the main room.

"Of course, that's really too much if he was abusing the children. You can't teach anyone anything that way." She nodded, rocking the baby.

"How long has this been going on?"

"They've been complaining for a while. And yesterday the youngest showed me his bruises. 'Well, that's just too much,' I said to them. 'We'll just have to talk to the *yanquita*.' "

"I'll tell you, Doña Justina. I could take Miguel away, and if you folks insist, I will. But the way I see it, these brigadistas come here to learn, too. If we take Miguel away now, just like that, well, that's like removing a problem instead of solving it."

"But the kids don't want to study with him anymore."

"Well, obviously, I'll have to talk to them and to Miguel, too. But I think he's willing to change. Maybe he lost his patience, but I doubt that he wanted to be so rough. How would it be if he kept giving classes, but held them here in the house, instead of over at Justo's? That way you could keep an eye on things and if there are problems, you could handle them personally."

"But Geraldo—"

"Like I say, I could bring Geraldo over here, but I'd really like to give Miguel another chance, for everybody's sake. And, really, right here under your nose, there's not too much that could happen, is there?"

She was looking strangely uncomfortable, gazing over my head toward the kitchen. Suddenly she leaned over close to me. "He was touching the girl."

"What?"

"He was fooling with my girl. That's right. We caught them at it last night. Lucas didn't want me to say anything, but I says, 'Lucas, this is something we can talk about between women, and it's better that the *yanquita* should know! So I'm going to tell you the whole thing." The baby was nearly forgotten on her lap.

"See, Lucas had this bad toothache and Miguel had given him some pills—who knows if it was maybe to drug him or what—anyway, yesterday night I'm hearing these sounds, and I say 'Lucas, what's going on?' and he says, 'Nothing, it's nothing.' But then he figures that he might as well get up and take one of those pills. So he's fishing for the flashlight, but before he can light it, suddenly there's a squeal, and it's Neli yelling, 'Mama! Miguel's here!' Who knows what would have happened if we hadn't woke up when we did?

"Well, you can imagine. Lucas wanted to kill him at first, but we kind of settled everything down, and the boy left in the morning, all embarrassed naturally. I didn't want anyone to know about it, nor did Lucas, because, well, you know how people talk. So I said, 'Let's just make up a little story and say that he was rough with the children. Except, just now I decided that we could trust you and that it'd be better to tell you straight out what happened. But please promise that you won't tell the other *profesora*. We just want to forget it."

"Of course," I assured her, for lack of a better response. I hadn't understood all of what she had told me, nor did I want to ask her to repeat it in greater detail. Was he raping the girl or merely kissing her? Was he forcing relations or sharing them? And how *would* it be viewed in the valley?

As I crossed the now darkening lowlands, I tried to figure out how to approach the problem, because I was all alone on this one. Miguel, as squadron leader, had to realize what damage his little follies could cause us; there wasn't much that could hurt us more, as outsiders, taking advantage. I turned the story over and over in my mind, thinking about all the oddnesses I'd noticed in Miguel and how deep they might go, about the culture I was in and what it expected—and what it said it expected—and how much gap there might be between the two—and if I knew enough to interpret correctly the things people told me. It was all a muddle and no visible plan.

The plan came after a restless night, as I walked to the schoolhouse for the new load of provisions. I'd confront Miguel without revealing what I knew and wait for his side of the story. If he was willing to talk about the "real" incident, we had a basis we could work from. If he denied it all flatly, the matter was more serious than I was willing to handle alone. It seemed a bit like the logic of the Salem witch trials, but it was the best I could devise.

After the brigadistas had all been issued their oil and sugar (and at last boots for more than half the group, together with two real Coleman lanterns for night classes), and the school was cleaned up and locked, I sat down with Miguel.

I offered him no clues, and he fumbled around for a while. "She doesn't know her own children...they tell her anything and she believes it..." I broke first, with a direct question about the girl. Miguel's face, which had been pale, turned red. I could see him turning over his answer in his mind, then, "Okay, I did have relations with the girl, but you don't know, *profe*, she wouldn't leave me alone. She was after me all the time. I told her I had a girlfriend and everything, but she still kept after me. Finally, like they say, 'If the hen lets her chickens loose'..."

It was only half an apology, his disclaimer based on all the fundamentals of machismo, but at least it was an admission of sorts. His forehead beaded with sweat.

I stifled my impulse to give a lecture on the rights of women, but tried to make him understand the situation—how glamorous the brigadistas seemed to these inexperienced girls, how few encounters they'd had with men, how Neli might indeed be tempted to throw herself at him, hoping to receive in return the only chance she might ever have to leave the valley. I explained how they as brigadistas must be prepared to deal with this, keeping in mind that a pregnancy, or even a misunderstanding, could do more damage to us than all the propaganda of Robelo and Somoza combined. He looked appropriately contrite, but then he knew that I expected him to. "Okay, Miguel, I guess you better stay at Don Justo's and just give classes there."

"Are you going to tell Chico?"

I had never thought that blackmail was my style, but there it was: "For the moment, I'm going to keep quiet, more for the sake of the family than for you. But at the first, slightest suspicion of other problems, I promise you that I'll squeal all the way to Grandma."

Night classes began at Doña María Elsa's and at Pedro Pablo's, using the new lamps. The math books arrived, not to be opened until the students reached Lesson 10 of the primer and passed the intermediate test. According to my mid-June statistics, that meant exactly 36 of the now 117-plus students. At Chico's suggestion, we began criticism–self-criticism sessions at the Saturday workshop, the first one, not surprisingly, resulting in universally hurt feelings, including mine. It would take a few more practice runs before we could learn how to give and receive criticism constructively.

Pablo led his family's mule into a deceptively deep brook with the month's supplies for four brigadistas. Twelve pounds of sugar dissolved into a hundred pounds of corn; twenty pounds of beans floated off with eight cakes of soap. The dunking also ruined my entire allotment of sanitary napkins. The only item salvaged was a liter of cooking oil per brigadista.

The rumor grew that Fidel Castro would be coming for the first anniversary celebration on July 19. Even the technical advisor began to weaken and talk of begging permission to make the trip to Managua for the day.

Don Rito González was picked up by the authorities. Of course, it was inevitable that Raúl would be there, as he had been—more or less—since he'd been run out of Don Luis's. Raúl walked out of his house one morning to find it surrounded by *compas*. *"Tranquilo*—easy now." I could just imagine him holding up his hands in mock surrender, flashing his crooked Raúl smile. There was another young brigadista staying there that night also, one from a bordering community. He deserted on the spot.

Don Rito, it turned out, was mixed up with the Democratic Armed Forces, a fancy name for an organization of dissident cattle producers. According to the Frente, they'd gone a great deal beyond dissidence—to the point of storing arms. Don Rito, as the story went, had made a sizable contribution. As the accusations became more concrete, they also became more serious. He had been paying some men in Muy Muy to carry out harassments—firing random shots at the police and army posts. The annoyances were intended to keep everyone on edge. Could it have been one of these nuisance attacks that had caught little Mario?

All this was still on the level of rumor; specific charges had yet to be filed. The revolutionary judicial system was brand-new, and while there was nothing like the disappearances and random murders that took place routinely before the triumph, there was plenty of disorganization. The habeus corpus law had just been enacted, and was still waiting final embellishments from the legal staff of the Council of State. Thus an accused person could be held for questioning without specific charges, and was frequently transferred from one command post to another without notification to the family.

Much of this I picked up from Doña María Elsa, who was Don Rito's sister. She cried telling me about it. "He was such a good boy, and he worked so hard after my father died. He's not a counterrevolutionary, I know he isn't. He's just a simple, trusting guy who maybe got in with the wrong bunch and was deceived."

I thought of the abrupt manner in which he had interrupted our meeting about Robelo. Deceived perhaps, but, if so, willingly. Don Rito was taken to Managua, and eventually found guilty. "Revolution and counterrevolution," an editorial shortly after the victory had read, "is a contradiction that's nailed in the heart of our revolution, and to remove it, sooner or later we're going to have to tear the heart apart once again."

These same contradictions were evident in the brigadistas, though more benign. Revolutionaries of high purpose one minute, rebellious cynics the next; half-guerrillas, half-children. It was impossible to comprehend the conflicts simmering in their heads. The only certain thing was that there were conflicts, and as our frustration increased, so did the explosiveness of the brigadistas' inner turmoil. Thus, without warning, we had an inexplicable spontaneous combustion at one of our Saturday workshops.

It began with the introduction to the new math primer. Here, too, the methodology was based on dialogue, in this case exchanges revolving around basic economic theory. The overall effort was to promote understanding of the economic base of the country and of the proposed changes in that base. At the same time, students would learn to count to one hundred, to write the numbers, dividing them into ones and tens, to do single digit sums and subtractions. The first lesson was based on the theme, "With the people and ENABAS, an end to speculation."

ENABAS, the national company for the supply of basic grains, was a major undertaking, and a major controversy. Nationalization of the banks, mines, and large haciendas had involved companies already huge and centralized. To put the basic grains under state control—

buying the harvests, regulating distribution, and controlling prices—meant major changes at every level of the economy, not just at the top. The idea was viewed with great mistrust, and not just by the wealthy. Years of living under Somoza had conditioned everyone to certain unwritten rules of survival—ways of accommodating to the system or circumventing it. The prospect of changes in these rules was unsettling.

We began the day's session by reading through the preparatory theme:

> One of the fundamental objectives of the government's political economy is to guarantee the normal supply of basic foods to the people. In order to achieve this objective, the revolutionary government has decided to intervene, together with the mass organizations, in the distribution of foods.
>
> The principal instrument with which the state will assure the supplying of the workers in both the country and the city is ENABAS, which will be assigned to buy up to 40 percent of the commercial production of basic grains and to resell them, principally to the poor barrios.
>
> ENABAS is created with the immediate object of combating speculation, hoarding, and the raising of prices....

Comments? We were sprawled around Doña Luz's small table, and the brigadistas seemed to share a common case of the fidgets. It was Freddy, serious, bearded Freddy—"The Bear," the kids called him—who first voiced the mood that was just beneath the surface. "This is bullshit. They're trying to brainwash us, that's all." His voice was charged with anger and resentment. I started at his tone, feeling other ears prick up at the challenge.

"What do you mean, Freddy? What do you think's wrong?"

"I'm just tired of the whole charade. Sandinismo here, revolution there. It's just a trick, that's all. And ENABAS is robbing the people like before."

"Yeah, it's just like before," chimed in another, emboldened.

"We come here to teach reading, and then they tell us that we can't go home or anything, like we're prisoners. And d'you think we'll get one word of thanks from anyone when we get out of here?"

"Yeah, yeah!" There were yells of agreement, and six conversations began all around me. My attempts to ask reasonable questions drowned in the din. "But the plan is—"

"And in Ocotal, the guy who runs ENABAS was just selling to his friends. I read it in *La Prensa*."

"Yeah, and in my barrio they sell at whatever price they want, and no one does anything about it. The leaders of the CDS are all Somocistas."

My voice went up a notch. "Let's talk about the problems as problems. Nelson, don't hang on the roof. Alejandro, come back in here if you have something to say. Just a minute, one at a time. Don't wave that book at me. Now, ENABAS—"

"They're just a bunch of rip-offs, and we're dupes."

"Yeah, my old lady works as a secretary and we're poor—not bourgeois like some of you people here—but then they started to denounce her as a Somocista and she almost lost her job. That's crap."

"How about your little family Mercedes if you're so down and out, Pineda?" In this free-for-all, there were no stable allies.

"Tomás Borge has one, doesn't he? How come no one denounces him?" Fend and parry.

"Well, I went out to fight and got my face screwed up, and all for nothing," Nelson said. "Now I can't even get work."

"I fought, too, and all last year I couldn't get a job."

"Now they're going to tell us we have to stay until October, and if we desert they won't let us back in school."

"Wait a minute! That's a stupid rumor and you know it." I grabbed desperately for the wild accusations, knowing as I did so that the larger debate was out of control. "And if you don't like the way things are going, you have to get involved and make them different." They were in no mood for such abstractions.

"They're just bigwigs, out for themselves, just like the others were."

"They want to take everything away from people who've worked."

"Listen!" Now I was angry. "You tell me how in a hundred years there's going to be change here if they don't shake up the ownership of land and the resources. You know that if that doesn't happen, we could come back here in ten years and see the same misery, the same poverty, and all this teaching won't have mattered a damn."

"Okay, okay." A peace offering from Roberto. "School's going to be free starting next year—I like that. And sure, we need change and all that. But I just want to make sure it happens, that we don't just get played for a bunch of fools."

"Well, I'm just here for my grades," Fernando blurted out in the clearest statement he had made in three months. "I don't like all the political stuff. I just want to get through so I pass."

"Yeah, and if you want to pass so bad, what were you doing

running off to El Tuma three weeks in a row with Raúl?" Poor Fernando, shot down by Friendly Fire.

"Come on," I pleaded. "Let's try to answer the questions honestly, and then look at the techniques for teaching the actual math." Taking advantage of the quiet, and hoping it meant that the rounds were spent rather than a pause for reloading, I hurried on. "Notice that they make a point of contrasting the math that people here have been doing for years in their heads with the idea of putting it on paper— something they don't know."

"*Profe*, when are we going to get more insignias?" Wonderful. Trash the whole project one minute; bemoan the deprivation of its symbol the next.

'We're not. I can't help it if three got stolen from the meeting."

"Quit looking at me that way, Chongo, I didn't touch them. I don't even have one."

"How about my pants? I never got even one pair."

"You gave them to Miguel, Elvis. If they didn't fit, that's one thing. But if you give them away, there's nothing we can do. Now, come on, please let's get finished."

"So ENABAS will buy everything and then sell it and keep the money just like always."

I refused to regard the remark as a taunt, though I knew it was. "No, it's not like it's private. Don't you understand the difference between private enterprise, where it all goes to one person, and state-owned, where the profits are used for reinvestment in public projects?"

"Well, my old lady had to put out ninety córdobas for a pair of boots, and my cousin says . . ."

In the middle of everything, the health brigade arrived—the medical students whose job in the crusade was to take care of the brigadistas. Within seconds the place was converted into a clinic. "Who's sick?" they asked. Everyone, it seemed, except me! Pills of five different colors were passed out like Halloween candies, followed by a lecture on building latrines and encouraging the peasants to boil the water. All very fine, but the presentation offered no hints about how to fight the customs of centuries here. The assembled brigadistas gave it less than their undivided attention.

When they'd all finally gone home and I had a moment to check the time, I was astonished to find that it was already two o'clock. What was with these kids? Was it because some of their parents had little shops or farms and felt threatened? Or was it just frustration in general—a resentment of the pressures to change? Was it youthful idealism, in which any flaw was an affront to their religious hope that this really *was* something different? Or was it impatience with the rain and everything slowing down? Or did they just enjoy baiting the *profe*? I had the recurrent feeling that they found me highly entertaining when angry.

But there in my afternoon visit was little José, who never came to meetings but who was always there with Don Roberto and his family in their now miserably damp little house. Anita Fley did not believe in pampering her *mozos*, even to the extent of helping them fix leaky roofs. Their house, with the children pale, the señora tired and the señor working but always without money, seemed the final punctuation to the brigadistas' cynicism.

Yet José Ramón was anything but cynical. A mere fourteen, he had been going through great changes in his political thinking, partly as a result of endless chats with Don Roberto, who had befriended him. Don Roberto had insisted that his wife and kids attend classes, and now José Ramón was giving me the only truly pleasant surprise of the week. The kids were learning, were actually *making their own words*! It was the first time I'd seen it done in any of the classes, and for overall miracle value, it ranked very high on my scale just then. Right above seeing Ramoncito himself, so proud and self-confident.

As June dragged on I suddenly remembered that I had to go to Matagalpa to reregister as an alien. To my delight, Doña Poldina decided to make the trip with me, to buy some material and a few other luxuries in scarce supply in Muy Muy. Wrapping our town duds in a knapsack, we set out across the muddy prairie.

The river was too deep that day to ford, so I cupped my hands and hooted "Goyooo" the way I'd been taught. Soon we saw his lean wiry figure slipping down the opposite bank toward his hollow-log canoe.

From Don Goyo's we cut sideways through an overgrown pasture that I didn't recognize. Some two hours later over hill and dale, Poldi in the lead, we finally emerged at a tiny hut with a Pepsi Cola poster out front. This I recognized from the last trip: we were at the highway to Matagalpa. Begging space inside to wash and change our muddy clothes, we emerged minutes later proper ladies in our town shoes and clean dresses, ready to board whatever vehicle stopped for us first—as it happened, the bus. Off we went to another world.

It was a world of miraculously firm ground, where people still walked around in light sandals, and when it rained no one got soaked. The main streets, so poor and spartan to me before, now beckoned with such a multiplicity of goods that I soon grew satiated, just looking and smelling.

There were big hugs from all the staff in the office of ANDEN, the teachers' union. Everyone was haggard and pale from a surfeit of meetings, statistics, and decisions. The other Matagalpa communities were coming along, I learned, but, like us, alarmingly behind the national average. I also got filled in on the progress of the groups I'd known almost nothing about—the urban Popular Alphabetizers and the Children's Rearguard.

Alphabetizing the City: The crusade in the countryside had captured center stage, but the literacy of those in the cities was not being neglected. Forty-eight percent of Nicaragua's population is urban-dwelling, and while the level of illiteracy was well under half that in the rural zones, it was concentrated of course in the poorest neighborhoods.

The Popular Alphabetizers, as the urban brigadistas were called, were from all levels of society. Many were students who were unable or unwilling to leave their homes. Others were workers, housewives, soldiers, professionals, anyone who could somehow manage to find two hours in their day to give classes. The basic organization was the same: afternoon or evening classes taught by volunteers, Saturday workshops and regular supervision by teacher-advisors. Although most of the Popular Alphabetizers worked in their own neighborhood or factory, there were those who had to move about. Crossing their towns and cities to reach the previously isolated poorest neighborhoods, they, too, were learning the geography of poverty.

The alphabetization in the city confronted a series of contradictions quite different from those which the rural areas confronted. The majority of city residents had had much more contact with letters and with the process of reading—be it street signs or scraps of newspapers—and so they were able to advance more rapidly through the beginning lessons. However, the urban alphabetization program didn't represent the novel and unrepeatable opportunity that it did for those in the *campo*. In the cities, there had always been programs of one kind or another—chiefly night schools—though the crusade was much more complete and convenient than anything to date. This, combined with the high level of other attractions in the city, meant a lower level of enthusiasm, more drop-outs and, as time went on, problems of absenteeism, both student and teacher.

With this counterbalance of advantages and disadvantages, the Popular Alphabetization in the urban outposts of Matagalpa department was keeping pace more or less with the progress in the rural zone.

A final appendage on the alphabetization mechanism was the existence of the so-called "rearguard." This was composed of programs for the primary school children, sons and daughters of working parents. Normal classes has been suspended all over the country so that the teachers would be available to collaborate with the literacy campaign. Nevertheless, in a country where daycare was unknown until the revolution and more than half the families are supported by a single parent, it would have been utter chaos to leave some 300,000 school-age children completely unattended. Thus, the *retro-guardia*, half-day programs of informal education and cultural enrichment under the guidance of teachers and volunteers, did its part, too, to help keep the country going while the alphabetization army did its work.

It was time to make a decision, or rather to carry out one we had already taken some weeks ago: Raúl and Guillermo were to be given the boot. Estela and I went over the evidence with Chico: repeated drunkenness, innumerable trips to Managua without permission, missed classes. Guillermo hadn't been getting along with the older folks at his house and had been more often absent than present. And the final straw was that Fernando was joining the gang.

"Now here's a kid who's weak but functional," I argued to Chico. "He can still be saved. But I guarantee you that if you give these two another chance, after the thousand they've already had, we're going to lose Fernando, too. And after him, who knows."

Strangely enough, we had a hard time convincing Chico. Despite all the threats, the apparent sternness, Chico didn't want to see anyone given the final sanction. "They don't understand," he protested, voice husky with genuine dismay. "This is going to hurt them for the rest of their lives."

Though I'd been pushing for their dismissal, I was now touched by his generosity. It seemed so like the generosity of the whole process, the same leniency that had astounded the world just after the revolution when, against all historic precedents, executions were banned.

From Wapá up to the national tribunals there was such a strong faith in human goodness, a belief in the power of education to reform the most hardened offenders. I saw all this reflected in Chico's face as the two brigadistas came strolling up to the school. And as I watched the scene, I felt a sweep of the same sorrow, and regret.

"I understand you've been having some problems, *compañeros*," Chico began.

Guillermo shrugged. Raúl lay down across the porch railing, red handkerchief protruding rakishly from his collar.

"Where were you last weekend?" Chico was trying to give them a chance, but not by sweeping it all under a rug.

Guillermo began to sputter a denial, but Raúl merely nodded his head gravely. "Yeah, man, we went to El Tuma."

"And it's not the first time, is it *hermanos*?"

The little drama played itself out rapidly, all of us hoping in the end that some new unthought-of-solution would magically appear. But it was impossible. Off they went at last to collect their clothes and turn in their equipment. Chico's tired sigh as he walked away summed up my own mood.

We met with Chico for "Propaganda and Theater Workshop," in which he delivered an excellent presentation: how to develop the skits they called sociodramas, how to reach the public, how to use children's games to present a message. But the mood of rebellion still reigned. The kids heckled and whispered as he talked, and finally one part of the group, led by Freddy, absolutely refused to cooperate on their assigned activity. Chico got angry, frustrated, the first time I had seen him like this. So it wasn't easy for him either. He was writing down names. We dissolved in disorder, with everyone complaining at once: Elvis that he was going crazy giving three shifts; Geraldo that Miguel wasn't even giving classes while he, Geraldo, was breaking his neck to cover both his house and Don Lucas's.

Finding Freddy alone at Doña María Elsa's one afternoon, I sat down to have a talk with him. At twenty-one, Freddy was very much grown up—reserved and introverted. His recent series of rebellions seemed, therefore, more serious than those of the younger brigadistas.

"Look, Freddy, what's going on with you?" I began, without the customary preamble. "Chico's mad at you for disrupting his workshop. Alejandro says you want to leave. I haven't been able to get a straight word out of you since before Mother's Day. Yet, of all the kids—and I told Chico this when he wanted to report you—you're one of the most reliable, and the hardest working. I don't get it."

It was hard to read the expression on his thick face, half-hidden behind his ferocious black beard.

"He wanted us to play children's games." His tone was defensive. "I wasn't trying to boycott his workshop; I just told him that I didn't know any games. I don't—I didn't play games as a child."

"Trouble in the family," I remembered Estela saying. "He's another one without a father.

"No, it's not that, specifically," Freddy amended, after a pensive pause. "It's things in general.

"Listen, if you have problems understanding the revolution, or with the alphabetization, let's talk about them, because you're doing a great job here. But I can't figure out when you're kidding and when you're not anymore. Are you mad at us about something? Or are you really unhappy here?"

Then he was looking at me straight on, across the short span of Doña Elsa's kitchen, with no masks, no bitter jokes. It took me by surprise, more so the abrupt intensity of his words. "For me," he said in a tone suddenly formal, "it's a great honor to be able to teach here, to teach our brother peasants. The only thing that really hurts me is that I can't do more. I'd already begun to give some classes to the *mozos* on my mother's farm, before the crusade even started. I went home in May, and they all begged me to stay, told me that the brigadista they had now wasn't doing such a good job. But I said no, my place is here and I have to go back. That's all, the rest is jokes. No, I'm not at all against the revolution—you've got me wrong. And to tell the truth, I'm happier here than at home. I'm only sorry that some of these people won't be able to finish, okay?"

I nodded at him, speechless. Who ever knows what's going on in the depths of another person?

Within ten minutes, Freddy was back, pestering me. "How do you say 'I love you' in English, *profe*? How do you say 'Why don't we get married?' Why don't we get married, *profe*? You could come and take care of my children."

"You have children, Freddy?" Half-believing.

"Sure, six of them, but that's between two wives."

A grand person, Freddy, I decided, turning away.

Goyo had left two weeks ago, after receiving an emergency message. "Brother hurt in an accident. Come home immediately." Now we had just learned that his brother had died, after a week in a coma, so Goyo wouldn't be back for a while. The hole he left would be more difficult to fill than most. He'd had a class of eleven—enthusiastic and dedicated students who had progressed well under his tutelage.

I conferred with Narciso. No bright ideas. Out of desperation, I would give classes there myself as long as I could. Real, direct activity for a change. It was an impossibly mixed group, sprawled everywhere in the tiny shack. A woman in the doorway on Lesson 4; a child at the blackboard on Lesseon 7; two bright teenagers racing through Lesson 9; Doña Petrona who couldn't see pencil marks, only the thick chalk letters on the blackboard. Indeed, it wasn't easy to keep the class in order. I fought to remember the ten steps of each lesson, and had to remind myself not to coax too much. I could almost hear myself criticizing the lesson as a dispassionate observer. But the joy, the pure joy of it!

The outside world went on, filtered through to us in morning broadcasts and infrequent newspapers. Robelo's campaign continued, as did the Frente's countercampaign, with the newspapers divided into obvious rival camps on the issue. Every facile criticism launched by Robelo had to be met with solid analysis; the real issues had to be explained to people—and the real problems. Again and again the message went out: "Don't just criticize, participate in the solution." The conscientious sectors responded—others merely looked on. And how many revolutionaries were there really? In Wapá I could firmly count Arturo and Don Petronilo, Chavelo maybe, Chico and Matías.

One Saturday I was sitting with Dõna Luz on the veranda of the Membreño house, waiting for the brigadistas to arrive. Apropos of nothing in particular, she glanced at the revolutionary posters which we'd plastered all over their walls for our Saturday workshops and remarked, "Yup, when Somoza was in power, we were with Somoza because what's a person to do? Now we got this new thing, so we go along with that." How many others thought as she did?

Then there was the international news. The exodus of dissident and maladjusted Cubans from Mariel was being given the expected twists in the wire services, while the existence of dissident and maladjusted Nicaraguans—the vicious remnants of the National Guard—was causing increasing alarm in the north of the country. The agony of El Salvador was increasing daily; we followed it as if it were our own.

And in a country no one I was living with could visualize very well, there were riots. "There's a revolt in Miami," people kept stopping me to announce. "They're killing the black people." And the questions I couldn't begin to answer: "Why do the blacks and whites hate each other?" "Is it true the black people can't live where the whites do?" "What's this 'Ku Klux Klan'?" And there was talk of the growing popularity of a presidential candidate named Ronald Reagan—something I could find no way of comprehending.

But for all the avidity with which we listened to the news, they were tales from another world. More and more, my world was the area between the three rivers, and my struggle was with the primers.

I realized somewhere inside that the "down" I was on was partly just me. "Why pay so much attention to the problems?" I asked myself. If you *look*, there are plenty of positive things to think about."

There was Matías, for instance, isolated out near the end of our territory, and with the largest class. Yet he was always there when I came to see him—serious and self-contained, helping Don Luis on his small parcel, struggling with his giggling students, studying himself, or "just thinking"—never asking for anything or complaining.

Ismael had recently returned and, weak and pale as he still was, insisted on going out to the field with Don Juan. "It makes me feel like a baby to stay behind." Mute in a political discussion, he nonetheless had *conciencia* up to the tip of his close-shaven head.

Then there was José Ramón, now an integral part of Don Roberto's family, and Marvin equally close to Don Amado, Luis showing Don Agapito the syllables for the tenth time, and Narciso cheerfully risking exposure to every contagious disease known to medicine with his daily trips over to the most miserable shack in the valley.

The three boys at the hacienda, not under my supervision, were doing a wonderful job, everyone said. Then there was Alejandro with his quiet patience, flaky Rolando trying to discipline himself, dark little Pablo in his jungle shanty with Don Goyo, sweet-tempered Jairo sticking by Don Chavelo through thick and thin, mostly thin.

I could see the progress in their classes, could see the growth in their outlook. Yet it just couldn't reach me as did Fernando's whine, or Freddy's scowl, or Nelson's sullen, "Estela told me she'd let me have permission if you would." And every brigadista I found *not* giving his class seemed to weigh so much heavier than those who did. With fifteen separate kids to supervise, I just couldn't be all the places at once that needed encouragement or help, to say nothing of the social relations that needed untangling, or the campesinos who needed firm encouragement to stay in their classes. As I criss-crossed the steamy prairie day after day, I found myself looking more at the mud and less at the good green things growing in it.

On Chico's next visit, he brought a copy of the documents from the First National Congress for circulation among the brigadistas. The Congress had been attended by some six hundred people who were divided into three commissions: technical/pedagogical; mass organizations, political and administrative groupings; and statistics, control, and logistic support. Within each commission they had studied the comments that had come up from the local and regional congresses, dividing them by categories and pairing each "difficulty" with one or more "suggestions" to resolve the problem.

In spite of my waterlogged spirits, I had to admit I was impressed. In my more cynical moments I had suspected that the careful programming of our own congress would be boiled down into broad generalities and the solutions would amount to exhortations to try harder. I should have known better. In each commission, the difficulties went on for pages, and from somewhere along the chain of contributions some solutions had popped up that were not only practical and feasible, but downright creative. For example, enlisting the parents themselves in the effort to curb absences and desertions. Those left at home would now have the clearcut choice between being part of the problem or an active part of the solution. The families would even be called upon to urge their brigadista children to attend the Saturday workshops—reaffirmed at the Congress as the backbone of the crusade.

It was very reassuring to leaf through the pages and see once again that we weren't alone in our problems. At every level and in every sphere there recurred the weaknesses that resulted from a country with too little money and too few experienced people trying to do the impossible.

It was also nice to see that there were some problems we *didn't* have. For instance, there were several references to right-wing religious sects that had done all they could to sabotage the literacy program in their communities. The suggestion in this instance was to call on the more progressive religious sectors to combat these ideological attacks. In our community there was no resident religious presence of any stripe. Once a year, a circuit preacher would come through and perform any services that needed performing—marriages, baptisms, communion. While the people of El Jícaro were as religious as any other part of this devout country, there were as yet no peasant catechists, no signs of a "base community" in formation. For religious ceremony, people had to content themselves with the occasional religious processions that took place in Muy Muy.

One entry made me squirm. The category was *"Diario del Campo"*—field diary—and among the criticisms I found: "The diaries have been very descriptive and not about pedagogical or political experiences or about integration into the community." They'd nailed me. Though I tried to remember what they wanted the field diaries for, there were times when I treated mine as my best friend, someone I could share my innermost feelings with. Well, I rationalized, if one read carefully between the lines, it was about integration. I made a mental note to remind the brigadistas to keep theirs up to date.

CHAPTER 15
Going Under

It's true that right now I don't like being here...but so many compañeros have fallen for this cause....For all those who never said they were going to die for their country, but who simply did, for them, I have to love people; for them, I have to continue the struggle.

FROM A BRIGADISTA'S FIELD DIARY*

June drew to a close, running rapidly as the now-swollen river and, like the river, carrying everything before it in no certain order. The statistics sheets, my only real hold on objectivity, showed us still hovering around Lesson 8. I carried the urgency around with me, heavy as my waterlogged boots, without being able to communicate any of it to the brigadistas. Matías was called to Matagalpa to defend one of his students who had been detained in a case of mistaken identity. Estela had stopped communicating with me altogether. Except for my warm and growing friendship with Doña Poldi, I felt all alone, dragging a burden that got heavier every day. I had watched so many classes with such intensity that I was dreaming in syllables instead of words.

Strangers in the house to buy the cows—medical expenses for Don Manolo had to be paid. Meanwhile, just up the path, Don Armado was trying to settle a year-old claim for pay and wanted help. It seemed the management of Babilonia had promised him 300 córdobas to clear a pasture—weeks of back-bending work in the rain with nothing but a machete—but when the work was done they'd only given him 200. Now there had been a change in administration, and they told him they'd pay him 250 and no more. I talked to him about channels for complaint, but most of all about getting promises put on paper in the future. Still, it didn't motivate him to attend classes.

Tomás Borge paid a surprise visit to nearby Matiguás. As the most eloquent speaker in the national government, he was there to help counteract the effect of Robelo's appearance. "He promised them a

---

*Quoted in Valerie Miller, *op. cit.*

new market and electricity," Doña Poldi reported. "And then he asked, 'Are we reactionaries here in Matiguás?' and everyone started screaming, 'No, we're Sandinistas, pa'lante, pa'lante [forward]!' " She'd caught it all on the radio, of course.

Meanwhile we were busy conducting a census of young children—candidates for a future school—and working with the CDS to promote the construction of a suitable building. Don Manolo had donated a small tract of land last year, more or less centrally located. Wood for pillars and beams was now being solicited, and we were in the process of begging two trees from the owner of Babilonia hacienda—trees which Don Alfredo would saw into boards. It seemed an ambitious project for our little community, and, privately, many expressed skepticism. "We'll never get a school here," they said, shaking their heads. "Even a revolution can't change things that much." Still, it was an issue around which everyone could unite. And we *were* moving ahead little by little.

Saturday workshop—this week the theme was the alphabetization itself. Suddenly it was all marvelous, wonderful, a great victory. The rhetoric made me want to scream. How could I get them to look at what was happening and evaluate it levelly? I thought of Manuel rising in the teachers' training session what now seemed like a century ago, before the whole thing began, and saying, "Though they've already planned it, right up to the victory celebration, we have to be very careful. It would be easy to do half a job and say to the world, 'See, we did it!' And only we would know. But we're not going to do it that way, and for that we need every bit of all of us."

June, June. The place in the river where we washed was accessible only by crossing a foot-deep mud puddle. I'd wash in the river from the knees up and, on returning, wash from the knees down. Every day there were more puddles, more swamps and less firm ground. It felt as if the whole earth was slowly slipping away beneath my boots.

I realized somewhere down inside that I was losing perspective. I was taking the whole thing too seriously, too personally, but I couldn't seem to stop myself. And at last the dam burst.

It was a day of mixed messages, of confusions and misunderstandings that took me to the school—only to find Chico and half a dozen brigadistas waiting to attend a meeting Estela had ordered. But Estela was not there.

"It's no loss," Chico said. He had wanted to talk to the squadron leaders in Wapá anyway. So he and I set off together across the familiar swamp, he without boots, trudging doggedly through the calf-deep mud. Easy casual chitchat—the camaraderie of mud and solitude.

And without my planning it at all, everything came tumbling out. Everything—the isolation, the problems with the brigadistas, the splits in the community, the mutinies on Mother's Day and on weekends, the problems of organizing a community, of organizing ourselves, the demoralization, the disappearance of Estela, the constant loss of class days, my self-doubts, the lack of support from Muy Muy. We crossed the lowland in front of Don Roberto's, the hills rising vibrant green on either side of us, and I talked on. Past the gate to Wapá through mud tramped to a thick soup by passing horses, and still I talked. This wasn't Chico's job, really, but I could no longer stop myself.

"I'm sorry, Chico, I know this doesn't really concern you."

"No, no, go on. Knowing the problems helps me do my work better. Really, I am interested." And so I did, encouraged by his silent, warm presence, and his attentiveness.

By the time we reached Don Ernesto's, I was spent. It was all out. Somebody knew everything, and though I didn't expect any solutions from Chico, I felt unabashed gratitude. I didn't even wonder what he thought of me; it was public now, Sheyla's going under in Wapá. I was no longer alone, it was someone else's problem, too. And if, as I suspected, Estela had been giving only positive progress reports in Muy Muy, the negative side had now been exposed. I could finally relax.

As I approached the porch of my house, I counted ten brigadistas sitting there. They had been working all day in the field and were waiting to be congratulated. I sent them all to find Chico, who had split off to see Ricardo. And I slept soundly all night, for the first time in weeks.

Technical Advisor's Bimonthly Report, End of June, Wapá

Alphabetizing: 115

Drop-outs: 36

New students: 15

Alphabetized: 20

Brigadistas reporting: 18

Illness: 1

Change of residence: 10

Absent or deserted: 2

Dismissed: 2

Progress Control:

Students in lessons   1–5:   5

  6–8: 46

  9–11: 20

12–15: 18

16–23: 26

BOOK FIVE

JULY
The Final Offensive

Do you know I'm not ignorant anymore? I know how to read now.
Not perfectly, you understand, but I know how. And do you know,
your son isn't ignorant anymore either. Now he knows how we live,
what we eat, how we work. And he knows the life of the mountains.
Your son, ma'am, has learned to read from our book.

DON JOSÉ, A PEASANT FARMER WORKER
TO THE MOTHER OF HIS LITERACY TEACHER,
JULY 1980*

It's a good thing emotions aren't cars. As June turned into July our
morale leaped from near idle to overdrive without passing through
the intermediate gears. It would have stalled a car; we—campesinos and brigadistas alike—just kicked into action.

And our fuel? First was time itself. During all of May and June
our days in the countryside seemed limitless; but by July everyone
was beginning to realize that the weeks were short. Second was
the nature of the pedagogy itself. Learning to read is a seemingly
endless process of small memorizing steps which culminate in a series of cognitive leaps. All over the valley, campesinos were reach-
ing that breakthrough point of comprehension. And finally, the
outside world was stretching out a hand. The data from the National Literacy Congress would result in a general plan for the
emergency final offensive, aiming special attention at Matagalpa,
the furthest behind of all Nicaragua's sixteen departments. The first
anniversary of the revolution was coming as well—a reminder that
victory was possible, and against much greater odds than ours.

We were now charged with the final offensive. It was time to
pull out all the stops. The victory was still far off, and time was
growing short.

---

*Quoted in Valerie Miller, "The Nicaraguan Literacy Campaign," in Thomas W. Walker, *Nicaragua in Revolution* (New York: Praeger, 1982).

CHAPTER 16
First Anniversary

If you see that the streets are wider now,
If you see that there are flowers everywhere,
If you see that in the children's hands,
There really is a bomb there—
The dream of all the fallen.
It's that today we're marking more than a year gone by.
It's that today we've grown just a little more.
It's that today our doors have been thrown open,
In this, our liberated Nicaragua.

"FIRST ANNIVERSARY,"
SONG BY NORMA ELENA GADEA

July came and all around it was green now, the green of the rainy season, the green of spring, magnified by water and sunshine. It almost hurt to look at it. All around there was growth. Paths that had been clear were covered in weeds. Pastures were knee-deep, then thigh-high in *zacate*, the sharp, wild grass that fed the cattle and rasped the skin. Cows were fat and corn was high. I could no longer see Arturo's shack from our house, nor Don Ernesto's from Dōna Luisa's, nor the school from the top of the hill. I began getting lost again.

But it didn't matter. At last, something was happening. An inaudible engine had turned over, an invisible gear slid into place. We'd reached the top of the hill. We were going to make it over.

I'd seen it first with José Ramón's class at Don Roberto's, but not until sometime later did I recognize the sudden surge forward as an overall pattern. A big change had occurred around Lesson 8 or 9, a kind of click. At that stage—sometimes several lessons earlier or later, depending on the individual—the logical pattern of the alphabet became evident. No longer was the learner performing an arbitrary act of memorization with each separate word and syllable. Instead, there was recognition of the actual relationship between letters and sounds, a relationship that in Spanish is utterly constant. Suddenly the pattern of the primer was falling into place. Each exercise brought a new consonant sound that combined with the familiar vowels to form new syllables. These syllables took their places alongside the known ones, and, with them, formed new words. The exercises began to take on new meaning and the whole process was infused with the excitement of discovery. Although almost half of the consonants and blends still remained to be studied, the foundation was finished. In Wapá, as we hit Lesson 10, the "clicks" could be heard like gunshot echoing through the valley.

"They're making progress, Sheyla, they really are," Matías confided wonderingly.

"Three of mine are about to finish," Roberto said. "Of course, they turned out to be superintelligent."

Elvis, with his low, serious murmur: "We're coming along fast at Don Chavelo's. Going through a lesson every other day. And I'm still trying at Dõna Jacoba's even though I can't get anywhere. Three shifts, Sheyla! Don't you think I deserve a few days in Managua for all my good efforts?" But he was smiling as he said it.

DIARIO DEL CAMPO

Sunday, July 6

We're gonna win, goddammit!
We are! We really are!

Acta #1

In the house of Don Manolo Zamora, Wapá; Community, El Jícaro; Municipio, Muy Muy; Tuesday, July fifteenth, nineteen-eighty.
Those present:
Sheryl Hirshon: Technical Adviser
Ramón Ocampo: Student
Roberto Ortega: Brigadista
Leopoldina Ocampo, Denis Ocampo, Jorge Luna: Witnesses

We are in the fenced-off corner of the porch where the zinc reflects the sun's heat directly onto the round table. The plastic blackboard with yesterday's lesson is still in evidence. We cluster around fifteen-year-old Ramón—skinny little Moncho—Doña Bernarda's youngest, as he gazes solemnly down at the square of newsprint: the final exam.

I give witness here that the student, without outside aid, demonstrated the capacity to read and write at a basic level, thus passing the final test.

The hands he uses for milking clutch the stub of pencil. A thin line of sweat appears on his upper lip. It's only the heat; he's confident, despite the row of faces. "I knew how to read a little, before," he says, "and Roberto helped me a lot. Now I'm really good." A cocky grin.

1. He wrote his name and surnames.

Line one, the line they would all complete with the greatest pride.

2. He read correctly and with expression the phrases of the test.

Solemnly, but easily, after a few moments study: "Illiteracy is a cruel heritage left us by Somocismo. Our glorious revolution proposed a war against it and won. Before, half of the Nicaraguans over ten years of age did not know how to read or write. The people with good conscience have carried out the alphabetization." The multisyllable words emerge slowly but completely, perfectly intelligible. We breathe a collective sigh of relief.

3. He answered correctly, in writing, the three questions of test item #3.

"Now in order to answer these questions, you may have to look back over what you've read. Answer according to what it says on the paper, not according to your own ideas. Okay?"

a. What was the task proposed by the revolution?

"That's easy! The alphabetization."

"Good. Now write down what you just told me." In his clear, thin letters, mouthing the syllables as he writes, he scratches out the words.

b. How many Nicaraguans were there who did not know how to read or write?

This is harder. From his first impulse to search for a numerical answer, he comes to the realization that the phrase, "Half of the Nicaraguans over ten years of age," represents the quantity required.

c. Who did the alphabetization?

A return of the grin. "The people" And this word, too, is carefully written onto the test form.

4. He completed the dictation without major errors.

The dictated phrase is "Now we know how to read and write." Moncho's mouth silently forms the shapes of sounds, as he makes deliberate pencil strokes. And it's done! Everyone's grinning and pumping Moncho's hand. Wapá has another new reader.

I sign this act in good faith confirming its veracity.

There were more over by the hillside, a few in Babilonia, Don Justo and his brothers, and two or three others—sixteen in all, their names proudly written out on cardboard and posted on the wall of Don Ernesto's. All of them had been slightly literate when we began; now they were reading fluently. The real test, of course, would be those who had known nothing, not even their own names, in March. They were the great majority, and even with the new surge of enthusiasm, I wasn't sure how many could finish in the month that was left.

Nevertheless, seeing others finish, knowing that it could be done, was having an effect. Those who had been vacillating decided to keep trying; those who had dropped to casual attendance began renewing their efforts to finish work on time and get to class. The brigadistas were seeing some results at last, too, and began to shake off their lethargy and respond with renewed dedication. And finally, enough Coleman lanterns had arrived to permit night classes in all the strategic locations. As before the bad news had poured in all at once, so now the wave of progress seemed to sweep over us in one solid rush.

Back in Muy Muy, my explosion with Chico had had its repercussions. On my next visit to the commission, I was questioned politely but pointedly by the new circuit directoress. I was then informed that my zone of responsability was to be cut to the plain of Wapá and Tierra Blanca, the other side of the hilly area where Don Luis Reyes lived. Estela, who had been overseeing a mere five brigadistas in El Jícaro, would be ordered to cover the near hillside, from Chico Barrera's to Don Agapito's.

Chico himself continued working with the brigadistas once a week—evaluation sessions, meetings with the squadron leaders, orientations, and the informal political talks that Sandinistas inexplicably call *chaguites*—banana plantations. Not all of his attempts were successful, but his words, and more, his example, were having an effect.

Meanwhile, the first anniversary of the revolution was approaching, amid constant reminders of its meaning. "Everyone to the plaza with the Frente Sandinista," was the jingle of the hour, a jingle echoed gleefully by Jorge. He was going to take Doña Leopoldina, he informed me, and Elvis was taking Don Chavelo, and others, too, were going to Managua to see Tomás and Fidel. "And to celebrate!"

Our orders, of course, were "no." It would mean too much of a strain on the scarce available transport, Chico said, "And, besides, it could be dangerous." Two brigadistas had been assassinated already, and there were more than a few active counterrevolutionary bands in the northern mountains. This would be a perfect opportunity for an ambush, an attack on one of the trucks as it descended through one of the poorly traveled feeder roads. How could we know? We couldn't take chances.

The brigadistas were unconvinced. They'd heard *"Patria libre o morir"** a few too many times to be successfully deterred by tales of danger. For my part, I was washing my hands of the whole issue. "This is your baby," I told Chico. "The only thing I got out of my Mother's Day attempts at discipline were scars." Estela agreed. "Our job is to pass on the information," she said. "I'm not responsible for what happens from there."

In anticipation of another mass desertion, we decided to hold our July 19 celebration a week early. There'd be a piñata for the children, with games and prizes. Then a commemoration and a grand fiesta. If that didn't get everyone out of their houses, nothing would. We dipped into our scarce funds to buy materials, begging an additional peso from each brigadista and each campesino family. That way, we figured, everyone would have a direct stake in the celebration. With the capital, we bought the clay jar, colored paper and hard candies we'd need to construct a properly grandiose piñata. And the shape? What else but a giant head of Somoza for the kids to whack at?

But the week had a few surprises in store. Tuesday and Wednesday we were called to Muy Muy for another marathon series of meetings. It was late on Thursday when I finally got home, to be virtually attcked at the door with the news.

"You'll never guess what!" Jorge announced, all in a rush. "We had a meeting with Chico when you weren't here, and it was the best meeting we ever had. Everyone came and everyone was serious, and nobody goofed around or anything."

"You did?" I stopped still, astounded as much by Jorge's obvious enthusiasm as by what he was actually saying.

"Yeah, no kidding, and he says that anyone who goes to Managua for the nineteenth can come back or not as they choose, but that they'll never get their alphabetizer's diploma and they'll have wasted

---

*"Free country or die," the slogan of the Nicaraguan revolution.

the whole three and a half months. So now no one's going, but we're going to have three days of carnival right here, 'dancing the hen,' and all kinds of games and three nights of fiesta. Then he signed kids up for the Juventud Sandinista. Lots of people joined, more than half. Geraldo did. I didn't, though; it's too strict about drinking and stuff. But, really, Sheyla, we had a good discussion. Everybody talked. You wouldn't have believed it."

Three of Doña Poldi's tortillas could have fit easily in my open mouth. "What on earth did Chico do to you all?" What, me jealous?

"I dunno. He's just got something about him."

Jorge wasn't exaggerating, as I confirmed the next day. On all sides they told me essentially the same story—and with the same grave conclusion. "*Profe, vamos a ponernos las pilas ahora.*" Loosely translated: "We're really going to finish by August."

I spent a few hours under my favorite tree, analyzing the new energy. Conclusion: the brigadistas' recent leaps of understanding were only the counterpart to the progress we were seeing in the students. From the beginning, we had understood that the crusade was as much to effect changes in the brigadistas as in the campesinos. Why should I have expected that one kind of change would come more easily than another? In this light, it was easier to see what had been going on. The activities that had involved the brigadistas in working to change others—the classes, the political meetings—had been embraced with enthusiasm. On the other hand, the activities which were intended to affect their own behavior—the discipline, the workshops, the criticisms—had been met with stubborn resistance, even resentment. And what were these but universal defenses against threatening change? As with the campesinos, though, something was finally happening to the kids. They, too, were moving past their middle lessons. The patterns were clearer now, the expectations less foreign. They could look back and see how far they'd come, and get a glimpse as well of where they were headed. What was called "revolutionary mystique" was beckoning, and many more than I would have believed were following the call.

The second surprise came Thursday, a brusque message for me from Humberto, director of the Muy Muy commission. "Be at the office early Sunday morning."

"Why? What's up?"

"Be at the commission Sunday. You're going to Matagalpa."

"I can't, Humberto. We have a piñata planned for Wapá."

"Estela'll have to take care of it. You're being 'emulated' this month."

"Against capitalist competition / Sandinista emulation," read the banner over the command post. The practice of emulation, a kind of collective positive reinforcement, had been mainly borrowed from the Cuban Revolution. What it meant, basically, was honoring the most exemplary member of a group—be it worker, student, teacher, soldier, or brigadista—so that others would be inspired to imitate the positive actions of that person. Instead of the negative rivalry implied by competition ("How can I beat him/her?"), it was intended to stimulate aspiration toward the best ("How can I be more like him/her?"). In practice, as I had learned during my work with the brigadistas, the line was often a fine one.

The delegation from Muy Muy left late Sunday afternoon: Chico; Oscar, a flute-toting brigadista from Olama, just across the river from Wapá; Gustavo, the bearded supervisor from the still remoter community called El Bálsamo; Lorena from the Muy Muy commission, and me. By early Monday morning we were filing into the hall, alongside representatives from each of the other ten municipalities of Matagalpa—all noisily cheering their own teams on. "Waslala! Waslala!" Sebaco vencerá!" "Muy Muy (clap, clap), Muy Muy (clap, clap)." There was a blackboard of obscure formulas up on stage, and a bulletin board on which the names of the various commissions would be posted in order of their achievement, from first down to eleventh place. Placements were based on a number of factors—the quantity of students alphabetized, studying and reintegrated in the program; the responsability and overall discipline of the brigadistas; the punctual delivery of reports and statistics; and the overall advance of literacy in the area. First-, second-, and third-place winners would receive a special banner for the commission office, and the others at least the satisfaction of knowing where they stood.

The second part of the emulation was for individuals. One participant from each category—advisor, brigadista, supervisor, and so on—would be selected for acclaim on the departmental level.

Emulations of this type had been taking place monthly throughout the country ever since the crusade began. While bearing a certain similarity to pep rallies, they unquestionably helped build morale, especially in the small-town commissions.

Muy Muy captured the banner for second place, thanks mostly to the flawless computations of Chino, the local statistics expert. More significant still, our own muddy Chico was emulated as the best zonal supervisor in the entire department. He deserved much more, in my opinion, after putting my gang in order.

And to polish off the week's triumphs: "I have your boots for you," Danilo, the supplies director, informed me on my return to Muy Muy.

Could it be possible? Overjoyed, I headed straight to the storeroom. Sure enough, there were the boots, but boots from the Korean children's brigade, apparently—tiny confections of blue and yellow plastic, the largest of which barely fit me.

"But we asked for 38s and these are 34s."

"Take them," Estela, also standing by, whispered gruffly.

"But—"

"Take them, I say. Look, I've been dealing with this place for months. These are our boots. We give them to the kids and they can do what they want with them—sell them, exchange them. At least they've got something and they'll shut up. We turn these down and we'll most likely never see another boot again, small *or* large."

And she was right. The boots shortly reappeared on the feet of the younger girls and boys of the community. I never asked what deal had been struck, but neither did I catch another word of complaint from those who'd been issued them. It was time to put all the worries away for a while and just celebrate. The first anniversary of Nicaragua's liberation was at hand.

It was to be one mammoth party, all over the country. Actually, there were three days to commemorate. On July 17, Somoza—after weeks of vacillation—finally abandoned the country for Miami, leaving it in the hands of a transitional government. This was the Day of National Joy. But it wasn't quite over yet. Francisco Urcuyo Malianos, the new figurehead, liked his promotion a little too much. Instead of decorously handing over the reins, as had been planned, he decided to set himself up in earnest as the next dictator. He summoned the remnants of the National Guard and resumed the bombings. Many who had relaxed their vigilance too early died. However, in the face of the massive popular insurrection, Urcuyo's pretensions didn't last forty-eight hours. By the morning of July 19, Urcuyo, too, was on a northbound plane. The last Guardsmen frantically scrambled for shelter in foreign embassies, stormed outgoing planes and commandeered boats. Guerrillas from all the fronts were rapidly converging on Managua to consolidate and celebrate the victory. It had been one of the most complete routs in history.

Now, one year later, it was time to celebrate. The newly constructed plaza would be jammed full of supporters, celebrities, visitors, and the curious. For us in the countryside, it meant doing the very best we could to commemorate, clarify, and just plain let loose.

And we were really cooking. By the time I got back from Matagalpa, Miguel and Narciso had organized the program, planned various fiestas, borrowed money, and bought all the materials. They'd even convinced Don Ernesto to move the beds out of his barnlike front room and turn it over to the dancers.

Thursday, July 17th: *Diá de Algería*—the day of joy. Get the phonograph from the Don Jaime (who somehow, sometime in his life had earned enough money to buy a small portable phonograph); round up donated chickens for frying; secure volunteers to make tortillas, run the cash booth and grind the corn; talk with Doña Luisa about contributing her famous rice pudding. Keep it simple, but spread the word well.

We kicked off the festivities by "dancing the hen." The poor victim, donated by Don Luis, was buried in the dirt with only its head protruding. Those who wished to participate in the game at a peso a head were blindfolded, spun around a few times, and handed a machete. Then the music was turned on and the contestant was expected to dance toward the chicken while the crowd screamed orientations, true or false. "Over there!" "No, no, more to your left!" When the time seemed right, he or she, still blindfolded, bent over and struck along the ground with the machete. If the aim was correct, the lucky butcher cut off the head and won the bird for dinner. If wrong, there was a lot of dust and screams of laughter. It was a kind of bloody "Pin the Tail on the Donkey," great fun for everyone but the hen.

It was completely dark when one of Doña María's sons finally put the bird out of its misery, much to the disgust of Jairo, who had spent his entire pocket money on the enterprise. Dancing was beginning, and in threes and fours the campesinos emerged from the night to take part. Holding their flashlights and lanterns in front of them, they crept shyly up toward our improvised dance hall, lit brighter than Broadway with our three new Coleman lanterns. Women were in their best dresses of bright polyester and the men sported immaculately ironed shirts. Inevitably, a cluster of excited children brought up the rear. Faces known and faces unfamiliar, they were coming in from as far off as Azancor Arriba and the hacienda El Jobo on the road to Matiguás. It was a big night.

The dancing went on until late by Wapá standards. There was the slow salsa that's danced separately, the folksy bolero that only Miguel had mastered, and the coupled box step. Brigadistas grumbled about the lack of disco music, but softly. Miguel and Narciso collaborated in keeping the event going—putting on the music, making jokes, overseeing the food sales and the finicky Colemans. At one point there was a brief speech and a lot of clapping. Somoza, the Last Marine (as he was called for his pro-American stance), is dead! Let's all dance on his grave!

Friday was our demonstration—complete with crepe-paper flags, speeches, and chants of *"Patria Libre!"* I couldn't decide whether our ragtag group of maybe seventy was beautiful or ridiculous as we solemnly marched through the thick mud from the site of the proposed school to Don Ernesto's. It was one of the shortest demonstrations I'd ever been part of and one of the smallest, but not by any means the least impressive. There was a seriousness in the dark faces, a conviction in the voices as they repeated the well-known slogans. *"Poder Popular!"* "The march to victory won't be stopped!" To finish off the demonstration, and the day, we hung our carefully prepared banner in front of Don Ernesto's. Simple words but, to us, significant: "Wapá celebrates the first anniversary learning to read and write."

Night brought the vigil to commemorate the dead. In the end the nature of the event wasn't completely clear. We arranged for Rolando to bring his very worn phonograph albums of the protest group "Pancasan," and we alternated their stirring political music with records for dancing. A weary Narciso heroically manned the refreshment stand, while Miguel, the only remaining brigadista with energy, pulled the delighted young girls onto the dance floor. I dutifully stepped my way through a few numbers, more dead than alive, then made a graceful exit out to the porch. There one of the young men from Tierra Blanca was playing the guitar. An eager circle of brigadistas and campesinos surrounded him, and everyone was singing or at least clapping out the rhythms. I took a seat on the shadowy fringes of the group and watched, mesmerized.

Jairo, above all, caught my eye. A round of "Tio Caiman" (Uncle Alligator) had begun, a song that involved everyone adding a set of couplets, preferably off-color ones. Seated just to the right of the guitar player, Jairo was leading the refrain. Long wisps of hair protruded from his green beret, and his half-child's face was lit with an incandescent joy. It was the joy of youth, of music, of creation, and of the naughtiness of the lyrics he was singing. Bouncing up and down while he clapped his hands to the guitar beat, laughter sparking from him like fireworks. This moment of complete transcendence would remain in my mind long after—an image of the crusade itself.

Saturday was The Day. I could see in my mind's eye the films of a hysterically joyful population pouring into the old square in Managua. Thousands upon thousands of *compas* mounted on the captured tanks had deliriously waved their red-and-black banners. *"Vencimos!"* "WE WON!" Miles and miles from Wapá, the scene was repeating itself now in a new plaza with an older, perhaps more sober, but no less joyful crowd.

For us, though, there were sack races for the kids and pin-the-tail-on-Somoza for all ages. There was also the "duck run," another bloody favorite in the Nicaraguan countryside. A live duck was greased thoroughly around the head and neck and hung upside down from a high branch. The contestants galloped underneath on horseback, grabbing at the head as they did so. The object, of course, was to pull it completely off and take the body home for supper. It was an event I chose not to watch, preferring to join the more pacific children's games.

Yet another fiesta swung into gear. I'd expected few customers this last night, assuming that the long walks and late nights would have taken their toll on enthusiasm and energy. But I was wrong. There were more people and more dancing than ever. Chico's "three days of fiesta" was a reality.

Sunday, July 20, was declared a day of commitment all over the nation, a reaffirmation of the goals of the revolution. Our commitment was to move forward on the school for Wapá. All of us go-get-'em-Sandinistas were out there with our machetes chopping the weeds, while the campesinos, working along at three times the pace, had the time of their lives trying to improve our style. "No, no, not like that! Lower! Bend lower!" The weeds would be back long before the school was ever started, but it didn't matter. We were out there to tell the skeptics that we expected action and that, eventually, they would have to be the ones to provide it.

Hundreds of thousands of people celebrated the anniversary in Managua and more than a hundred in Wapá. I missed Fidel's speech, even on the radio, but Don Justo's was almost as eloquent as he took his final test.

I climbed the long hill up to the deserted house. Matías, beside me, was the very picture of the guerrilla-brigadista, with an embroidered red star on his grey *cotona* and the whole outfit tucked tight into a webbed military belt hung with canteen. Alert and erect, he had that special look in his black and glowing eyes. It was a look I'd come to know. Penetrating, direct, and proud, it was the look of one who can't be bought or crushed. More unwavering than menacing, it was nonetheless a look you wouldn't ever want to see if you were a tyrant. It was in the eyes of the thousands who fought, many of whom died. And now it had passed to others. Wordless, it spoke of the dream and the decision.

We gazed down on the valley rich in fruit and spun plans for it: bridges to span the rivers, a school at each end of the valley with scholarships for those who wanted to go on to secondary school in Muy Muy, an access road to the highway, a really functional clinic, irrigation equipment so they could reap two harvests, land cooperatives.

Maybe Matías was trying to impress me just a little, as we looked down from the rock at the top of the hill and talked of revolution and sacrifice, struggle and meaning. But it didn't matter. The point was that he was an example of the best that this revolution, or any revolution, can hope for—young and visionary, serious, stubborn, utterly impoverished, and totally committed. What happens to him— and to our dreams for little Wapá—*is* the Nicaraguan revolution.

The little guy they called "Chino" had promised to meet us at the school to help fill out the statistics reports. While I waited for him and Estela, I decided to drop in on the Murillos, whom I hadn't seen in several weeks. It was a joyous reunion. After a while, the conversation once again turned to Don Chico, senior, and the books he had written. "Would you like to see one?" Doña Guillermina asked me. They had a good copy of one of the many notebooks he had filled, and a cousin who lived in the city had had it ty

Who knows what I expected to see, but this v different. A collection of stories, adventures, ref tain innocence, naturally, a lack of polish, but the pages woven through with remarkable skill and imagination. In the best, "The Wizard-Woman," he meets a fairy princess, or perhaps a witch, who takes him flying off to India, to exotic mountain castles. The steep Himalayas are lovingly described—the clouds, the jungle with its animals. Where did he get these ideas, this campesino who had never seen television, who had probably read very few books and fewer storybooks? "He'd work in the fields all day, then come home, wash himself, and write and write and write," Doña Chenta told me. "He never in his life went to school."

Something in me wanted to say, "What a waste!" But then I pondered. If you write books to show to a few friends and give away as gifts, one here and one there, and die happy at eighty-eight, looking out over the cornfield you've planted year after year, have you lived any less the life of a writer than any other writer? If so, then less what?

Saturday again—somehow they seemed to come more frequently than they had before. I arrived at the workshop to find the faithfully punctual waiting for me: Ismael, Matías, Narciso, Elvis, Jairo. This was normal. What was not, though, was the sudden appearance of the rest. There was Jorge, Geraldo, Ricardo, hurrying up from Doña Bernarda's where they'd been visiting, Marvin and Luis crossing the corral toward us, Pablo further off but visible. Even José Ramón.

"What do you know? We're all here today!"

"*Puño en Alto*'s been saying that if you miss a Saturday workshop you don't get your diploma." Hm, clearly the National Congress meant business.

"So what, idiot. I came because I wanted to. We've got to get some things settled here." Choleric Roberto, unable to bear his own compliance.

"Anyway, it's good to see you. There are only a few announcements and the important one I'm going to save until the end. So that just leaves the news that we're ending in less than a month and you should be preparing your groups for the final test. Also, we need the money you collected from the raffle on the nineteenth."

"Anything else?" Their quiet attention was making me nervous. "Narciso?"

"*Profe*, could you pass me the list of those in my group who owe ney. I'll take care of the collecting."

re, Narciso." I looked over in muted surprise at the new, authoritative tone, and noticed something else unusual. The two squadrons were sitting grouped together on the benches, each with its leader, instead of sprawling in clusters of two and three as far away as they could legitimately get. They looked like a group, and their leaders looked like leaders. More than half of them even had notebooks and pencils in their hands.

"Let's get on, then, to the week's evaluation." A pause.

"May I speak, *profe*?" Miguel's voice. "As squadron leader I have to visit my group and report on their progress." This wasn't exactly news to me, but it was certainly the first time it had happened. "We have six *alfabetizados*, counting Don Justo, who just took his final test. I visited everyone but Freddy and Luis last week and everyone's working and trying to finish. Geraldo needs a new mantle for his lamp. And, uh, the indiscipline this week was Elvis, who was in Muy Muy on Wednesday."

"What time, López? You tell me that." Elvis was on his feet, face scarlet. "I went to do an errand for Doña Peta in the morning because there wasn't anyone else. And I was *back* in my class, in *both classes*, on time. I even skipped lunch to make it." He was angry all right, but he wasn't denying Miguel's right to call him to order.

Narciso stood up, his stocky figure breaking off the discussion before it could get going. "Come on, you guys. Elvis should have asked permission all right, but on the other hand he did get back on time. I saw him go by." Both accepted the peace pronouncement. "For our part, the main news is that Goyo came back." An exchange of smiles on all sides. It was a last-minute return, but Goyo had been a valuable member of the team and we were all glad to see him pitch in again. "On the bad side, Fernando's still screwing around and we're going to throw him out of the group if he doesn't stop, because he's making us look bad." (Fernando looked more alarmed at this than he's looked at any of my far more extravagant threats.) "We have four alphabetized, but we'll have a bunch more in about fifteen days. And we need chalk." He sat down, then stood up again. "Oh, and I have to report on our participation in the July 19 activities. Everyone cooperated, especially Rolando. We have fewer members than the Ernesto Castillo squadron, but we did more."

Miguel opened his mouth, then closed it again. Roberto handed a cigarette to Geraldo, but quietly. No whispers, no bickering, no fidgets.

"All right, my observations I've already discussed with the people in question. Matías, you're really trying hard, but you've got to work more with the whole group and less with each individual, because you never get around to them all in time. Pablo, your group is finishing. You should get it together so you can go help out somewhere else. Goyo, I know you've been gone for a long time, but don't forget to review with the syllables chart, or how to help the students form words. And you'll have to work Saturdays and Sundays."

"*Profe*, the radio says all of us should be working Sundays now. Is that for real?"

"Yeah, Ismael. I'm going to get around to that when we talk about the final offensive."

I waited for the clamor of protest.

"Well, I don't mind, but I don't think my students will do it."

"Sure they will, Baldy. Tell them they won't graduate if they don't." Roberto flicked the ash off his cigarette as if to say, "There. Problem solved."

I was beginning to realize I'd become a victim of my own low expectations. This new mood had me lost; I'd gotten used to spending Saturdays in near riot.

"Goddammit, Geraldo, you just finished one cigarette and now you want one of mine," Miguel mumbled.

"Shh," I waved them down, smiling. At least they hadn't all become saints.

"Okay, I'm going to read anyway. Should I read the selection, *profe*?"

I nodded. It was time for the week's political theme, based around the photo and dialogue content of the lesson. "We're on Lesson 18, Geraldo."

We're forming brigades to construct and improve our housing

Lack of adequate housing is one of the most serious social problems that the Sandinista revolution inherited. For many years this sector hasn't been adequately attended; as a result, in the countryside and in the poorest barrios the majority of our brothers and sisters lived in conditions unfit for human beings, in filth and overcrowding.

The Revolution has a project to resolve definitively the housing problem but this can only be achieved with everybody's efforts and over a reasonable period of time....

The current housing plan is based in the following concepts—new housing is a public works for the government on one hand and for the community on another. The government can provide through long-term credits the materials, the planning and direction, but it will have to be up to the community to provide the labor force that the project requires.

Lección 18

"Okay, Geraldo, that's the first page. Now, comments?"

"I like these themes. They're a lot easier to understand, not just blah, blah. Anyway, my cousin worked on one of these projects out behind the arena. Now they've got their own house."

"Yeah, that's fine for the city, but where's the land going to come from for the campesinos?" In forty seconds, Elvis had seen through to the other side of the problem.

"Something's got to be done, though. Don Luis keeps saying how they're poor and all—and they are. But you know what? They live better than we do. The only thing is we have electricity. Aside from that, my sister's house, where we all live, is in lots worse shape." It was rare to hear Matías speak up in a meeting, much less make a personal comment. It seemed that the general air of serious attention had impressed him, too.

"But I mean it. What about the land?" Elvis was insistent.

"They should just take it away from people who aren't using it and give it to other people to build a house on. Like here, for instance."

I looked around nervously. Doña Luz, not far away, was probably catching this confirmation of her worst fears about us. "Well, how are you going to approach this in your classes, then?"

Goyo, gone six weeks but still our master teacher. "There's a problem here, *profe*. Because the dialogue's supposed to be about people's experience, right? Well, most of the campesinos won't understand what this picture's about, because they've never seen buildings like this."

"Sure they have. There's lots of them in Matagalpa."

"Not everyone here can get to Matagalpa like Doña Angela, stupid."

"You're stupid. Anyway, anyone can tell you what this is."

"Remember, *compas*, Chico said we should stop calling each other names. And remember, Jorge, lots of the women and kids never get out of here. It's all right to tell them what it is, isn't it?"

I nodded, speechless. Where had these brigadistas fallen from? Of course, Marvin was fidgeting, Jairo daydreaming, but they were silent, thinking, and the rest were talking like adults, like thinkers.

"No, in the country you can't even talk about housing until you talk about land reform."

Like revolutionaries.

"*Profe*, it's 10:15 and we always have a break at ten."

And yet, like kids.

CHAPTER 17
The Final Offensive

July 21, 1980

The National Directorate of the FSLN, together with the chiefs of staff of the Popular Alphabetization Army call on their combatants in the countryside and the city and on our people in general to ignite the Final Offensive on July 22—an offensive that will permit us to eliminate the last remnants of illiteracy from our country.

The combined actions of our various combat entities should guarantee the victory in each community, town, and department, making use of all means of struggle within our reach and realizing, among others, the following tasks:

1.   Increase by two hours daily the number of class hours;
2.   Obtain 100 percent attendance, discipline, and punctuality on the part of the brigadistas;
3.   Make sure that each brigadista and advisor prepares and delivers the necessary statistical material;
4.   Work with the mass organizations to obtain 95 percent attendance of the students in the literacy classes;
5.   Establish Sandinista Review Sundays in all study groups to increase the rate of assimilation;
6.   Assure that the advisors visit each group at least once weekly to help solve any problems that arise;
7.   Make full use of the Saturday workshops to explain the use of the final test;
8.   Be sure that all are listening to the current orientations broadcast by the program *Puño en Alto*;
9.   Begin preparing the sustainment phase, the phase that will follow the departure of the brigadistas;
10.   Avoid leaving the area for anything but absolute emergencies; suspend leaves of absence and all meetings that do not relate directly to the learning process.
11.   Plan political and cultural celebrations for each area declared Victorious in the alphabetization.

This was it then, the final offensive. What had been the last push in getting rid of the dictator was now the final battle against illiteracy. The announcement was official—there would be no extension of the crusade.

The plans for the final offensive had been reached using the data from the National Literacy Congress. While the crusade as a whole was progressing satisfactorily, there were alarming setbacks in key areas, chiefly the department of Matagalpa.

In the Pacific zone, where the land is flat and relatively well-settled, the literacy crusade had met with few obstacles. Brigadistas abounded, and access to the small communities was easy. Likewise, in the coffee- and cotton-producing areas, the concentrated populations of the large haciendas provided easy access to the classes and brigadistas. At the other end of the scale, the furthest removed areas—chiefly the vast department of Zelaya on the Atlantic Coast, with an illiteracy rate even higher than Matagalpa's—had received special attention. It was there that the university students were concentrated. Furthermore, the sparse and ethnically diverse populations of the Atlantic zone tended to live concentrated in small settlements along the myriad rivers, making the logistical job of alphabetization somewhat easier.

The northern mountain areas and foothills of Matagalpa and Jinotega were far more difficult. Dispersed populations, rising rivers, insufficient personnel—it was the same all over the zone. And the Matagalpa area was twice hard-hit: not only did it have the highest rural population in the country, and therefore the high illiteracy rate, but also the highest percentage of absolute illiteracy. Many peasants were totally unfamiliar with letters, even with pencils, making the task easily twice that of teaching one who knows at least the basics.

All these factors combined to form the special emergency of Matagalpa. Of the 61,000 in the censused illiterate population, 10,000 had finished by July 19, and another 7,000 were past Lesson 16—well on their way. But some 32,000—52 percent of the total—hadn't yet passed Lesson 10. My own alarm of May and June had found its echo. It was *"Patria alfabetizada o morir"* for everyone.

Communiques flew thick and fast from the commission, reiterating the points in the July 21 message, and adding that brigadistas should be relocated from finished or hopeless classes to critical, but hopeful, areas.

There were also new orientations for speeding up the lessons. Fewer words in Step 6 and in the dictation. Repeat less. Have the students write out the words but not the sentences. Put the K and the W— which occur only in a handful of Miskito and English words assimilated from the Atlantic Coast region—together. After Lesson 15, there are blends instead of syllables; put these together. The final exam should be given as soon as the student has finished Lesson 19—or whenever the student is ready to pass it—instead of waiting to finish the book.

"Remember, compañeros campesinos," they announced daily on *Puño en Alto,* the crusade's official radio program, "in three weeks the brigadistas will be going back to their homes. You must make every effort to prepare yourselves as fully as possible while there's still time."

So we surveyed the situation of each brigadista. Who, exactly, is studying with you? What lesson are they on? Who has finished? Who has dropped out? Who might be coaxed back? How many will be finished by August? We counted the lessons and exercises that remained for each student and divided them into the time remaining, emerging with a rigid day-to-day schedule, and, for my part, an overview of our possibilities.

There were three clear categories of students: those who would definitely finish; those who would definitely *not*; and the doubtful. The definite noes were those who had suffered the delays of illness or lost brigadistas, or the slow learners like Doña Bernarda, who had proudly struggled her way to Lesson 6. These would have to come in on the next round.

The battleground lay within the "doubtful" group—fifty percent of Jairo's class, the same percentage of Geraldo's, Doña Jacoba's daughters, the Barreras. For the most part, these were pupils of normal ability and enthusiasm who had been receiving classes from brigadistas just a little too *"tranquilo."* If they could be pushed over the mark, I figured, we'd at least reach our quota of 75 percent—*"Territorio Victorioso"*—if not the 90 percent we needed to become *"Territorio Libre,"* Free Territory.

"You gotta get down and *do* it now!" The frazzled coach was exhorting those who still seemed to lack fire. All I needed was a locker room and a cigar stub in my mouth. I made out a schedule for Geraldo, one of those shortest on initiative: two shifts daily; extra time with the two at Don Lucas's who just might finish if we pushed them enough; night classes at home. "But those kids at Lucas's don't want to study, *profe.* I know them. They won't finish."

"You've got to try with them, Geraldo. Because if you don't, you're not going to have a single diploma to give out. And God knows if they'll give *you* your diploma." Anything to get him moving.

For the most part, bullying wasn't necessary. We were united now against the common enemy—time. Time, the mental capacity of our students, and the social disorganization of the valley itself.

Another Gothic Interlude. Things had not been static on the manor. Following a visit by Don Alfredo, Don Manolo's wicked brother, who had gone off with a mule and a number of cattle to pay, he said, for Manolo's "treatment," the situation had become very mysterious. Don Manolo's whereabouts, for instance. Doña Angela had been strangely vague after her return from nights of vigil in Matagalpa. "He's in Managua, in the hospital." "In the psychiatric hospital?" "Uh, no, they say it's some kind of clinic." "But he is in Managua?" "Yes, in Managua, with some family of his, a niece."

Carlos visited Managua and returned encouraged. "Yes, I saw my father. Yes, he's a little better." Carlos with his oversized head and slow, deliberate speech. "But he kept asking me for money. They say they don't give him any for fear he'll just take off."

Doña Poldina, like all classic family servants, at the center of everything, sketched a seamier side. "Who knows what's happening, Sheyla? Those people are up to no good. He's with a daughter of this Don Alfredo, and who knows how they're keeping him. Angela doesn't want to make the trip to find out, and Carlos—well, you can tell Carlos anything. This brother's capable of anything. They say he killed a whole family once in order to get his hands on their land. And he for sure had his own sister-in-law run off when his other brother died. These people'll have Angela out in the street if she isn't careful. The farm's in Carlos's name, but the rest of that clan doesn't know it. With Manolo so helpless, they could pull anything—brainwash him, kill him even. And him and Angela aren't married, so she's got no right to anything, except through Carlitos."

The scene could have been written by Tennessee Williams. No one knew how to run things on the farm in Manolo's absence. Doña Angela certainly hadn't the faintest idea, and Carlos, poor Carlos, with his Matagalpa education, didn't know anything at all. The only ones who knew were the *mozos*, and they weren't being paid, and so were quietly looking elsewhere for work. Fences began to sag; one group of calves was sold and then another; the bean crop was washed away in a rainstorm. Only the daily milking went on as always, and the corn, as corn will, kept growing.

Secretly, I watched Doña Angela, thinking about her life, her sixteen years as companion to this gruff old farmer. She had begun by picking coffee with her mother, and now she had a house in Matagalpa and a 200-300 acre farm. It had been her one break in life, economically speaking, payment for having been born with light skin and blue eyes. How high was the price she had paid? It was difficult to say, for she wasn't a person to confide much in others. But at the moment, she was clearly less upset about Don Manolo's illness than worried for her and Carlito's future.

With the money from the cows she sold, a few luxury items appeared in the house. A new food grinder (the Nicaraguan equivalent of perhaps a new washing machine in the United States); a watch for Carlos; dolls for Carolina, the adopted five-year-old daughter. It was a fling of financial independence after a lifetime of dependency: sell the cows and buy the things you've always wanted without having to ask anybody. Even if all your sisters and neighbors do shake their heads and mutter, "Ruin!" And even if the few *mozos* you have left haven't been paid in weeks.

And what did this gothic soap opera have to do with revolution? Perhaps it stood as a kind of historical marker, "Where we started from." The web they were spinning here necessarily hung on a feudal land system. Family intrigues, dependency relations all around, suspicion and the ever-present threat of violence. It was all part of the struggle to survive when the rules are written with money and privilege.

Upper middle-class farmers like the Zamoras would be the last of the old order, and the last to grasp the new. They were too small to be confiscated or controlled, too comfortable with what they had to seek out the benefits of the new laws. The revolution was passing around their generation, affecting them, but not changing them.

Not so their *mozos*. Already they were talking change, tired of hearing their children coughing in the rainy nights. "When the corn is in . . ." Don Goyo and the others would threaten. "There's no work here; there's nothing without work."

"Then what'll Angela do?" Doña Luisa lamented. "She can't run that farm without *mozos*." And she summed up the entire class struggle in an old countryside expression: "Where there's money, there's no peace in the house."

Doña Luisa, the accumulated wisdom of sixty-odd years; wisdom of the moon, the shifts in the clouds, and the plants that surround you. You'd tell me what the weather was going to be, each time I passed by. "It's going to rain in a few minutes, Sheyla, you'd better hurry." "There's a good wind coming and it's the new moon. If it doesn't rain tonight, it'll be dry for the next week." You were wrong only twice that I can remember.

You don't have any land of your own to plant, but the tiny plot you squat on is full of sprouting trees and small plants. You used to go out yourself and seed the crops, Doña Poldina told me; one of the few women who did. Not because you didn't have willing sons or a man to do it for you—you did—but because you loved the work.

Your tall, spare figure is pure Ocampo, as is your intense interest in the world around you. Sitting by the table in your kitchen—straight gray hair in a braid around your head—you hang on the words from your radio and wait for passers-by to share them with. Sixteen years in this valley; a lifetime in the rural zone between Matiguás and Muy Muy. Never the city. "What for?" you asked me. "The city bores me. And everyone's corrupt there. It's better here, even if we are poor." You've a directness in your words, not arrogance, really, but a sureness that you've thought about things and that you're right. You usually are.

Four children living—a very small family by campesino standards. "That's because my husband was half Yankee," you explained. "They're not very good breeders." Still, all of your sons have turned out fine, as you're fond of saying. Socorro's in the Army and Guadelupe's a little crazy, but not lazy or a drinker. And Arturo—well, Arturo's as much as anyone could expect. "It's because they had a good father. He always took care with the children. After your man died of a fever—"In those days there wasn't anyone to tell us what fever it was"—you raised the children alone, running a small shop and at times selling moonshine to stay afloat.

You're too old to study properly, you say, so you content yourself with learning to write your name and adopting a squadron of brigadistas. They're around your table day and night—Narciso, of whom you're inordinately proud, Nelson, Jorge, Pablo, and usually one or two others as well. They aren't exactly begging, but they certainly keep hungry eyes on your stove. You're also one of the best cooks in the valley, and the combination of skill and generosity is one the kids are quick to sniff out. And, increasingly, I'm there, too, gratefully drinking cool lemonade in the hot mornings, coffee in the rain-chilled afternoons. But more than that, I'm there listening to you, learning about the valley and its history, about the Ocampos, about the corn and the movements of the moon and about the rich and the poor. I'm there learning about the revolution.

In a memo to Estela, I mapped out the last relocations for brigadistas whose students either had finished their exams or obviously would not. None of them wanted to move from their homes, particularly those who were scheduled to transfer all the way to El Jícaro. Rolando had been telling me for weeks that he had new pupils, that a new administrator had come to the hacienda who wanted to finish the literacy course, that he had finally convinced the three girls to come back. They were stories that evaporated in the light of day.

Pablo's deception had had more success. "No, I'm nowhere near finishing," he assured me week after week. "The señora's on Lesson 10, and Don Goyo's just finishing. Then there's their son, too, and he's going real slow."

But finally my faithful spies blew the game. "Don Goyo already knows how to read," they informed me. Pablo's smile—and Don Goyo's—as they denied it, were just a shade too mischievous. I waded across the moat to watch a lesson. The señora was on Lesson 10 all right, but she was reading through it like a storybook. Pablo, apparently, had taken my advice about reviewing a little too seriously. I skipped to the end of the book—a refreshing change—and, sure enough, with only the slightest hesitation, she could read through the very last passages. So much for that. And Donato, their son? For the first time, I looked carefully at this dark, skinny kid. How old was he, anyway? An abashed smile from the señora. "Well, he'll be eight or so, soon." Eight? Pablo, brother, you know that the crusade's aimed at kids of ten or more. "Yeah, but *profe*, they wanna learn the math, and—aw, shoot!—I like it here." Sadly, he, too, had to be sent onward. "You took a vow to alphabetize Nicaragua," I reminded my reluctant émigrés, "not just your favorite friends." I waved Rolando and Pablo off on Tuesday. Two forlorn figures with bulging backpacks, trudging off to the other end of the community, now so very far away.

Turning back, I passed the study circle, hard at work in Don Ernesto's shady vestibule, serious, thoughtful, absorbed, working out the meaning of the pamphlets and questions that Chico had passed them. I hovered nearby for a few minutes, feeling like an interloper, but unable to resist watching. When had this change occurred? Jairo—quiet, attentive; Jarvin—reading his answers to the group; Carlos—firmly and justly moderating the meeting. Afraid of the disruption my presence might cause, I merely waved at those who noticed me and walked on.

I also thought with gratitude of the strange Membreño family. What manner of quirkiness made them so stingy with their workers, so ambivalent about the revolution, yet so generous with their home, which stood square in the well-trafficked center of Wapá? With all the new meetings thrust upon us, it seemed that the Membreño living room or porch was always adorned with a cluster of brigadistas. When there weren't revolutionary posters fluttering from their walls, there was a growing list of campesinos who had passed their final examination. "So now we go along with the revolution," Doña Luz had said, noncommitally.

It was time to get serious about the final exams, the definitive statistical proof of a student's literacy. These completed test forms would serve both as a control on the number of diplomas issued from the municipality and as correlation of the statistics at the national level.

Here it must be said that despite its emulation for good statistical preparation, the Muy Muy municipal commission in practice was working extremely badly. It was the extension of a general problem— the best-trained elements were in the cities, the most conscientious were in the countryside, and, in large part, those who were neither were in the small towns. Problems with the commission had gradually conditioned those of us in the surrounding areas to look elsewhere for support. Now, though, with the exams as the most obvious manifestation of the pressures of the final offensive in general, the differences between "us" and "them" were about to come to a head.

It was a simple conflict—the national and departmental offices were clamoring for their statistics, while we needed every day right up until August 15 to prepare our students. The result was mounting pressure, beginning in late July, to "produce" the test results we didn't have yet. At best, this tension merely added another strain to the difficulties of the last weeks; at worst, it almost turned the final offensive into a pitched battle between the Muy Muy statisticians and those of us in the field.

Little by little, the administration of one or two of these exams had become a part of my daily routine. These first ones were administered carefully, individually, with pride and with love. Faces confident, faces nervous, the special tension of tests everywhere. It was a luxury we weren't to enjoy for long.

On Wednesday, I stopped in to give the exam to Alfredo, one of Roberto's students. We were just finishing the last sentences of the reading when two mounted forms appeared at the door. It was Estela and Pedro, one of the assistants from the Muy Muy commission. Their faces were tight; something was up.

"How many final tests do you have?"

"Final tests?" I was bewildered. "Well, I'm finishing one here, and tomorrow or the next day I'm going over to Babilonia to collect the ones there, then over where Pablo was."

"They want all the tests tomorrow. Everyone who's in Lesson 19 or further."

Estela gave me the eye as I sputtered my protests. "I told him how it was here," she backed me up, "but he insisted on coming." From their unbending postures, I gathered it had been a stormy journey from El Jícaro.

"Send all the brigadistas to collect tests on their students," Pedro ordered. "If you pass the word now, they'll be able to get their tests to you early in the morning. Easily."

"And the order that we're to supervise each one of the tests?" I countered.

He looked slightly uncomfortable. "Uh, you can trust your kids, can't you?"

He was clearly edgy, backing slowly off on his horse. I choked down my resentment. After all, why argue with him? He was only the supplies assistant, here to deliver the message.

"I'll do my best." My best would mean at least two days of solid running, passing the word, doing tests I was doubtful about, explaining to others how to do them, finding and testing the campesinos whose brigadistas had been relocated, getting the packet of tests delivered to El Jácaro.

"And why tomorrow?"

There was no answer.

Thursday was our weekly meeting with Chico, and everyone was present but the star himself. The river was high and no one was coming in or going out. I accompanied Geraldo back to his house and found the walls still bare of syllables charts. His clever excuses failed to calm me; I was becoming positively choleric in my old age.

Ah, but then there were the first ears of corn over at Don Lucas's. Sweet, sweet taste of the sun and the rain. Of course, I raved over them, but in a tiny corner of my mind, I thought, too, of farmstands on New England Sundays. Smell of early fall afternoon. Sweet corn.

Saturday's workshop was the best one yet. As we were leaving, Doña Luz motioned me over to give me a glass of watery *pozol* and to complain about Jairo.

"That boy's nothing but a vagabond, Doña Sheyla. He moved over to the other house so he could play cards all night, that's what."

"But your classes are coming along well, now, aren't they? I watched you all on Wednesday and thought you were making really good progress."

She sniffed, scorn radiating from her stiff figure. "Huh! When we *have* classes. Too bad, I say, that it turned out this way. We were really excited about studying."

Spies from the other camp claimed that it was a smear campaign. "She's just taken a dislike to the poor kid," Doña Luisa told me. "He's working hard there now." Poor Jairo, trying so hard and receiving so little for his efforts to be a good brigadista to the Membreños. They were still smarting from the court ruling in Don Jaime's favor, and now there were new laws against moneylending as well. And grumblings were growing in the valley that the sugar they had brought in from Matagalpa was being sold at well above the legal prices.

Doña Luz just knew that we were somehow responsible for all of it. So I was glad she was mad at us. Perhaps we *had* scratched a small change upon the land. Strange family, I said again to myself for the eleventh time.

A group of Salvadoran refugees perished in the Arizona desert. There was a military coup in Bolivia. The Shah of Iran died. The Cuban revolutionary Haydee Santamaría committed suicide. And in Nicaragua, yet another brigadista—Marta Lorena Vargas—joined the list of martyrs. It was all real, somewhere out there.

For us, though, it was the corn and the *zacate*, now scratching our faces instead of our legs. And the ever-expanding list of names on the wall of Don Ernesto's. Large shaky letters, but clear and fully legible. The words wore proud grins: Luis Fermin Gonzales...Celestino López Hernández...Celso Hernández Polanco...Alva Rosa Cruz Gonzales...Justo Valle-Leiva.

The moon filling, the tenderest of white shadows touching the night. Donã Angela had gone at last to Managua to see what had become of Don Manolo. We sat on the front porch, listening to the silences: Denis and Roberto stretched full-length across the benches, drowsing,

Jorge slumped beside them, I crouched in my corner beneath the lantern, and Doña Poldi erect by the banister, looking out across the dark waves of grass.

A quiet sigh escaped from Poldi. "Yup. Next month this time, we'll be all alone."

The thought went through me like a needle. Could it really be true?

"Seems just like yesterday we were talking about the brigadistas who were supposedly coming, wondering if they'd really come here, if we could trust them."

"I can't imagine this valley without us."

"Bernarda was afraid to offer her home 'cause the rumor was that they'd make her take down the saints' pictures. Now she's not going to know what to do when Roberto goes."

"Parties, man! It's gonna be pure Carnival in Managua." Jorge made no pretense about counting the days.

"It's going to be like a funeral here," Poldi continued, refusing to hear him.

"Well, we'll be here through most of August. Then, who knows? Maybe we'll all just stay."

"Are you crazy? August 15 and it's 'Managua here I come.' No one's gonna hold me back."

I could hear Leopoldina's sigh echo my own. We fell silent again. The night, subtlest guerrilla army of all, had taken the valley. And the moon poked softly from ragged clouds, lighting this last night of July. Forty-six *alphabetizados* in Wapá.

Fifteen days to go.

BOOK SIX

AUGUST
Territorio Victorioso
and Goodbye

FLASH! Nandaime, department of Masaya, has been declared the first victorious municipal area with a total of 708 new readers, 92.7 percent of the 764 who are studying. We raise the flag of triumph over the town and salute their efforts.

MORNING BULLETIN ON THE RADIO
STATION, VOICE OF NICARAGUA,
AUGUST 2, 1980

CHAPTER 18
The Sustainment Plan

The Literacy Crusade taught us two things. One, what our own children are capable of doing and of becoming. Two, what our country is like and how gentle and how poor our people are in the countryside.

A MIDDLE-CLASS MOTHER
OF THREE LITERACY TEACHERS,
MANAGUA, AUGUST 1980*

It had long ago been announced that the literacy crusade would be followed by a plan of primary studies for adults. Obviously, the crusade was only the first of many steps toward a fully educated population. Left as a single gesture, it would rapidly have become a futile one as the newly learned skills fell into disuse and then oblivion.

The problem was that the adult study program was nowhere near ready for immediate implementation, and the date of the brigadistas' departure was rapidly approaching. Continuity had to be maintained in order not to lose the achievements and the momentum of the crusade. Immediate follow-up was crucial. A so-called Sustainment Plan, then, became the priority for August, perhaps even more important than the actual work of finishing the alphabetization.

The sustainment plan responded to two pressures. One was the need at least to maintain the new readers in contact with the printed word during the interim. The other was to include a program for those who wouldn't finish by August—a population that, unfortunately, looked as though it would be larger than had first been hoped. It was a phase that was to last from the day the brigadistas left until January, when the first materials for "Level One" of the Adult Education Program would be ready.

All through the months of the crusade, the pedagogic team in Managua had been grappling with the problem of designing the sustainment plan. Now the manual was ready. As I read it through, I began to grin. They knew what they were doing all right.

---

*Quoted in Valerie Miller, op. cit.

The introduction was written in an informal, simple Spanish for those who had just learned to read. Amid cartoons and jokes, it began:

The National Literacy Crusade put into your hands the primer, *Dawn of the People*. When you finished this book, you took one step further in your real education.

You have, then, a commitment to yourself and your neighbors. You've got to keep on studying and you've got to help your comrades who haven't yet finished the primer.

You must give them a helping hand as we did in the war. They, too, should soon finish their lessons, so that, like you, they'll be able to read, write and continue studying.

Remember that the tasks of the revolution are tasks for everyone.

In this manual, we're going to tell you about a few things that you have to do to help maintain the education in your community. You and your comrades will be inventing other things with the help of the mass organizations, the departmental and municipal offices and the Ministry of Education.

Onwards, then, *compita*, and remember that the brigadistas will be going home soon and it will have to be you—with effort and creativity—who finish the mission; you who make your own education.

Given the conditions and traditions of the countryside, bringing all the adult students into large, centralized classrooms was not feasible; neither was finding teachers, even migrant ones. And prolongation of the crusade was out of the question. So where was the solution? It lay, as have so many others in this impoverished but practical and trusting revolution, with the people themselves. The sustainment plan would work within the structures already set up and count only on the native resources. "To finish the mission ourselves," as the manual put it.

The Literacy Units—the group of students surrounding each brigadista—would remain intact, but would now be known as CEPs, or Collectives of Popular Sandinista Education. The most advanced or most willing pupil in each CEP would be trained to assume the brigadista's role, becoming "coordinator" of his or her group. From each group of ten or so coordinators, a "promoter" would be chosen to do liaison work with the commission, arrange materials, and conduct the Saturday workshops. If sufficiently skilled, the promoter could also fulfill the role of technical advisor; in places where this wasn't feasible, the town commission would have to do it. These commission offices, then, would not be dismantled at the end of the crusade, but would be converted immediately into offices of adult education, permanent centers of organization and support.

It was not only an obvious way to continue the learning process for both the coordinators and the pupils, but also a way to continue the political work that had begun with the literacy crusade. The sustainment plan, and later the adult education program, would maintain the network of organizations that reached from the humblest, most farflung shacks to the centers of the towns and cities. The Saturday workshops would be a kind of cement on community consolidation, a way to pass literature and orientations to the brightest and most active who would then, in the natural way of country people, pass their ideas on to those around them. If the main goal of the Freirian method was to convert the peasantry from passive recipients to active agents of change, the sustainment plan was the obvious culmination of this process. Those who had completed the course were now being graduated into leadership, a process having both psychological and political implications.

And all this would be carried out within the traditional structure of the countryside—the extended family and the nearest neighbors. This was the only group all campesinos had experience with—the only group that most of these newly literate could accept easily, without being handicapped by the severe self-consciousness they call *"pena."*

All that remained was to explain and to convince. This was *our* final exam. If we'd done our job well, we should be able to form the necessary nuclei and recruit the coordinators without difficulty, leaving the community in good order. If we couldn't do this, it would mean we had failed, no matter how impressive our literacy statistics looked.

So my rounds now took on a dual character. I continued the perpetual progress checks—what lesson, what exercise, what advances? Can we push harder? Can you get in more hours? Is there anything we've neglected to do for these students? Probe and prod. But I also found myself facing the campesinos again as a petitioner, much as I had during the initial census. Do you think you could? We need your help. Feeling naked again in my need for their support, I passed from shack to shack taking names.

The brigadistas themselves did the recruiting of the most enthusiastic: Don Chavelo, of course, and Jaime, Doña María Elsa's son. Julio, Don Luis Reyes's grandson, had been an instructor with the old radi and Doña Beatriz over in Babilonia had had some experience in a primary school; both were happy to take up the challenge again. Myriam, Doña Jacoba's oldest daughter, approached me of her own accord to ask about working with the Espinozas, a desire that may or may not have had to do with their handsome teenage son, but who cared about purity of motive? Daysi I recruited easily, letting Arturo off the hook for once. Then there was Pablo from Don Agapito's, Migdonio from the Quinteros, Juana Barrera... We were in business.

"And how about you, Doña Poldina? We need someone to work with Ambrosia next door and to keep reviewing with the kids." It was the first time I'd directly tried to recruit her for anything, despite her obvious capabilities. Now I held my breath. Her answer was particularly important to me.

"Well, Angela won't like giving me the time off for those Saturday meetings."

"We'll work around that, if we can. Or Moncho can come over and repeat the stuff with you."

"And if they start killing us like they've been killing the brigadistas?"

"Aw, come on. Who else can I get here? Carlos?"

A pause. "Well, okay, I'll try, Sheyla. With the kids, anyway, and with Ambrosia if he wants."

"Poldi, that's wonderful!" Another step. I went off smiling to myself.

The only area that wasn't falling into place was the back corridor where Miguel, Geraldo, Nelson and now David had been working. No one there wanted the job of coordinator, they reported, and those who wanted to keep studying weren't capable of reading the supplementary materials. It was yet another repercussion of their apathetic approach to the task. Then there was the problem of Doña Justina's giggling foursome, none of whom, I'd been assured, was going to finish. Who on earth would take over that thankless mission? I made a note to investigate the matter thoroughly and went on to other concerns.

EL DIARIO NUEVO,
August 1, 1980

Elements identified as ex-National Guard members, carrying war arms, struck another criminal blow in the afternoon hours of Wednesday, assassinating two young brigadistas and wounding another three persons, including one other brigadista and a young child.

It's known that the outlaw assassins crept into Jinotega department from Honduran territory and committed this outrage in the community of

La Pita, along the banks of the Coco River, where they shot the two brigadistas to death.
The names of the two young alphabetizers are Noel Gadea Pastora and José Antonio Chacón Morazán, both residents of the city of Jinotega. . . .

The new materials were promptly delivered for once—a bundle of magazines for the newly literate. Titled "July 19th," the magazine's simple illustrated readings accompanied by writing exercises would form the basic material for the sustainment phase. There were readings titled "Increase Production, Defend the Revolution," "War Against Malaria," "The Revolution Encourages Sports." There was a poem by Ruben Darío, photos to stimulate creative writing and miscellaneous questions to answer.

The accompanying manual explained the methodology to the new coordinators. First, the students should read the test silently, taking as much time as necessary. When they were finished, the coordinator would initiate a dialogue—a directed discussion of the photo or drawing that accompanied each text and of the topic in general. "What importance does this theme have for us?" Next, the passage would be read aloud and analyzed, paragraph by paragraph. "Of course, the most advanced readers may have to help the least advanced in this step, but, remember, always with patience, compañeros." Finally, various direct activities would be undertaken by the group. "Write about the sport you like best." "Talk with the CDS about a way of promoting sports in your community." Emphasis here was on what Freire calls "transformation"—the movement from understanding to activity. Each group was to have a bulletin board, preferably a small one for each CEP and a larger one for the Saturday workshop. These would be used to display the groups' written efforts and stimulate interest on the part of the community.

Days of running to distribute the magazine, explaining, intensifying the recruitment. Moncho agreed to work with his mother, Doña Bernarda; others were slowly persuaded through means that occasionally left the plane of revolutionary ideals: "The lamps and blackboards will be immediately reallocated to those groups where the CEPs are functioning."

Amid all this, a completely different kind of harvest v
The corn was up all over the valley, thin yellow tassels v
phantly as banners.

Atol in the morning—fresh ground corn cooked with milk and sugar to form a sweet thick pudding. *Guirilas*—tortillas of tender corn, dense and chewy. *Elotes*—the fresh ears, roasted over the fire. And *chilotes*—the tiny immature ears—in soup. Sweet tamales—wet dough wrapped back in the rebellious cornhusk and boiled. Tamales, steaming hot and sweet, drenched with slightly soured cream. Taste of new growth in our mouths.

Making tamales was a task for the dextrous: fold, pour, bend, and tie. Doña Poldi laughed as mine exploded, spattering me with the thick, yellow paste. "Don't feel bad. Bernarda can't do it either, after all these years."

Roasted, boiled, steamed, ground, fried, corn was everywhere—in all the houses, on all the fires. We were made of corn now; we *were* corn. Pale yellow particles dotted the hair of the children and glistening cobs lay in piles outside the door. Xilonem, the Mayan god of corn, reigned over the valley of Wapá. And we were all gaining a few pounds.

The "Militant Investigation" and the "*Diarios del Campo*" remained to be pried from the brigadistas. The former was to be an investigation of every aspect of the community—its location, history, production, migration, health problems, education, housing, social organization, state agencies, communications, and folklore. Like all the work of the alphabetization, the task cut two ways. On the one hand, it was meant to stimulate the brigadistas to investigate and reflect on their surroundings; on the other, it would furnish a file of detailed information on each of the countless communities in the country—information that could then be made available to any agency needing it. The work itself was based on a lengthy questionnaire in the back of the teachers' manual. Some of the questions—most common type of home construction, distribution of housing, means of communication, etc.—could be answered easily. Others, touching on the specific history and cultural traditions of the community, required research and personal interviews with the oldest settlers.

The trouble, of course, was that the brigadistas, as typical students, had left it all until the last minute. Now the commission was clamoring at us, and we in turn were clamoring at them to deliver up the reports.

"Aw, *profe*, I had it half done, but it was in my notebook and the baby spilled it out into the mud. But I did it, honest."

"Marta says that to get your diploma, you'll have to show the investigation *and* your diary," I reported, feeling awkward in my sudden complicity with the authorities after five months of laxity with the brigadistas.

The histories that emerged for our area were pure mainstream Nicaragua. Land purchases and land fights, intermarriages and family feuds, sellouts and grab-outs and rivalries among the first families of settlers. All on a minor scale, though. Wapá was small pickings, left for the only slightly ruthless. The land simply didn't have the value of the coffee or cotton areas, lands where the Somocistas had clustered like army ants.

The ancient history held the most promise, though no one knew much about it. The falls at El Esquirín had a certain local fame, with their curious rock formations visible in the dry season and the accompanying legends of phantoms. Nearby was a large rock, curiously carved with primitive designs that the locals went over with chalk every so often to make them more visible. Like the pottery fragments that many kept in their homes, they were a source of pride and curiosity. "Yup, those Indians were a funny people; they knew a few tricks we don't."

We referred our discoveries and what pottery we could collect on to Muy Muy where a young woman was now working full time in the field of documentation. Someday the artifacts, legends, poetry, histories, songs, and handicrafts being discovered all over Nicaragua would become part of a new national museum, along with the documentation of the crusade itself. For now, there was time only to collect the data, taking maximum advantage of the brigadistas' presence. Processing and ordering it all would take years. Someday, perhaps, the origin of the artifacts in El Esquirín would be discovered. For now, they could only be reported and filed away.

The collection of the diaries was next on the list. The diaries were supposed to have been read and discussed at every Saturday workshop, and a weekly resume written up by each squadron. In actual fact, we had neglected this task. Week after week, everyone "forgot" his notebook, or only one or two remembered, or the diaries were the last item on an overlong agenda. In the end, I had just let it go. After all, I had *my* journal, and I wasn't about to read it to the group.

But now here was Lorena from the commission at our Saturday workshop to inform the brigadistas that she would be collecting their diaries during the next week. There was a stir. Jorge raised his hand.

"Uh, Lorena?"

"Yes, Jorge?"

That sweet, sincere voice: "The thing is, my diary's kind of personal. If I give it to the commission, it'll just get lost, I know it will. So, if you don't mind, I think I'll just keep it."

Light was dawning in everyone's eyes. "Yeah, my diary's *mine*. I'm not giving it away. They're my own personal thoughts, not for anyone else." "Yeah, Lorena, they're our only real souvenir of the crusade."

Lorena was wrinkling her brow in warmhearted sympathy, and I was staring hard at my muddy boots, trying to keep a straight face. I *knew* that no one had written a page since April.

"But you really have the diaries?" Lorena pushed.

Righteous indignation on all sides. "Of course we have them. They're just private, know what I mean?"

"Oh." A pause. "Well, how about if you just write out a summary of what you've got, like one or two pages for each month with a short account of what happened in your classes and everything. Really, I understand your problem, but we're supposed to collect these diaries for the museum. How does that sound?"

"That seems fine to me." Nodding of heads, countenances of sober mien.

It wasn't until the walk home that I let the giggles out. Not for nothing had they been practicing sociodramas.

On Sunday eight persons came to my first coordinators' workshop, with five more hovering on the fringes. And they were all women! It was the first active participation I'd seen by the female population here, with the exception of Doña María Elsa. We went over the ten teaching steps, the basic methodology of the crusade, and they were fascinated by it. They were now seeing the forest instead of being one of the trees.

Again I was swept by that feeling that always came when I realized that this was being mirrored all over the country. Little by little, just like the corn, the kernels of the new Nicaragua were being planted in tiny plots until now, suddenly, there were *chilotes* everywhere, maturing in the revolutionary sun from Puerto Cabezas to Corinto.

But the battle for *alfabetizados* in Wapá was by no means over. The offensive was still in high gear. Despite expanded hours and intense motivation, victory remained uncertain. It simply wasn't a mechanical issue, solvable by increased hours. It was a matter of many separate lights of understanding—would they dawn or wouldn't they?

Then there was the struggle with the personnel of the town commission, which had become a personal issue. Muy Muy seemed obsessed with collecting a large number of final tests—presumably with the goal of gaining departmental emulations. The reality that we in the field were living had apparently long since ceased to matter to them. On our side, their incessant clamoring for data had ceased to move us very much either.

Sunday evening I decided to bathe from the bucket, too tired to face the river in the rain. Just as I was finishing, I heard a stir from the front of the house, and peeked around to find Estela and Migdonio, water coursing from their ponchos onto the legs of their horses.

"Muy Muy just sent the message that they want all the tests tomorrow for everyone who's in Lesson 15 or past." Estela had a look that said I don't like the message any more than you do, and I don't like riding over here in the rain either, so spare me your grief.

"But I just passed them my schedule," I sputtered, feeling my temperature rising. "We'll be finishing on the fourteenth. And the students in Lesson 15 can't *pass* the test. You know they can't."

"Humberto says to turn all the tests in now."

My patience-duct burst again, splattering the yard with bile. "I won't falsify the test, if that's what they want," I announced brusquely, "and I'm not going to kill myself for the greater glory of Muy Muy either. I don't work for them. I'm working for the revolution, the crusade, and the community...and Humberto and his commission can just go to hell. The exams will be done when we're ready," I concluded on a histrionic note.

Alas, everyone looked more amused than impressed. I delivered over the three tests I had, unbent long enough to promise a collection mission in the morning, and retired to the kitchen. Doña

Poldi served me a grin with supper. I decided she liked seeing me explode as much as the kids did.

There was a new battle plan passed down from Matagalpa: organization by groups. The newly alphabetized formed Group I; they were over the hump and required no more work for now. Group II were those currently studying in Lessons 16 to 23; they would take the test immediately. Group III, those who were in Lessons 13 to 15, would be tested on August 8. Group IV, those currently in Lessons 10 to 13, would have theirs on the fifteenth. And Group V, those who hadn't yet made it to Lesson 10, weren't going to make it. Counting our candidates, we had sixty-nine possible diplomas in my sector of Wapá. I'd long since lost contact with El Jícaro, and now I was losing count of the hillside groups since Estela had taken charge of them, too. But I couldn't worry about that now. My only concern was how those who were in Lesson 11 on August 5 were going to make it to Lesson 17 on August 15.

Amid this chaos, our local gothic serial took a new turn. Doña Angela reappeared after a pilgrimage to Managua. "He's disappeared!" Gasps from the audience. "Shhh, don't let Carlos hear. I told him that I'd seen his father and that he was better. He gets so upset. But I went to the house and Manolo's brother wasn't there anymore, nor the woman, nor Manolo. 'And where are they?' I ask a second cousin, or niece or something. 'They moved,' she tells me, 'but I don't know where.' 'Well, I find that very strange,' I say, 'that you don't know where your own family moved to.' So then I told her that I was going to talk to a lawyer in Matagalpa and that I'd be back on Monday."

Doña Luisa nodded her head sagely when I related the news. "I told that sister of mine not to get mixed up with those people." Personally, I was far more enthralled than preoccupied. It gave me a good opener on my daily rounds. Had he been lost? Stolen away by the evil Don Alfredo? Murdered and secretly buried in Managua? I'll let you know Monday, I assured my audience. Now, meanwhile, let's talk about your future CEP.

Eyeglasses had finally arrived, after months of promises; at least they'd be there for the sustainment phase. No such thing as oculists, of course. "We let them try on several pairs, and they can keep the one that feels best."

Last general meetings, last statistics. Muy Muy inexplicably dispatched us Chino, the statistics nut, and Gustavo, the supervisor from El Bálsamo, to collect our final tests. "What do they think we've done?" I inquired acidly of no one in particular. "Buried them somewhere?"

From Gustavo I confirmed the rumor that they'd finished in his community—a week early and with 95 percent of the community literate. "You really alphabetized everyone? And they can really read?"

"Yup," he nodded, not missing the insinuation. "They can all really read."

"Well, how did you do it? Your kids had the reputation of being even more delinquent than ours."

Gustavo grinned. "Yeah, they were a bit degenerate. But when they put their minds to it, they really moved."

Later that night, as we watched Chino inflate a huge air mattress for himself that had been sent as part of the international aid, he whispered, "Hear the latest slogan?"

Catching the conspiratorial tone, I leaned closer. " 'Who's the bourgeoisie of the alphabetization?' 'The commission!' "

I tried not to laugh too loud.

I bowed to defeat in the back corridor. There would be no follow-up there, unless one day the people woke up to what they were missing. Whose fault was it? Three households barely literate, one still semiliterate, one well literate but unstable, and one literate and indifferent. No volunteer coordinator. Nothing more to be done but turn my attention to the other areas of Wapá where the organization was surging ahead.

Then suddenly Chico was gone, sent to zones of even greater difficulty. Johnny, his replacement, wasn't a bad talker, but he lacked that special air of the hero. It was true, though, that the important work had been done here. We would make it on our own now. Still, we'd all miss him a lot, I realized.

Squadron reports were compiled by the group leaders, a laudable effort somewhat complicated by Miguel's bad report on Elvis, due to the fact—I learned belatedly—that he, Elvis, punched him, Miguel, in the face during an argument over I-preferred-to-know-not-what.

On Wednesday another surprise awaited me at the old ranch. Don Manolo was back, thin as a rail and drugged to the teeth. It seemed that he'd broken out of house arrest and taken off on his own for "the mountain," some part of the countryside where he had family. The niece in Managua had been afraid to tell Doña Angela that they weren't really sure of his whereabouts. Now found, or partially so, he wandered the house in bewilderment, with that terrible look of mental patients everywhere scratched on his grizzled old face.

One week and a day—what was I going to do out there in the world?

It had become a major refrain, one that began as soon as I lay down on my *tijera*. "You're going, you're going, you're going." It seemed impossible to leave all these people, to disappear back into the city, mission accomplished. We weren't ready to go—*I* wasn't ready to go.

One more week. I tried to picture the city. Movies, restaurants, electricity. No more green-forested hills, no more muddy paths. Eyes everywhere, streetlights, and... *how could we just leave?*

CHAPTER 19
And Goodbye

Lamps and blackboards had to be counted and readied for collection. One of each per brigadista—or no diploma.

"Collective Texts" was the theme of the last workshop for the campesino coordinators who would be carrying on the sustainment phase. It was one of the main activities for reinforcing new writing skills and an excellent pedagogical device at any level.

"Instead of my explaining it, let's try it." Eyes of these young women shy but eager, their faces sweet in first bloom. Paula's proud red hair was carefully tied back from her face; Alva Rosa sat carefully in her immaculate white pleated skirt; Doña Beatriz, some twenty years older, still had the sweetness remarkably intact in her dark face.

"First we're going to choose a theme. Then I'm going to ask each of you to write a sentence on that theme. Okay?"

Giggles. Don Chavelo, not the least unnerved at being the only man present, nodded assent. "You tell us the theme."

"No, you tell me. What would be a good topic for today?"

Silence. Then Doña Beatriz: "The brigadistas' leaving." That got a general nod of approval.

"Okay, now let's get started. Everyone write one sentence in your notebook about the brigadistas' leaving, or maybe about the party we're going to have for them today." More giggles. Those immaculate dresses weren't just for this workshop. Already, at ten in the morning, there was a festive air around Don Ernesto's. Sweeping and cleaning were beginning, and there was a general gathering of food and women in the kitchen. The men, temporarily left out of the action, clustered on the other end of the benches, eyeing us curiously. Despite the embarrassing surfeit of attention, the group was going to try.

The writing of a sentence. Brows wrinkled and lips formed words. So many syllables. Even in Spanish, with its consistent phonetics, it's no easy job to order all the parts of all the words, record them correctly, divide the words up where they should be divided, remembering about capital and small letters and always keeping in mind what it was that you wanted to say in the first place. The advanced were finished within ten minutes or so. Miriam, Paula, and Gladys were still struggling.

"Now, each one's going to write her sentence on the blackboard here, and together we're going to correct the errors."

Daysi's was the most elegant: "Next Sunday, the brigadistas are going to be leaving, so today we're having a party to thank them." Doña Beatriz: "The brigadistas are finishing their work in our community." Miriam: "We want to say 'thank you' to our brigadistas." Paula, after a half hour of struggle, had managed: "toda therl be a parti." One by one the phrases went up on the board. Our participants were overwhelmed by the circle of people now surrounding them. Faces scarlet, lips moved as the new readers proudly tried out their skills on this fresh test.

"Now let's make some corrections. What needs to be fixed in the first sentence?"

"Uh, isn't that Sabado, S-a?" said Daysi, catching her own error. She'd been as far as third grade. But I was amazed at the response from everyone. They were so exemplary it almost hurt.

But soon the participation began to diminish. There were just too many people staring. And the smells issuing from the kitchen were growing irresistible. "If this were a real situation," I explained, "we'd finish the corrections and then arrange the sentences in the best possible order, combining any that are the same. Then we'd copy out the whole text and hang it on our bulletin board. For today, let's just leave it. You've done fine." We stood up and stretched, proud of ourselves. And now it was party time again.

Don Alfredo had told me about the fiesta some time back. "We want to do it for you all. Don't worry about anything—it's a present." But in the confusion of the last week, I'd paid little attention to it. Vaguely, as I made my rounds, I'd been aware of collections being taken up—food, money, utensils. However, I'd in no way realized the extent of the celebration. Now, poking my head into the kitchen, there seemed no end to the bubbling pots. Pieces of the kitchen fire had been reproduced in various spots on the dirt floor, creating three or four annexes to the regular stove. There were dressed chickens everywhere. Rice was cooking, pineapples and potatoes were piled to one side, yuca salad was steeping in vinegar, raw rice was being milled for drinks (with Jairo loyally manning the grinder), hands were slapping tortillas into shape. It was the biggest gathering I had seen of Wapá's female population—a forest of skirts, all bent over separate pots in Don Ernesto's cavernous kitchen.

And there was *chicha** at Don Toribio's, they told me. Judging by the pink cheeks of the Murillos and the ebullience of the rest, they weren't being stingy with it either. The music was starting, and the party was already merry. It was a busy Sunday in little Wapá. They'd come from El Jícaro with Estela, and from as far off as Azancor Arriba. At last, amid cheers and giggles, I got my round on the dance floor with old Don Toribio. According to him, he had fought with Sandino in the 1920s. So now the old veteran had made his peace with the Yankees—or at least with one of them.

I wasn't paying much attention when the fight started. "Come out quick," one of María Elsa's brood tugged at me. "They're fighting!"

The crowd was already streaming toward the outside porch, which offered a sheltered view of the spectacle. No, it wasn't brigadistas, as I had feared at first, but one of the Rojas sons with another from the state hacienda. Both on horseback, they circled each other menacingly while their women wept and various community members attempted to pull them apart. "Don't worry," old Don Alfredo whispered to me, "as soon as I saw things getting ugly, I took Daniel's machete out of the case and hid it. The other boy doesn't have anything."

Despite the screams, the only real danger was that one of the spectators might be wounded by flying hooves. Or that Juan Ocampo and Roberto, in their persistent and inebriated efforts to make peace, might be crushed between the two combatants. Circle and retreat and circle back again, until at last the sky cooperated: a heavy cloudburst brought the fight and the fiesta to a quick, neat end.

"Things used to be different before," Doña Poldina told me on the way home. "Now they just threaten and maybe hit each other. Before—pap-pap!—they'd pull out pistols and one or both would end up dead. And they never think once about the women and children they leave behind. Just after the war the *compas* came through and made everyone turn over their arms. That's the best thing this revolution's done. I don't care how much some of the men complain about it."

---

*Nicaraguan home-brew, made from fermented corn.

The next day it was back to tying up the loose ends, final tests on the stragglers. The brigadistas who had been off sick or who had had family problems at one time or another were now paying for the time they'd lost—three or four hours of classes, Saturdays and Sundays. The students who stuck with them in this marathon would make it. Don Chavelo's house became the first *"Casa Libre de Analfabetismo"*— house free of illiteracy—and was festooned with a special banner to commemorate the fact. Marta from the Commission lent me her camera to take a picture of the graduating family: the shyly smiling señora with her new baby, Don Chavelo with his pack of thin children all proudly clutching their primers. The nine-year-old had learned, too, in defiance of the age limit that no one enforced anyway. There were eight in all, all reading, and now, all smiling. Click!

"Juan Gato"—Juan-the-cat—bright-eyed son of Juan Espinoza and Petrona, and heartthrob of more than one local *muchacha*, had run off to join the Popular Sandinista Army. Poor Doña Petrona cried so long and so bitterly that Ismael couldn't take it and moved over to our house to spend the last week. "I told him that the army wouldn't take him if he didn't have his diploma from the crusade," a disappointed Ismael moaned, "but he wouldn't listen."

Now my work was almost exclusively with the CEPs, watching the future coordinators give their first classes. They were shy and blushing, but their first attempts were no worse than I'd seen from the brigadistas themselves. Brothers and sisters looked on in awe while the now paternalistic brigadistas grinned as proudly as if they had personally invented the entire plan. I discovered accidentally that Doña Beatriz had been working all this time with Pedro, the only one of her sons who hadn't finished the primer when Rolando left. Rolando had reported him hopelessly stuck in Lesson 6. Now Pedro had reached Lesson 12, the real comprehension stage for him. I was amazed at her success and told her so, while she blushed with pleasure. "I tried to do the best I could with him." After ten children, she still looked like a young girl when she smiled. "You're the proof," I told her. "You tell the others that they can do it too."

And as suddenly as it had begun, there was now nothing left for me to do; the last exams were being slowly collected. The urgency was over; the commission had finished whatever it was they were rushing to do. "Just get the names in in time for us to fill out the diplomas," were the new instructions. We made little banners to hang on the houses, *"Casa Libre de Analfabetismo"* where all had learned to read, or *"Casa Alfabetizada"* where the majority had. And the students, along with finishing the tests and the primers, were being asked to write letters to the national government thanking them for the crusade.

This latter idea was borrowed from the Cuban literacy crusade, at the end of which the newly literate wrote thank-you letters to Fidel. In Nicaragua, where the policy of all the top leaders was one of extremely low profile, the assignment was more difficult. Who to address the letter to—Sandino? Some opted for Tomás Borge, the most recognizable figure and the most eloquent. Others addressed their letters to Father Fernando Cardenal, the director of the National Literacy Crusade. Still others just thanked God and their brigadistas. All, though, were small works of art, the crude rounded letters as eloquent as the calloused hands that shaped them. "Nowe that I can rede and rite, I wan to thank therevolution."

Nothing to do but pay my last visits and silently watch the last lessons in progress.

Lesson 23

The Sandinista Revolution extends fraternal ties to all peoples.

Fra ternal

Fra Fre Fri Fro Fru

fra fre fri fro fru

Actually the photograph for this lesson was now a rather embarrassing one, consisting as it did of Alfonso Robelo and Violeta Chamorro applauding the primier of Vietnam. "You have to be honest when you do the dialogue with this," Chico had explained. "Be very clear about why they're in the photograph—who they were and who they are now and why things have changed. And answer all the compañeros' questions."

Let's read and write:

fraternidad   frente   frijoles   frontera   fruto

The Sandinista National Liberation Front frustrated all the enemy's plans. The Nicaraguan conflict had world-wide repercussions.

Let's write with our best letters:

LET US LIVE IN BROTHERHOOD

I crossed paths with Estela on my final visit to the houses on the hillside. There at Doña María Elsa's generously laden table we compared notes. Thirty-odd new readers from this area and almost as many in El Jícaro; with the 60 or so from Wapá, we had topped 120— *Territorio Victorioso*. And there, speaking of victory, third to the last on Estela's list was Don Agapito's name. He'd done it, that crusty old codger! As if he'd heard, in walked Luis, Don Agapito's brigadista, felt hat tipped rakishly over his eye. Marvin limped in his wake, the result of a fall off a horse several weeks earlier. "Yup, he goes at it slow, but he can read all right," reported Luis. My thoughts traveled backward, to a baked shack on the hillside and the gruff assertion that brooked no denials: "It's fine for the kids, but I'm just too old."

Estela also filled me in on the plans for the demobilization. There would be a community assembly at Don Ernesto's on Sunday to give out diplomas and say our final goodbyes. Then we were to march out to El Jícaro where there would be another ceremony, followed by a fiesta. We would all be spending Sunday night there, because early the next morning we were expected in Muy Muy for the closing act and the raising of the flag over the town. The resplendent new flag of the alphabetization—yellow circle of sun against the matched triangles of red and black. Then there would be yet another fiesta and parade in Muy Muy, and Tuesday the nineteenth on to Matagalpa to repeat the same process with all the department's 1800 brigadistas. And at last, on Wednesday morning, the brigadistas would be bused triumphantly into Managua.

The return of the brigadistas to their homes would be choreographed even more carefully than their departure, and with more precautions. None of us knew at this point just how many brigadistas had been killed, but the number seemed more than sufficient. Caution was the word. The original plans had called for the simultaneous arrival of all the brigadistas—a recreation of the victory celebration of July 1979. Logistics, however, had made this impossible. Instead, the alphabetization fronts would be returned to Managua one by one, and the final concentration in the plaza would be a commemoration, not an arrival.

"We've got to wait for Sunday now?" was Jorge's response. "I thought I'd be home by the fifteenth." He quickly cheered up, though. "Wow! Party in El Jícarco, party in Muy Muy, party in Matagalpa, then there'll be a party in my neighborhood, party at school, party at home, party in the plaza. It's going to be one hell of a carnival, man!" He'd been ebullient these last few days, like most of the brigadistas—proud of himself and looking forward to the end. They would be coming home heroes, every one. Home to applause and admiration, cheers and celebrations. Home victorious. "Boy, those kids who deserted must feel like dirt now. I'm sure glad I stuck it out. God, I felt *awful* those first few days."

The brigadistas' excited anticipation was in direct contrast to the mood of the campesinos, so much so that at times I wished I could hush the kids up. For those who were staying behind, it would be more wake than party. The loss of a now-loved brother, son, teacher. An end to the laughter and richness that these strange city kids had brought into their lives. Over and over I heard the echoes:

"I'm sure going to miss Narciso. He never forgets to bring me back fruit when he goes out."

"I don't know what I'm going to do without Roberto. Truth is, he's been better to me than my own sons have."

"Yup, when Matías goes, we're going to be all alone."

And to me, "It's going to be strange not seeing you go by every day. We've gotten used to seeing you—walking, always walking."

The campesinos had done more than learn that they could learn. They had also learned that urban secondary students—a category held almost in awe—were paragons neither of virtue nor of knowledge. Like the first Indians to kill a horse, they had learned that the other side wasn't nearly as strong—or they as weak—as they had thought.

The students had learned something as well. For them, it had been a move from intellectual to physical and emotional commitment. Fighting for an abstract idea wasn't the same as fighting for a lived conviction. Here the problems were not abstract; here there was nowhere to go but forward. And the campensinos were now no more an abstraction than their conditions; they were loving family.

I, too, was feeling more sorrow than jubilation. Yes, we'd won, more or less, and, yes, I'd be going back to that incredible far-off world where there was solid ground, even when it rained, but what would I do? I'd miss the utter frenzy of it all, the songs and jokes, the wide eyes of these brigadistas, the soft manners of the people I'd come to love. How could I leave this valley behind me?

The worries still chattered inside me as I watched the thin moon. Why had we barely alphabetized 75 percent? Could we have done more? Had we laid a strong enough base of organization? Would the community slide back? When would the revolution catch hold here?

How? At whose expense? Would Denis be saved the misery that Doña Poldina had had to face? Had we helped enough? Had we understood enough?

Saturday the puppy cried and the cats fought and it rained and rained while I lay in the folds of my *tijera*, not believing I could really leave. Time to organize, time to get my things together. I couldn't seem to keep my mind on it.

Came the morning, the final morning, and I still couldn't get a grip on it. Goodbye visits combined confusingly. Suddenly it was well past one—time to be heading home to get ready to go. But as I passed Doña Beatriz's hut, she appeared in the doorway. "Look at that black cloud coming! You'd better come in and wait for the rain to pass."

"I can't. I'm in a hurry."

"Well, could you just take a quick look at this wound my boy's got on his foot? I think it's infected."

Indeed, it was seriously infected. And in the time it took me to examine it, a cloudburst to end all cloudbursts swept the valley. It threw me into a state of complete confusion and worry. How would Estela and the people from Muy Muy get across the creek with the diplomas? How would we get across to El Jícaro? Would we be going today or not?

After almost an hour, the rain stopped. I rushed full speed back to the house, realizing vaguely that it was now some hours past the time I was supposed to be at Don Ernesto's with my things. Jorge and Ismael were still at home, waiting for me. "Are we going, Sheyla?"

"I don't know." It was like one of those dreams where you are caught by terrible paralysis in the face of something that needs to be done. "Well, I guess we ought to go see what's happening."

"Just a minute, Sheyla, I've got to get Rolando's shirt on him," said Doña Poldina.

I turned with heavy heart to say goodbye to everyone, but there was only Don Manolo. Everyone else was going with us. And for the last time, we were Sandino's own army crossing the prairie.

DIARIO DEL CAMPO

Sunday, August 17

They're all there! As we splash up to Don Ernesto's, soaked with rain and mud, I can see the milling forms of what look like hundreds. The whole community's come, and all the brigadistas and Estela and Soila, one of the few dedicated workers from the commission, and Don Alfredo leading a packtrain of horses. And it's *over*. They've given out all the diplomas and everything and they were only waiting for us. Through a buzz of dazed exhaustion, I hear Soila's voice. "And now, we want to present someone who's worked very hard for all of you, and who encountered a delay which prevented her from coming earlier, but who'd surely like to say some words of farewell."

I'm looking at the blur of faces: Don Luis, Migdonio from my first home in El Jícarco, Doña Bernarda's sad blue eyes, Don Toribio, Don Agapito, Daysi, Arturo, Paula's red hair, the twenty eyes of Don Chavelo's brood, all my brigadistas with their little brothers and sisters clinging to them, and more than one pair of eyes suspiciously red.

I open my mouth to say something and my voice cracks. All I can do is mutter, "Oh, hell, I hate to cry in public!" and turn my face to the wall.

I collect myself in time to say something at last, and then everyone's yelling, "Come on, come on, it's late," and my pack's ripped from my back and loaded on a horse, and Soila with her kind voice leans over, "Sheyla, we really have to go now."

Handshakes, kisses, clenched hugs, eyes glistening bright with tears. How can I tell you what I feel? What I want for you? What I'm remembering as I look at you? Your hands—calloused hands of the men and women, squat hands of the children already toughening. Those hands wrapped painstakingly around pencils. Your fragile letters on twilight newsprint, and the red light shining holy on your dark beautiful faces.

"Sheyla, come *on*!"

"Doña Poldi!" I've found her in the crowd and we're both blubbering like a pair of idiots. "I'll be back, you hear?"

But the first brigadistas are already out of sight, and the procession of horses is moving off beyond the corral where the low vegetation of the pastureland blends into the forest, where the land drops down to the creek, where I first saw Don Manolo, where I first crossed into the valley. I'm running, as well as anyone can in clayey mud with wet rubber boots. The path, or what's left of it, doubles over the hill. The house fades back into the vegetation, and we're gone. *Territorio Victorioso, adiós.*

There was a wet scramble to El Jícaro and a last night in the ancient leather bed at Doña Chenta's. More goodbyes and more songs and speeches and parties and congratulations. The flag went up on the tower of Muy Muy. They roasted a cow for us, and we moved on to Matagalpa. Suddenly we were parading through the streets, each municipality winding into town from a separate entrance. Little by little we began to converge. We became a hundred, two hundred, a thousand, tens of thousands. We packed the main streets; we filled the stadium to bursting; we were an army of gray *cotonas*, worn sombreros, and muddy pants. Chickens—the last, the most precious gifts of our campesino families—hung from our belts. In Matagalpa, Tomás Borge spoke. Fernando Cardenal spoke. The band played and we cheered and screamed and danced and WE DID IT! All over the department, all over the country. We're a force, we're the EPA, and we did it! We taught 400,000 people to read. We've reduced the illiteracy rate to under 13 percent and there'll be no stopping us now! There'll be no stopping this revolution!

A wet street dance and the last night I slipped into an exhausted sleep on the floor of the school we were staying in, while hordes of brigadistas marched through my dreams, beating the drums they'd made and chanting: *"Ya nos vamos!"*—Now we're going! Then it was morning and we were loaded into the shiny new buses that had arrived in the country while we were looking elsewhere.

"Aren't you coming to Managua?"

"Sunday, Narciso, not today."

Clutching their cheese, parakeets, chickens, tortillas, knapsacks. Clutching their dreams and their memories of the home in front of them and the home behind them. I kissed each and every one of them—Matías last—and turned abruptly off up the city streets of Matagalpa so as not to cry again.

Comandante Carlos, we've finished the mission. We also taught them to read.

*"The panel of judges
designated by the Director General of UNESCO
to grant the 1980 prizes
for distinguished and effective contribution on behalf of
literacy...
has unanimously chosen for first prize—
the National Literacy Crusade of Nicaragua."*

UNESCO, PARIS, FRANCE,

SEPTEMBER 1980

REFLECTIONS, JANUARY 1983

The story, of course, didn't end there. Three years have now passed since the Popular Literacy Army first set out to do battle with ignorance. The story of these three years would make another book in itself—and that one with no end either.

The revolutionary process, so new and untried in that first year, is now more firmly established. Without losing its dynamic creativity, it has broadened and deepened its structures all over the country. The mass organizations—the Sandinista Youth, the neighborhood Defense Committees, the teachers' and workers' unions, the small producers' association and the farmworkers' union, the women's organization—are spread all over now, as are the FSLN party structures themselves, grouping the best elements into the grassroots power structures. Each of these organizations develops programs and makes decisions on a local level and also elects representatives to the national Council of State, which makes and ratifies the laws of the country. Some of the delegates now serving learned to read only during the crusade.

The health system is being restructured, with regional hospitals and village clinics combining forces to offer at least minimal care for all Nicaraguans. The emphasis is on preventive education, using a very similar system of brigadistas in short-term crusades, all through an outreach push of the Health Ministry. By now, almost every community has a minimally trained health brigadista, selected from the communities themselves. There have been massive vaccination and hygiene campaigns conducted through the network of neighborhood defense committees. The incidence of tetanus, measles, and malaria has been cut drastically, and in 1982, as a result of these efforts, there was no reported case of polio in the entire country. The latest project, scheduled for April of this year, is an antirabies vaccination campaign. "Even our dogs are Sandinistas," explained one proud member of a CDS.

More basic still has been the agricultural reform, initiated in earnest in 1981. While most of the land remains in private hands, and most

of the Somocista properties are run as large state farms, the re.
is based on peasant cooperatives working on basic grain production.
The goal, in this fundamentally agricultural country, is to end imports
of basic foodstuffs. Those who are interested—including those who
own less than fifty acres as well as the totally landless—can organize
into groups of eight or more families, and have assistance from the
technical team of the Ministry of Agrarian Reform. After a year or
more of experience working together and the consolidation of the
cooperative structure, they are offered titles to cooperative plots—
near their community when there is state land available, farther away
when there isn't. By now, 60,000 people have received titles to land
under the cooperative program. Of the 2.6 million acres of public
lands, 740,000 have been earmarked for redistribution to cooperatives
by July of this year. Little by little, this is changing the political geography of the country.

Matagalpa, like Managua, like most of the cities, gleams with new
construction, housing, schools, hospitals, and highway projects. While
none is terribly impressive to visitors from developed countries, all
are startling changes in the context of Nicaragua and what had been
before. These social projects are even more impressive in light of
Nicaragua's continuing economic crisis.

Society, in short, is gradually being reshaped, with all the pain,
errors, dislocations, misunderstandings, confusion, and outright opposition that the process of radicalization, even slow radicalization,
brings. But that, as I say, is another story.

The literacy crusade never really ended. One day after the mass victory celebration in Managua, the offices of the small town and city
commissions were once again open, with reduced but dedicated staff,
determined not to allow the spirit of the crusade to falter. At the same
time, offices were being opened for the planning of the new literacy
crusade in other languages—English, Miskito, and Sumo, the written
languages of the Atlantic Coast region.

The CEPs have been consolidated, under the format that was explained to us at the end of the crusade. The "popular teachers," many
of them alphabetized in the original literacy crusade, give classes to
their neighbors for two hours daily, supervised by promoters from
the same community who pass on the necessary material and collect
data, much as I did. The promoters in turn receive help and guidance
from the technicians in the town commissions, a chain that goes on

v and elegant primer for those still learning to read,
teachers' guide, appropriately titled *El Machete*, after
th͟e of peasants throughout Latin America. Furthermore,
the curr͟i͟c͟u͟l͟u͟m has been building year by year until it now covers
from first to fourth-grade level, roughly a primary school education.
Experts have said that without that level of attainment, it is easy to
forget everything. Each level has a math and a language book for the
student and a manual for the teacher. Coordinators receive a subsidy
of approximately $20 a month and promoters $50—not much, but a
recognition and a stimulus to continue. And in 1983, for the first time,
a formal program of training was begun for these semivolunteer teachers so that one day they can take their place in the tiny country
schoolhouses that have been popping up like mushrooms all over the
country.

The days of silent, humble peasants are passing fast, as are those
of the isolated shack full of fear and misery, and the pot-bellied children who run and hide at the sight of a stranger. Cultural patterns
cannot be eliminated in three years, and severe economic limitations
still exist. However, one can pass through any part of the remote
countryside and find the seeds of change—campesinos open, alert,
curious, eager to talk, and to read whatever printed material the visitor
may have brought. The most involved among them have increasingly
formed part of the education, health, and union structures, as well
as the people's militia. They are determined that no force—either
ideological or armed—will take from them what they've won in these
three years.

Isolated little Wapá and El Jícaro, of course, have been a part of all
this. Just after the crusade ended, there was a rash of migrations—a
natural reaction to the stagnation of land relations in the valley. Don
Chavelo Cruz moved with his family to the state farm on the other
side of our territory. His children are beginning to look rosy, and
baby Elvis, now three, is fat and healthy. Don Alfredo Castro, María
Elsa's husband, moved the whole brood to the city, but she didn't
like it much, so he bought property near Río Blanco, far beyond
Matiguás, and they all, together with Daysi and Arturo, went off to
work it. Arturo and Don Goyo sued Don Manolo for all the vacations
and Sundays they were never paid for, as well as for his refusal to

rent the ox-cart so that they could all get the harvest in. They ended up with $150 apiece and, presumably, a sense of vindication. Don Goyo, the owner of the log canoe, has gone to Río Blanco as well, to work on a new road there. Migdonio, the son of the family where I first stayed, left for parts unknown, and any number of the more active young girls—Miriam, Nelis, Paula—left for domestic jobs in the city.

The undernourished baby of Doña Santa is dead, as is the swollen-bellied two-year-old in the house where I was shyly given the green peppers. And Nubia had a girl.

The Ocampos are still there. Juan Ocampo fell from a tree and fractured his ribs, and with María pregnant again, who knows how they'll get by. Don Manolo more or less recovered his balance, during which process he and Doña Angela suffered a final breakup. In a messy legal battle that lasted well over two years, she and Carlos received the farm, and he the animals. Doña Leopoldina resigned as cook, washerwoman, and cheese-maker and built her own shack over by her sister, Doña Luisa, where Denis, now sixteen, ekes out a precarious living for them. He's in the volunteer militia now, as is Juan Ocampo, his uncle, and as are Moncho and Alberto, Doña Bernarda's sons, Don Chavelo, and several of the Quinteros over in El Jícaro. This group had also organized the base of a cooperative, working the year before on land Doña Angela lent them and waiting to make a decision on land offered them by the government in an isolated area substantially further west.

Alva Rosa, Don Chavelo's daughter, is not only a health brigadista, but also a CEP coordinator. Last year she taught two campesinos to read, and this year she's matriculated more. Carlos, Doña Angela's slightly simple son, gave classes as well, as did Doña Beatriz in Babilonia, Don Luis Reyes's son Julio and Don Roberto Cruz. Not only that, there were two Cuban teachers, one in El Jícaro and one in Wapá. A total of seventy graduated from the first grade last year in the valley. And finally, finally, the legendary school in Wapá now lacks only a roof.

Of the brigadistas I know less. I've seen many of them in their homes in Managua, now plump again and back in school or graduated. I visited Matías once, in his home in the city, and was shocked. Ramshackle boarded hut, alone in its small bare clearing, a sister's naked children with their small swollen bellies. It is hard to remember that the realities of urban poverty are as crushing as those of the *campo*. Matías wasn't there. He had a job chopping weeds, and it was Saturday—payday. I was sorry to have missed him. I wanted to find a way to tell him that even though he was not outstandingly brilliant or musical or outgoing, and that even though he comes from a culture where even now his darker complexion is considered *feo*—ugly—I wanted to find the words to tell him how beautiful he was.

Most of the brigadistas have been back to visit their campesino families at least once, but the many tasks the revolution has demanded of its youth—picking coffee, organizing health campaigns, studying, working, and, now, defending the country—has left precious little time for the long trip into the country. All are alive. Most have remained active, incorporating the insights of the literacy crusade into their maturing perspective.

And I'm still here, too. Now a technical assistant in the mountains north of Muy Muy, I am still struggling with my Nicaraguan compañeros to bring the 40 percent illiteracy rate left in the department of Matagalpa down to the level of the rest of the country. My brigadistas and co-workers are no longer anxious students from the city but mostly young campesinos from the zone. Yet, interestingly enough, there's the same restlessness, the same idealism, the same craziness, and the same love. Their faces, their eyes, their hands in the late afternoon light, still give me the shivers.

This year, despite the floods of the year before, the coffee and cotton harvests reached record proportions. The DPT and polio vaccinations were about to begin again. Primary school enrollment was a record high, as was enrollment in secondary schools, in the university and in the adult education CEPs. And the battle for the fourth grade was declared.

FURTHER REFLECTIONS

In March 1983, thousands of well-armed counterrevolutionaries crossed from Honduras into Nicaragua and—with the active help of both the United States and Honduran governments—briefly penetrated deep into the country, until they were driven back across the border by the volunteer Sandinista militia. They concentrated their forces in the small villages of the north, seeking to accomplish by terror what they could never accomplish by persuasion. And so a quiet war broke out in the mountains of Matagalpa—a war whose aim was and is to overturn all we've struggled for, during the literacy crusade and since. Many campesinos who couldn't be bought off were terrorized, kidnapped, or killed.

There were targeted victims, too—the land reform technicians, the CEP teachers, the foreign doctors—by now the Georgino Andrades have been multiplied by several hundred. The Cuban teachers, particularly obvious targets of the *contras*, were removed for their own protection. Two youths—one a CEP coordinator—were slaughtered in Azancor Arriba, the community just up the hill from Wapá; seven were killed during an adult education workshop in Esquipulas to the south; seventeen members of the Sandinista Youth were killed in Río Blanco, a technical assistant in Boaco, a French doctor in Rancho Grande, and a German doctor further north. And these were the specific civilian targets; they do not include the *compas* who have volunteered by the tens of thousands to defend their revolution.

And in isolated Wapá, seeing the counterrevolutionary bands pass by on the crest of a hill, the community members who weren't off fighting hid the books and fled to sleep out in the brush where no one could ambush them. "I hid the photo of you and Jorge out in the hills," Doña Leopoldina confided shortly afterward. "I would have felt too bad burning it." Photos of two smiling figures in gray tunics—souvenirs too dangerous to keep. Books of language and arithmetic, a peril to your life.

These *contras* will not win. The people of these mountains can no more turn their backs on the last four years than they can become illiterate again. The new slogan in the country is "All arms to the people to defend the revolution!" Yet it doesn't hurt any the less to see the blood flow again, to wonder how many of our teachers, our students, our ex-brigadistas must pay with their lives to defend their newly won freedom. And there is a special pain in knowing that the arms used to slaughter them come from my own country.

The *contras* continue their attacks along the Honduran border. And now in May, there are attacks from the south, from Costa Rica, by other counterrevolutionary groups. It is a somber note to end on, but then again, it's not really an end. We go on in this new country we're making. The people are going on with notebooks and pencils, and as long as they're necessary, with rifles. We are going on with hope and determination. I recall the words of a brigadista I ran into on the first anniversary of the crusade:

"We'll be there to help El Salvador when they have their crusade, won't we, *profe*? They're going to win soon, I know it."

Right, Domingo, *Puño en alto!*

And If You Wish to Know More

The Nicaraguan literacy crusade has received scant attention in the English-speaking world. A good general account, brief and to the point, is Valerie Miller's "Nicaraguan Literacy Crusade," published in *Nicaragua in Revolution*, ed. Thomas W. Walker (New York: Praeger Publishers, 1982). A longer, scholarly account is contained in the same author's Ph.D. dissertation, *Nicaraguan Literacy Crusade: Education for Transformation* (University of Massachusetts, 1983). George Black and John Bevan's *Loss of Fear: Education—Nicaragua Before and After the Revolution* (London: Nicaragua Solidarity Campaign, World University Service, 1980) presents a polemical point of view.

For an introduction to Paolo Freire's thought, see his *Pedagogy of the Oppressed* (New York: Continuum, 1970).

For specific details on the aims, organization, and materials used in the crusade, readers are referred to the following Spanish-language publications:

Aleman, Luis, et al. *Vencimos: La Cruzada Nacional de Alfabetización de Nicaragua*: Libro Abierto para Americana Latina.

Assman, Hugo, ed. *Nicaragua: Triunfa en la Alfabetización: Documentos y testimonios de la Cruzada Nacional de Alfabetización*. San Jose, Costa Rica: Departimento Ecumenico de Investigaciones, 1981.

Castella, Miguel de. *Educación y Lucha de Clases en Nicaragua*. Managua: Publicaciones del Departamento de Filosofia, Universidad Centroamericana, 1980.

Chacon, Alicia, and Pozas, Victor S., *Cruzada Nacional de Alfabetización*. Nicaragua, 1980.

———. *Documentes: Primer Congreso Nacional de Educación Popular de Adultos*. Managua, August 1981.

Encuentro 16. Revista Universidad Centroamericana.

For information on the course of the Nicaraguan revolution, the best, most comprehensive guide in English is George Black's *Triumph of the People* (London: Zed Press, 1982; available in the United States from Littlefield Adams, 81 Adams Drive, Totowa, N.J. 07512). Also informative is the previously mentioned *Nicaragua in Revolution*, ed. Thomas W. Walker (New York: Praeger Publishers, 1982).

For continuing reports on the revolution, the best contemporary source is NACLA *Report on the Americas*, a bimonthly available from the North American Congress on Latin America, 151 West 19th Street, New York, New York 10011.